THE ROHINGYA IN SOUTH ASIA

The Rohingya of Myanmar are one of the world's most persecuted minority populations without citizenship. After the latest exodus from Myanmar in 2017, there are now more than half a million Rohingya in Bangladesh living in camps, often in conditions of abject poverty, malnutrition and without proper access to shelter or work permits. Some of them are now compelled to take to the seas in perilous journeys to the Southeast Asian countries in search of a better life. They are now asked to go back to Myanmar, but without any promise of citizenship or an end to discrimination.

This book looks at the Rohingya in the South Asian region, primarily India and Bangladesh. It explores the broader picture of the historical and political dimensions of the Rohingya crisis, and examines subjects of statelessness, human rights and humanitarian protection of these victims of forced migration. Further, it chronicles the actual process of emergence of a stateless community – the transformation of a national group into a stateless existence without basic rights.

This volume will be of great interest to students and researchers of human rights, migration and diaspora studies, race and ethnic studies, refugee studies, politics and international relations, discrimination studies, and peace and conflict studies, as well as to international organizations, those in law, media and journalism, civil society and policymakers.

Sabyasachi Basu Ray Chaudhury is a Professor in the Department of Political Science, Rabindra Bharati University, Kolkata, India. He is also

Honorary Director, Centre for Nepal Studies, and is the founder Head, Department of Human Rights and Human Development at the same university. He has been the Vice Chancellor of Rabindra Bharati University since 2012 and is a member of the Calcutta Research Group. His areas of interest include international relations, South Asian politics, refugee studies and human rights. He is among the few experts in India on the Andaman and Nicobar Islands. He is a regular contributor to academic journals, periodicals, dailies, news channels and portals. His publications include *Indian Autonomies: Key Words and Key Texts* (co-edited with Ranabir Samaddar and Samir Kumar Das, 2005); *Internal Displacement in South Asia: The Relevance of UN's Guiding Principles* (co-edited with Paula Banerjee and Samir Kumar Das, 2005); and *Rights after Globalisation* (co-edited with Ishita Dey, 2011).

Ranabir Samaddar is currently Distinguished Chair in Migration and Forced Migration Studies, Calcutta Research Group, Kolkata, India. He belongs to the critical school of thinking and is considered one of the foremost theorists in the field of migration and forced migration studies. His writings on the nation state, migration, labour and urbanization have signalled a new turn in critical post-colonial thinking. Among his influential works are *The Marginal Nation: Transborder Migration from Bangladesh to West Bengal* (1999); *Beyond Kolkata: Rajarhat and the Dystopia of Urban Imagination* (co-authored, 2014); and *Karl Marx and the Postcolonial Age* (2017).

THE ROHINGYA IN SOUTH ASIA

People Without a State

Edited by Sabyasachi Basu Ray Chaudhury and Ranabir Samaddar

Routledge
Taylor & Francis Group

LONDON AND NEW YORK

First published 2018
by Routledge
2 Park Square, Milton Park, Abingdon, Oxon OX14 4RN

and by Routledge
711 Third Avenue, New York, NY 10017

Routledge is an imprint of the Taylor & Francis Group, an informa business

British Library Cataloguing-in-Publication Data
A catalogue record for this book is available from the British Library

Library of Congress Cataloging-in-Publication Data
A catalog record has been requested for this book

ISBN: 978-1-138-74345-8 (hbk)
ISBN: 978-1-138-61101-6 (pbk)
ISBN: 978-0-429-46767-7 (ebk)

Typeset in Bembo
by Apex CoVantage, LLC

CONTENTS

ILLUSTRATIONS

Figure

Tables

CONTRIBUTORS

Sahana Basavapatna is an advocate practising in Bengaluru, India, and is a Partner at Factum Law. She is now engaged in a number of civil litigations on arbitration, family law, intellectual property rights and child sexual abuse. Previously she has worked in a number of capacities (from 2006 to 2015) in the field of asylum law and migration, including as a Coordinator of the Burmese refugee programme in the research consultancy The Other Media, New Delhi, and as a legal representative of refugees before the Office of the United Nations High Commissioner for Refugees in New Delhi.

Madhura Chakraborty is a writer, researcher and activist. Her research focuses on migration and gender. Her published work deals with Afghan refugees and Bengali migrants in Delhi's informal sectors. She has also worked with waste workers and policy research in Kashmir, Bihar and West Bengal. She currently works as the lead researcher for Video Volunteers, a community media organization working across India.

Sabyasachi Basu Ray Chaudhury is a Professor in the Department of Political Science, Rabindra Bharati University, Kolkata, India. He is also Honorary Director, Centre for Nepal Studies, and is the founder Head, Department of Human Rights and Human Development at the same university. He is the Vice Chancellor of Rabindra Bharati University since 2012 and a member of the Calcutta Research Group. His areas of interest include international relations, South Asian politics, refugee studies and human rights. He is among the few experts in India on the Andaman and Nicobar Islands. He is a regular contributor to academic journals, periodicals, dailies, news channels and portals. His publications include *Indian Autonomies: Key Words and Key Texts* (co-edited with Ranabir Samaddar and Samir Kumar Das, 2005); *Internal Displacement in South Asia: The Relevance of UN's Guiding Principles* (co-edited with Paula Banerjee and Samir Kumar Das, 2005); and *Rights after Globalisation* (co-edited with Ishita Dey, 2011).

Kriti Chopra teaches English at the Cambridge group of schools. Her research interest has largely been in migration and related areas. She has published two papers in the journal *Refugee Watch Online*, apart from writing extensively on this issue.

Suchismita Majumder is a doctoral candidate in the Department of Sociology, University of Kalyani, West Bengal, India. Her areas of interest include diaspora studies, medical sociology, gender studies and religion.

Charlotte-Anne Malischewski is Associate in Litigation Group, Toronto, Canada. She maintains a bilingual general litigation practice which includes civil and professional liability, class actions and complex commercial litigation. She has represented clients before the Ontario Superior Court, the Ontario Human Rights Tribunal and the Supreme Court of Canada. She is actively involved in a number of civil liberties, immigration and criminal law matters.

Ranabir Samaddar is currently Distinguished Chair in Migration and Forced Migration Studies, Calcutta Research Group, Kolkata, India. He belongs to the critical school of thinking and is considered as one of the foremost theorists in the field of migration and forced migration studies. His writings on the nation state, migration, labour and urbanization have signalled a new turn in critical post-colonial thinking. Among his influential works are *The Marginal Nation: Transborder Migration from Bangladesh to West Bengal* (1999); *Beyond Kolkata: Rajarhat and the Dystopia of Urban Imagination* (co-authored, 2014); and *Karl Marx and the Postcolonial Age* (2017).

Shuvro Prosun Sarker is Researcher at the Centre for Regulatory Studies, Governance and Public Policy, West Bengal National University of Juridical Sciences, Kolkata, India. He is Assistant Editor of the *Asian Journal of Legal Education* and former mentor at the Legal Aid Society of National University of Juridical Sciences, India. He is also the author of *Clinical Legal Education in India* (2015).

Sucharita Sengupta is a doctoral candidate at the Graduate Institute of International and Development Studies, Geneva, Switzerland. She was associated with the Distinguished Chair in Migration and Forced Migration Studies at the Calcutta Research Group (CRG). Her research interests pertain to forced migration and border studies in the context of Asia.

Priyanca Mathur Velath is Assistant Professor and Postgraduate Coordinator of the Master's Degree Programme in the Department of Political Science at St Joseph's College, Bengaluru, India. She is a recipient of the Schomburg Fellowship, Ramapo College, Mahwah, New Jersey, USA; a Junior Research Fellow in Finland as part of their Indo-Finnish Exchange Programme, hosted by the Tampere Peace Research Institute (TAPRI), Tampere, Finland; and the Commonwealth Scholarship by Queen Elizabeth House, University of Oxford, UK (2002). She also received a grant from the Charles Wallace India Trust of the UK.

ACKNOWLEDGEMENTS

This book is about the Rohingya – a million-plus community, mainly living in the Arakan region in northwestern Myanmar as an ethnic minority, many of them stripped of their citizenship, and therefore rendered stateless. There is already a handful of publications dealing with the displaced Rohingya, but this book is probably the first of its kind to focus on the Rohingya in India in the larger context of the statelessness of the Rohingya in South and Southeast Asia. As such, this book may also be viewed as a companion volume to Calcutta Research Group's (CRG) work on statelessness in South Asia (*The State of Being Stateless: An Account of South Asia*, 2015).

This volume is part of the CRG-Taft Foundation research on the Rohingya, which was undertaken as part of the First Research Workshop on 'Interrogating Forced Migration Studies', supported by the Indian Council of Social Science Research (ICSSR), Maulana Abul Kalam Azad Institute of Asian Studies (MAKAIS), Kolkata and the Taft Foundation. We are grateful to these three institutions for their support of our research initiative.

We also thank all the participants of the two workshops held in Kolkata and Darjeeling, where parts of the research outputs were presented and discussed. We sincerely thank, in particular, Subhas Ranjan Chakraborty, Anup Sekhar Chakraborty, Paromita Chowdhury, Samaresh Guchhait, Ravi Hemadri, Roshan P. Rai, Amar Singh Rai, Nitya Ramakrishnan, Suhita Saha, Srimanti Sarkar and Ragini Trakroo Zutshi.

We also thank Meghna Guhathakurta of the Research Initiatives, Bangladesh; Amena Mohsin of Dhaka University; Sanlaap, Kolkata; the United

Nations High Commissioner for Refugees (UNHCR) offices and staff in Delhi and Dhaka; the *Daily Star*, Bangladesh; and Asif Munier, International Organization for Migration (IOM), Bangladesh.

We convey our gratitude to Additional IG (North), Adhir Sharma and other officers of the Correctional Homes in West Bengal for their utmost cooperation in conducting the research. We are also thankful to Sourabh Sen and Gaurav Bansal for their overall support and help in facilitating the research.

Our thanks also go to the six young researchers who supported each other in this research work during the entire research period and made this research possible; also to our colleagues, Suhit K. Sen and Subharanjan Dasgupta, who went through the chapters and made improvements on what was initially a collection of reports. Finally, thanks are due to Paula Banerjee, Director, CRG and the entire staff and colleagues of CRG for their comments and support in shaping this research.

INTRODUCTION

Sabyasachi Basu Ray Chaudhury and
Ranabir Samaddar

This book is on the Rohingya in South Asia with a focus on their situation in India. While there are studies – mainly reports and articles – on the Rohingya in Myanmar and on their situation as refugees in Bangladesh, there is to date no such study focusing on the Rohingya in India. Also, the literature on stateless communities in South Asia, particularly India, is still very inadequate. The exceptions are two books. First, *State of Being Stateless in South Asia*, edited by Paula Banerjee et al. (2015), offers a detailed account of different stateless communities in India, but does not deal with the situation of precarity faced by the Rohingya. The second, Deepak K. Singh's book, *Stateless in South Asia* (2009), is on the statelessness of the Chakmas living in India's northeast, and leaves out other stateless communities in South Asia. This book covers two major gaps: it deals with the Rohingya, one of the most persecuted minority communities in the world today, and their situation as a displaced community in India; second, it describes and analyses the process of the production of statelessness, one of the fundamental situations of rightlessness in the world today.

When the image of the body of Aylan Kurdi, a toddler, brought ashore in Turkey in the first half of 2015, went viral on the social media network, the world woke up, almost overnight, to take stock of the crisis of migrants/refugees/asylum-seekers in Europe that has been persisting for some time. The picture, released by a Turkish news agency, started spreading worldwide on Twitter under the #KiyiyaVuranInsanlik ('humanity washed ashore') hashtag. The disturbing image of a boy lying face down on the beach sparked an international outcry over the human cost of the crisis. Europe, indeed, has not witnessed so many people moving from one place to another since World War II, except during and in the aftermath of the Balkan wars in the 1990s. But is Europe alone witnessing massive migrations?

Almost four decades back, the stories of Vietnamese boat people looking for shelter hit the news headlines. After so many years, the migrants/ refugees/asylum-seekers/stateless persons are still paying high prices for space aboard unseaworthy ships, with small food supplies and terrible sanitary conditions, to flee their respective home countries. As a consequence, after their weeks-long journey on rickety, overcrowded vessels, the displaced and stateless Rohingya were either brought ashore to Thailand, Malaysia and Indonesia, where they were placed in the camps set up by the governments, or they were denied shelter in alien lands, perished in the seas and found their end in mass graves. Thousands of Rohingya, a persecuted ethnic minority from Myanmar, crossed the Bay of Bengal and the Andaman Sea in recent times towards treacherous, precarious and uncertain futures. This is a high risk the Rohingya take to escape their statelessness in conflict-ridden Myanmar. But can they really escape the condition of statelessness? The answer is an emphatic 'No.' Rather, they are landing in a situation of precarity. However we brand them, whether as refugees, migrants or asylum-seekers, they remain stateless in the world of nation states. In countries marked by post-colonial societies, torn apart by the delineation or re-lineation of borders and boundaries, the Rohingya are among the excluded. To grasp this sordid saga of the Rohingya, one first needs to go back to history of this community.

The new boat people

India, Bangladesh and Myanmar were united or closely linked historically and shared a past before borders divided them into separate independent nations. The borders dividing these territories, however, have largely remained porous, and the more governments try securitizing them, the more migration, be it 'legal' or 'illegal', takes place. Therefore, it is not surprising that the Rohingya of Myanmar, in a milieu of 'well-founded fear of persecution', cross the Naf River to enter Bangladesh in search of a safe place to live. On the other hand, the second or third generations of the Rohingya, already settled in either refugee camps or makeshift settlements in Bangladesh, are taking to the sea to seek jobs in the Southeast Asian countries. Rohingya are migrating not only as asylum-seekers but also as economic migrants from Bangladesh to mainly Southeast Asian countries over the high seas.

The nature of migration is thus mixed. Despite the high risk of travelling in rickety boats with the assistance of middlemen, the accessibility of the sea, compared to land, seems easier. They are also trafficked to Southeast Asia, West Asia and even Australia. The precariousness of their journey to find a comparatively secure territory needs to be underscored. It has landed them in border-detention camps, often on the road to death, or turned them into bonded labour. The 'pull factors', conventionally called so in economic literature, have trapped them in a trafficking nexus that involves many actors.

Recently, the international media publicized several reports and video clippings of the precarious situation in which the mixed and massive flows of population from Bangladesh and Myanmar are taking place involving deaths and torture on high seas and in detention camps. Followers of the situation may find a close similarity between the recent Rohingya exodus and that of the Vietnamese boat people in the late 1970s. The term *boat people* was first used to describe Vietnamese refugees. They fled in small, often fishing, boats. The Vietnamese during that time sought refuge elsewhere before being accepted into Europe, North America and Australia.[1] It was only after some graves were unearthed on a remote and rugged mountain in the border district of Sadao in Songkhla, Thailand, that the enormity of the Rohingya problem started capturing public imagination.[2]

However, even after that, persecution of the Rohingya within Myanmar continues. In fact, salt has further been added to the wound of the Rohingya as Myanmar's military defended its crackdown on the Rohingya Muslim minority in early March 2017 as a lawful counter-insurgency operation, adding that it was necessary to defend the country.[3] General Mya Tun Oo, chief of the General Staff of Army of Myanmar, said: 'I want to say that I am very sad because of these kind of reckless accusations and neglect of the good things that the government and the military have done for them,' referring to the reports in the media quoting Rohingya residents describing the alleged abuses such as burning of houses in the area.[4] Meanwhile, in late 2016, an estimated 21,000 Rohingya sought refuge in Bangladesh, as Myanmar's forces launched a terrible, bloody crackdown against the million-strong Muslim minority that became evident from the testimony from refugees, satellite imagery compiled by rights groups and leaked photos and videos from inside the Arakan state of Myanmar.[5] The latest troubles began in early October, when police said three border guard posts were attacked by Islamist militants. Interestingly, Aung Sang Suu Kyi, the messiah of the democratic upsurge in Myanmar, the Nobel Peace Prize winner, who came to power in the country after the polls in November 2015, does not display any willingness to address the Rohingya issue.

The Rohingya are now the world's most persecuted minority without citizenship. Currently around 32,000 Rohingya are registered with the United Nations High Commissioner for Refugees (UNHCR) in Bangladesh, living in two camps in Kutupalong, and Nayapara near Teknaf. However, unofficially around 850,000 unregistered refugees are living in conditions of abject poverty and malnutrition outside the formal camp areas. Being unregistered, they do not have formal access to food, shelter or work permits in Bangladesh. In search of a better life, some of them are now being compelled to take to the seas in perilous journeys to the Southeast Asian countries.

It is quite difficult to enumerate the Rohingya in India, given the large number of unregistered refugees and stateless persons in the Indian sea of humanity, thus there are many estimates. According to recent and 'official' data publicized in July 2015, there are nearly 6,684 families of Rohingya settled in Jammu and Kashmir, while 1,755 are reported to be in Andhra Pradesh. The number of families settled in different states of India is 10,565, spread all over the country as follows: Jammu and Kashmir 6,684, Andhra Pradesh 1,755, Delhi 760, Haryana 677, West Bengal 361, Rajasthan 162, Uttar Pradesh 111, Punjab 50, Maharashtra 12, and Andaman and Nicobar Islands 3.[6] The former chief minister of Jammu and Kashmir, Mufti Mohammad Sayeed, said that over 5,000 Rohingya refugees were living in many settlement colonies in Jammu. 'There are about 1,219 Rohingya (Burmese) families comprising 5,107 members who are staying in Jammu,' he said. Nearly all of the refugees live in the Jammu district alone, most of them in the Narwal area of the city. 'Out of the total Rohingya refugees living in Jammu province, 4,912 members are having United Nations High Commissioner for Refugees (UNHCR) cards and 186 members are without the cards,' said Sayeed. Their children are reportedly being provided education in six *madrasas*(Islamic seminaries) in many city areas.[7] According to Mohammad Rafik, a Rohingya refugee in Jammu,

> We have been forced to be scrap dealers as there are no employment avenues available. A large number of refugees here is unregistered as there is a long process to get your name registered with UNHCR who provide a registration card.[8]

Children of these refugee families support their families by collecting and selling recyclable materials, and some women work in walnut factories up to twelve hours a day, cracking shells and removing nuts.[9] Interestingly, none of the available figures includes families staying in Manipur. In any case, if one goes by various available figures the number of Rohingya in India could be somewhere between 40,000 and 50,000, assuming that each family on an average has four or five members. However, if we take into account the unenumerated refugees and asylum-seekers (on the basis of estimates of other unregistered groups of foreigners compared to the registered groups of those foreigners), the total number can go up to 100,000 or more.

Labelled 'Asia's new boat people' and compared to the Vietnamese exodus, the fate of thousands of Rohingya depends on countries willing to help and provide them with shelter. But on several occasions, the Rohingya and Bangladeshis often riding the boats together are abandoned in the sea by traffickers. In May 2016, an estimated 6,000 Rohingya and Bangladeshi refugees were stranded at sea, as the Malaysian authorities turned them away. The then deputy home minister of Malaysia said: 'We have to send the right message that they are not welcome here,' after 1,000 refugees landed on the shores of Langkawi.[10] There are already Rohingya refugees in Malaysia, many of whom are being detained under horrible conditions in detention centres.[11] An estimate indicates that, as of the end of October 2016, there were more than 150,000 refugees and asylum-seekers in Malaysia, of which some 54,856 were Rohingya.[12] In this context, the prime minister of Thailand also claimed that their country lacks the resources to host the refugees. And the least said about Australia, the better.

The process of smuggling Bangladeshi nationals along with the Rohingya in boats has been going on for a little more than a decade. There were police reports of young boys missing in areas adjoining Cox's Bazar, but the reasons for it were unknown. Recent media reports give us an idea of the extent of migration that has taken place through the past ten years. The fact remains that labour migration from Bangladesh to Malaysia was a practice recognized by both the governments of Malaysia and Bangladesh. Rohingya from Bangladesh began going to Malaysia probably because the latter was a Muslim country, and they felt that there was a huge labour market with high demand for labour. Consequently, the traffickers burnt the midnight oil month after month to lure Rohingya along with Bangladeshi nationals. The Bangladeshis were included as they were likely to pay more than what the Rohingya could afford.[13] Sucharita Sengupta's account in this volume gives the details of the population group that has now come to be known as the *boat people*, evoking comparison with the Afro-Asian groups often perishing in the Mediterranean and other seas while to trying to reach European shores.

In retrospect

The contributions to this book require a historical perspective. Here we present the historical perspective in some detail. It helps us to understand different aspects of the present phenomenon of statelessness of the Rohingya.

Apparently, the word Rohingya is derived from *Rohang*, the ancient name for Arakan. Historically, the Rohingya belong to a community that developed from many stocks of people including Burmese, Arabs, Moors, Persians, Bengalis and others – all adhering to Islam. Although the naming of *Rohingya* seems to have come about only recently, around the beginning of the 1950s, the Muslims in Arakan have a long history since the beginning of the MraukU dynasty (1430–1785) of Arakan. There is a possibility that they resided there even before the emergence of the kingdom. However, because Arakan and Tenasserim were occupied by the British after the first Anglo-Burmese War (1824–6), the confrontation between the Muslims residing in the northwestern part of Arakan and the Buddhists as the majority in central and southern Arakan became tense because large-scale Indian immigration was subsequently encouraged by the British.

The defeat at the hands of the British forced Burma to sign the Treaty of Yandabo in 1826, which resulted in the absorption of Arakan to the west and Tenasserim, Burma's southern coastal strip, into the British Empire. Eventually, Burma became a province of British India, and the porous border between Bengal and Arakan facilitated a variety of cross-border contacts.[14] Over time, numerous Bengali Muslims, some of whom were Chittagongs,[15] moved into northern Arakan and began to merge with the Rohingya community. In this way, the distinction between these ethnic groups became blurred following the ease of cross-border and inter-community interactions.

The immigrants coming into the Arakan included many Muslims from Chittagong. They were classified as the Chittagonians or Mohammedans by the British officials. The confrontation came to a head during the Japanese occupation period (1942–5), when Japan armed the Buddhist Arakanese in order to fight against the British and the British used Muslim forces for a counter-attack. The situation did not change even after the independence of Burma in 1948. But before coming to the present, we need to explore the past a little more.

Arakan, the westernmost state of Myanmar, is now officially known as the Rakhine State. The Rakhine or Arakan State of Myanmar (Burma), the traditional homeland of the Rohingya community, is situated on the western coast of the country, bordered by Chin State to the north; Magway Region, Bago Region, and Ayewardy Region to the east; the Bay of Bengal to the west; and the Chittagong Division of Bangladesh to the northwest. Rakhine has four districts, 17 townships and 3,871 villages, according to a government report of Myanmar published in 2001.[16] The province, with an area of more than 36,000 square kilometres, is a narrow strip of coastal region at the crossroads of rivers, mountains and valleys.

Rakhine is on the frontiers between the Islamic and Buddhist cultures of Asia, as it is located in the tri-junction of Myanmar, India and Bangladesh. This has a huge area of swampy plains and estuaries along the coast, bordering a long range of deep mountains to the east. These mountains are perceived to have kept Rakhine, or Arakan of the past, comparatively isolated from the affairs of the central region of the Republic of the Union of Myanmar. Even today, despite its maritime potential and easy access in the north to Bangladesh, Rakhine remains connected to central Burma only by a handful of barely motorable roads. Therefore, till recently, Rakhine remained a forgotten and impecunious remote place within the country – but not anymore.

In fact, of late, China has been involved in the development of infrastructural facilities in Rakhine State. It has invested its resources for this purpose in Kyaukphyu, where the CITIC Group Corporation Ltd, formerly the China International Trust Investment Corporation, a state-owned investment company of the People's Republic of China, won a contract to develop the multibillion Kyaukphyu Special Economic Zone (SEZ) that involves building a deep-sea port and industrial park. In December 2008, China and Myanmar signed a deal to construct an oil pipeline at Kyaukphyu.[17] Similarly, in November 2010, the China Development Bank and Myanmar Foreign Investment Bank signed a $2.4 billion loan deal to construct the 1,060-kilometre pipeline from Kyaukphyu to Kunming in the Yunnan province of China.[18] In other words, this region has turned critical for China's energy security.

On the other hand, in April 2008, India signed the Framework Agreement for facilitating the Kaladan Multi-modal Transit Transport Project with Myanmar as a major part of its 'Look East Policy'. This project would connect Kolkata to Sittwe port in Myanmar via the Bay of Bengal, then Sittwe port to the inland water transhipment terminal at Paletwa town in Myanmar through the Kaladan River, connect the Paletwa River terminal to the India-Myanmar border at Zorinpui at the southern tip of Mizoram in India's northeast, and finally construct the 100-kilometre road from Zorinpui to the Aizawl-Saiha Highway (the Indian National Highway 54 at Lawngtlai). NH 54 is the part of the larger East-West corridor connecting the rest of India with India's northeast. Therefore Sittwe, the capital of the Rakhine State of Myanmar, has also become a critical point of India's connectivity policy.

A number of minority ethnic groups in the course of time settled in Rakhine (then Arakan), including Chin, Mro and Khami (mainly Christians now), Kamans in the coastal areas (largely converted to Islam), in addition to the Buddhist majority groups, and other Muslims. The Rakhines usually speak a dialect of Burmese, like the Tavoyans of Lower Burma. The people of Rakhine have claimed political autonomy from Myanmar. As a result, there is a history of long-drawn conflict between Rakhine leaders and Burman rulers or governments in Mandalay, Rangoon (now Yangon) and central Burma. This situation has continued until today. However, the cultural and ethnic dissimilarities between the Buddhists and Muslims or Rohingya and other Rakhines as clearly perceived today were not always quite as clear in the past, and the fact remains that Muslims and Buddhists in the past lived on both sides of the Naf River that marks the present border with Bangladesh.

The Rakhines used to practise Theravada or Hinayana Buddhism, the influence of which generally dates back to the eleventh century when the Burman king and unifier of Burma, Anawrahta, overwhelmed the kingdom of the Buddhist Mons in Lower Burma and moved hundreds of monks and scholars to Pagan, the capital. Subsequently, the Rakhines started challenging the supremacy of the Burman kings, and a number of powerful Buddhist rulers arose in Arakan, with proud cultural and political traditions similar to the Burmans, Shans and Mons in the east. The Royal Court at Myohaung or MraukU, established by King Narameikhia in the fifteenth century, turned into a seat of power for Arakan.[19]

Comparatively speaking, the Islamic influence in Arakan seems to have come from a number of sources. Many historians have shown evidence of the Muslim presence along the coastlines of Arakan from the ninth and tenth centuries. It is argued that the Arab traders and proponents of Islam arrived first in this region. Thereafter, as the Muslim influence under the Sultanate and later the Mughal Empire extended deep into Bengal and Chittagong in particular, the situation began changing. This became more evident during the rule of King Narameikhia in the fifteenth century. King Narameikhia, after taking shelter in King Ahmed Shah's kingdom of Chittagong during a conflict with the Burman kings, took Muslim titles after reclaiming his throne. Some say that Narameikhia converted to Islam although it also could be that, he simply used these titles as royal honours, which were of great prestige in the region. Be that as it may, as the Arakan kings started reasserting themselves, Chittagong became a bone of contention between local rulers in Arakan and Bengal for the next two centuries. As a consequence, this territory also changed hands several times until it was picked up by the Mughal emperors in 1666.[20]

When the first census of Burma was taken in August 1872, British Burma consisted of the three provinces of Arakan, Pegu and Tenasserim. The Muslims were categorized either as Burman Muslims or Indian Muslims. Two-thirds of the total number of Muslims recorded in the territories of British Burma at that time, around 64,000 people, lived in the Arakan.[21] The Census of 1891 included most of the recognized territory of Myanmar today. It recorded Muslims under the categories used for the broader India census. Thus the Muslim people were divided as Shaykhs, Sayyids, Moghuls, Pathans and other groups, including Arakanis, Panthays, Shan Muslims, Turks, Arabs and Choulias. According to Moshe Yegar, many Arakan Muslims who were offspring of intermarriages between the Indian Muslims and Burman Buddhists were registered as Shaykhs in the census. By 1921, there were over 500,000 Muslims in a population of over thirteen million.[22] Muslims of Indian origin came from several different provinces of India.

According to the 1931 Census, the category of Indian Muslims constituted the great majority of Muslims in Burma, particularly in the urban areas. But of more than one million Indians recorded in Burma, the majority was Hindu.[23] There was a geographical concentration of Muslims in Arakan that accounted for a sizeable section of the total Muslim population of Burma.

Henceforth there would be both regular mingling of different ethnic and religious communities as well as conflicts, especially around the Naf River border. The Rakhines had earned notoriety for coastal raids into Bengal, and therefore they received the epithet of Mags or bandits, and accordingly, Arakan was popularly referred to as Magermuluk (in Bengali) or the Land of Mags. Cox's Bazar also turned into a Rakhine majority town till the withdrawal of the British Indian administration in 1947.[24] Meanwhile the coastal Kamans adopted Islam. Many Bengali traders and craftsmen started visiting the Royal Court at MraukU. Many of them settled in the coastal areas of Akyab (Sittwe), where one of Rakhine's largest mosques, the Jame Mosque, was constructed in the seventeenth century.

In 1784, the Burman King Bodawpaya invaded Arakan, ousted the last Arakanese king Thainada and took away the Mahamuni image to Mandalay. Thus Arakan's historic independence came to an end. Later, over 20,000 Arakanese, led by their king, took shelter in British-controlled Bengal and requested assistance and protection. This finally brought the British into Burma, and it culminated in the earlier mentioned first Anglo-Burmese War.

During British rule, labourers, merchants or administrators migrated to Burma from outside. They included Hindus and Muslims, Nepalis and Tamils. Similarly, many migrated to the Arakan towns of Maungdaw and Sittwe or Akyab from Chittagong. Some of them were seasonal workers to help local rich landowners during harvest time. However, it was the activities of Chettiyar moneylenders from southern India which caused the greatest resentment amongst impoverished rural farmers in central and lower Burma. This in turn fuelled the growing tide of Burmese nationalism, and there were violent anti-Indian communal riots in 1930–1 and again in 1938 in which several hundred Indians were killed. As a consequence, there was a growing tendency of clubbing the Indian Muslims and the indigenous Muslims of Arakan together.

Against this backdrop, during World War II a huge number of Indians, including Muslims, fled Burma. Some followed the departing British administrators, but others were brutally chased out by nationalists of Aung San's Burma Independence Army. Thousands also died of starvation, disease and in military attacks, accounting for one of the darkest episodes in modern Burmese history. In any case, the simmering discontent continued in Arakan even after World War II and after the departure of the British rulers from the region. A number of different armed and communist groups of Rakhine, spearheaded by a former Buddhist monk, U Seinda, fought against both the British and later the first post-independence government of U Nu after General Aung San's assassination. At the same time, the Muslims of Arakan started demanding autonomy for the Muslim-majority Mayu Division adjoining the Naf River border.

Since Burma's independence in 1948, the political demands of both Muslim and Buddhist communities in Arakan were entirely overlooked by the central government in Rangoon. Arakan was not even granted provincial autonomy. In 1962, General Ne Win seized power in a military coup and imposed his Burmese Way to Socialism, which set off a new wave of social unrest and insurgencies in the country. Under the 1974 Constitution, Arakan was granted statehood and was given the official title of the Rakhine State. The name of the state capital Akyab was changed to Sittwe. Many Muslims in the Rakhine State feel that this was the beginning of a long-term policy to exclude their culture and people from Arakan. After all, in both governmental and Rakhine terminology, a Rakhine must be a Buddhist. The attempt to eliminate the Muslim voice from everyday business and political affairs of Arakan after 1962 was backed by intense military pressure. Under Ne Win, a draconian military operation known as the Four Cuts policy was introduced. The Burmese army targeted the entire region and began relocating villagers in relentless military operations in order to flush out insurgent forces and their sympathisers.

In 1978, a military operation codenamed 'Ye The Ha' was launched in the mountains of north Arakan around the Sittwe plains, together with an unusual census operation known as Nagamin or King Dragon, to check identity papers in the border region for the first time. The Nagamin census operation generated controversies amidst widespread reports of army brutality including rape, murder and the destruction of mosques. As a result, about 200,000 Muslims took refuge elsewhere. The state-controlled media of Burma blamed the 'armed bands of Bengalis' or 'Muslim extremists' for attacking indigenous Buddhist villages. Moreover, it was also argued by the military junta that many of those who fled in 1978 were in fact illegal Bengali immigrants who had entered Burma as part of a general expansion in the Bengali population in this region of Asia. The counter-argument was that many displaced persons had either never had national registration cards or they had been confiscated by the immigration authorities during the 1978 operation. That the Rohingya were deliberately being discriminated against was further strengthened after a tough Citizenship Act was passed by the Ne Win government in 1982. Under this act, three categories of citizens were created: national, associate and naturalized. Full citizenship in Burma was only for national ethnic groups such as the Burmans, Mons or Rakhines, or those who could prove their ancestors resided in Burma before the first Anglo-Burmese war.

For many Muslim residents, this was a near impossible task. There were no such records to be found and, in fact, such a law was discriminatory according to international law and covenants. In any case, many Muslims have since been forced to apply for naturalized citizenship, if they had not already applied for citizenship under the earlier 1948 Citizenship Law, in which case they now found themselves reclassified as associate citizens. Many Muslims complain that this second-class status is deliberately used as the basis for every kind of petty harassment and economic or social discrimination. In fact, this turned into a long-term government plan to drive Muslims out of Burma. Since the early 1980s there have been continuing reports of anti-Muslim persecution throughout the country. The result was a continuing flow of Muslim refugees, including holders of national registration cards, out of Arakan to countries such as Egypt, Saudi Arabia, Pakistan and other parts of the Muslim world where they were referred to as Asia's 'New Palestinians'. Therefore, after 1982, the continuing destruction or uprooting of Muslim villages and mosques was reported in several parts of Arakan, from Sandoway to Tongup. This was the backdrop to the mass exodus of 1991–2.

From the middle of 1991, several new regiments as well as a local border police militia known as the Na SaKa were deployed in the northern border region. In response, local Rakhine, Mro and Chin populations began to complain of forced relocations and military harassment. Subsequently, over 250,000 Muslim refugees from Maungdaw, Buthidaung and Rathedaung fled to the Cox's Bazar area of Bangladesh. However, the state-run *Working People's Daily* claimed in January 25, 1992 that the 'Rohingya problem is no more than the problem of unregistered illegal immigrants'.[25]

The Rohingya became a stateless population in 1982 with the revised Myanmar Citizenship Law that excluded them from the list of 135 national ethnic groups. The category of *non-state persons* has come into existence with the concept of citizenship, which on the one hand indicates certain rights, and on the other hand increases the miseries for those who are deprived of citizenship rights.

Sahana Basavapatna's chapter touches on various aspects of the legal situation of the Rohingya in India. One of the most important aspects of the Rohingya is their statelessness. Statelessness is one of the most pressing humanitarian issues of the twenty-first century. In law, statelessness is the lack of any nationality, or the absence of a recognized link between an individual and any state. There is not only a lack of systematic attention given to collecting reliable statistics but also a lack of consensus on whom to include when counting stateless people. There is a general agreement that ade jurestateless person is someone who is 'not considered as a national by any state under the operation of its law'.[26] However, there are millions of people who have not been formally denied or deprived of nationality but who lack the ability to prove their nationality or, despite documentation, are denied access to many human rights that citizens enjoy. These people may be de facto stateless – that is stateless in practice, if not in law – or they cannot rely on the state, of which they are citizens, for protection. Although individuals who have legal citizenship and its accompanying rights may take both for granted, what they enjoy is one extreme of a continuum between full, effective citizenship and de jurestatelessness, in which individuals have neither legal citizenship nor any attendant rights. In between these extremes are millions of de facto stateless persons denied effective protection.

People can be stateless for a variety of reasons, including inequitable laws (such as marriage laws), transfers of territory between countries, flawed or discriminatory administrative practices, lack of birth registration and the withdrawal or renunciation of citizenship rights. Conservative estimates of the current number of stateless persons in the world range from about eleven million to fifteen million who live without a nationality – in a legal limbo.

One of the main reasons why people are denied or deprived of nationality, and thus rendered stateless, is racial or ethnic discrimination. The denationalization and expulsion of tens of thousands of black Mauritanian citizens in 1989 was racially motivated. In Estonia, ethnic Russians have struggled with statelessness since independence in 1991. Likewise, Rohingya, a stateless minority, are also victims of ethnic discrimination. Ethnic and national identities have been effectively merged in Myanmar, with words like Burmese, Burman and Buddhist often being used interchangeably. Myanmar, as described by Brown, is an 'ethnocratic state', and Ne Win, head of state from 1962 to 1981, believed that one's 'Burmeseness' is something that Burman people are naturally endowed with. In an official message to fellow heads of mission, the Burmese Consulate General in Hong Kong said 'in reality, Rohingya are neither "Myanmar People", nor Myanmar's ethnic group . . . their complexion is "dark brown" . . . They are as ugly as ogres.'

For decades, the Muslims in Arakan, and particularly the Rohingya, have been subjected to excessive violence, human rights abuses, and forced resettlement both within Burma and across borders, which has created hundreds of thousands of refugees and internally displaced persons (IDPs) and has led to a protracted humanitarian crisis. Often compared to South Africa under the apartheid regime and the current situation in the West Bank, the situation has resulted in substantial political, social and economic marginalization of the Rohingya. Rather than addressing the underlying issues of historical interactions, political and socio-economic inequity and military aggression, there is a tendency by the Myanmar government to view the Rohingya themselves as the problem.

According to Van Hear, under the Constitution at the time of independence the Rohingya had a good claim to citizenship, yet today they are considered 'resident foreigners',[27] even though their families have been there for generations. As identified by Chris Lewa, the distribution of citizenship is often highly politicized, reinforcing hierarchies of power, which is clearly the case for the Rohingya.[28] Unlike the preceding 1948 Citizenship Act, the 1982 law is essentially based on the principle of *jus sanguinis*. Very few Rohingya can fulfil the requirements of citizenship.

In 1989, colour-coded citizens scrutiny cards (CRCs) were introduced: pink cards for full citizens, blue for associate citizens and green for naturalized citizens. The Rohingya were not issued any cards. In 1995, in response to UNHCR's intensive advocacy efforts to document the Rohingya, the Burmese authorities started issuing them temporary registration cards (TRCs), a white card, pursuant to the 1949 Residents of Burma Registration Act. The TRC does not mention the bearer's place of birth and cannot be used to claim citizenship.

Let us now briefly introduce the chapters of this book. In the first chapter, Sucharita Sengupta primarily traces the migration of Rohingya as asylum-seekers from Bangladesh to mainly Southeast Asian countries in boats and examines the reasons for the same. She shows how, in order to seek a better life, the Rohingya are compelled to take to the sea in perilous journeys to Southeast Asian countries like Malaysia, with Bangladesh and Thailand being the main transits. Despite risks, the accessibility of the sea as compared to land has ushered them into being trafficked to the Southeast and Middle East, and also to countries like Australia. The focus in this chapter is on their evolution as 'boat people' and the precariousness of their journey to seek out a secured territory. She points out that many do not even make it to the destination, perishing midway. The chapter traces the history and context of these maritime drives, arguing that the phenomenon is not new. Reasons that allure them to take to the sea from Bangladesh, reactions of the recipient countries, and also the recent media attention to the phenomenon generating mass awareness of the issue internationally, especially in Bangladesh, and to some extent in India are highlighted in this chapter. They are known as 'Asia's new boat people', and their plight is being compared to the 'Vietnamese exodus by boat in the 1970s'.

In the second chapter, Sahana Basavapatna looks at the dimensions of Rohingya refugees' lives in India. Variously represented as foreigners, Muslim, stateless, suspected Bangladeshi nationals, illiterate and impoverished, a large number have been and continue to be arrested for violation of the Foreigners Act, 1946, and the Passports (Entry into India) Act, 1929, among other legislation. A majority live in deplorable conditions in slums or unauthorized colonies. Unlike other mandate refugees, Rohingya are spoken of in the same breath as Bangladeshi nationals. Lastly, their proximity or collaboration with some Muslim organizations may have provided them with material advantages but not the credibility needed by a community seeking asylum from persecution. Against this background, the chapter approaches the Rohingya migration into India from a legal perspective. The primary focus is the way in which laws view the Rohingya in India, and in doing so the chapter provides a fragmentary account of Rohingya lives in Delhi, Jaipur, Jammu and Mewat. It is foregrounded in refugee experiences, analysing the plenary powers of the government of India vis-à-vis foreigners, the place of the new legal developments in the broader context of 'refugee law' and the extent to which being recognized as a refugee has secured rights for Rohingya. It also seeks to analyse developments in refugee law, one in which a state-led status determination mechanism appears implicit.

The third chapter, by Priyanca Mathur Velath and Kriti Chopra, seeks to document Rohingya in Hyderabad through primary interviews and establish the situation of refugees/stateless persons in India. The process of addressing any refugee issue has been hindered by the lack of an effective legal framework in India. If issues have been dealt in the past they have often been politically motivated, or actions have been taken mainly to improve diplomatic relations with a particular country. The existing laws in India, like the Foreigners Act of 1946, are completely outdated in the twenty-first century. In India, refugees are placed under three broad categories. Category I refugees receive full protection from the Government of India; Category II refugees are those who are granted refugee status by the UNHCR and are protected under the principle of non-refoulement; and Category III refugees are those who are neither recognized by the Government of India nor the UNHCR but have entered India and assimilated into the local community. There is a lack of clarity on the legal framework within which refugees and stateless persons stay on Indian soil, and hence people like the Rohingya will always be living in a state of limbo. These are some of the aspects that this chapter intends to explore through examining various aspects of the condition of the Rohingya in Hyderabad including their living condition, insecurity and the support structure.

The fourth chapter, by Suchismita Majumder, focuses on the Rohingya detained in the Correctional Homes of West Bengal, India. Through testimonies, narratives and analysis of the data gathered from February 2015 to July 2015, she tries to understand the lives of the Rohingya – how they live amidst persecution, what they do, how they migrate and what they need at present to have a life of a human being. The research is based on both primary and secondary sources of data. With these objectives the study conducts in-depth interviews with 100 Rohingya in the Correctional Homes. The data used in this study was collected in the above manner.

The fifth chapter, written by Madhura Chakraborty, focuses on media representations of Rohingya in Bangladesh and India to highlight how the Rohingya refugees enter into and shape popular discourse on asylum, refugee and infiltrators in these two countries. It also draws from primary interviews conducted in Bangladesh and Kolkata. The chapter examines how public opinion shapes the response of the nation states towards various stateless population groups.

The sixth chapter, by Charlotte-Anne Malischewski, looks into laws relating to statelessness. In this chapter, she has explored certain key concepts and their legal implications in India, for instance who is an 'illegal migrant' in India and how is citizenship defined in the context of India. She has also delved into questions like what is meant by right to nationality in international law, factors that give rise to a precarious condition of statelessness, the legal aspects of these concepts and so forth.

In the final chapter, Shuvro Prasun Sarker has examined the laws on statelessness in the Indian context, citing case laws and referring to parliamentary debates. He has pointed out that there are two UN conventions on statelessness, but these two cannot make India liable to go by their terms and conditions as India has not signed them. Therefore, the condition of people, turning stateless *de facto* on account of the arbitrary partitions of the Indian subcontinent, and due to the more recent exclusionary citizenship laws of a few South Asian nations, residing in India and elsewhere, is becoming more and more precarious.

In 2014, the UNHCR launched its campaign to end statelessness by 2024. In fact, a child is born stateless every ten minutes, and over a third of the world's stateless population are children, according to the UNHCR, which launched the 'I Belong' campaign. The UN Secretary-General and former UN High Commissioner for Refugees Antonio Guterres said: 'Statelessness makes people feel like their very existence is a crime.' Most situations of statelessness are a direct consequence of discrimination based on ethnicity, religion or gender. The largest stateless population of the world is in Myanmar, where more than one million Rohingya are refused nationality. Statelessness affects the enjoyment of all the rights which most of us take for granted, for instance the right to work, the right to vote, the right to welfare benefits and a child's right to education. Statelessness exacerbates poverty, creates social tensions, breaks up families and can even fuel conflict. Stateless people are not recognized as nationals by any country and are deprived of the rights most people take for granted. They often live on the margins of society where they are vulnerable to exploitation. Statelessness prevents people from moving and increases their chances of arbitrary arrest or detention with no adequate remedies. In short, it marginalizes people and makes them feel worthless with no prospect of their situation ever improving, no hope for a better future for themselves – in short, a situation of precarity.

International law provides a framework for action in respect of the stateless. Despite the existence of two significant legal documents, namely, the 1954 UN Convention Relating to the Status of Stateless Persons and the 1961 Convention on the Reduction of Statelessness, the critical mass to end statelessness is beyond our reach after so many years. Article 1 of the 1954 UN Convention relating to the Status of Stateless Persons defines a stateless person as 'a person who is not considered as a national by any State under the operation of its law'. The 1954 Convention establishes minimum guarantees in areas such as education, health care, employment and identity as well as travel documents. While it does not oblige states to provide nationality for stateless persons in its territory, it asks them to facilitate naturalization.

The 1961 Convention sets out important safeguards that can be incorporated into nationality laws to prevent statelessness, for example in relation to acquisition of a nationality at birth or loss of nationality on marriage, or as a result of prolonged residence abroad. In addition, international human rights law plays a significant and complementary role. Its guarantees apply to all persons, with very few provisions restricted to nationals alone. Key human rights standards include the obligation to ensure birth registration, the prohibition on arbitrary deprivation of nationality, guarantees of equal treatment for women in relation to nationality laws and protection against arbitrary detention. In regions where ratification of the UN statelessness conventions is poor, standards in human rights treaties that enjoy higher levels of participation assume importance.

Despite quite a number of global initiatives taken so far, new risks of statelessness have emerged. Moreover, low levels of ratification of the UN statelessness conventions raise questions about their impact and continued relevance. The Rohingya were and are being chased out of Myanmar. They were chased out of Bangladesh. Some of them reached India in phases. The UNHCR identity cards given to the registered Rohingya refugees are often not recognized as they are not issued by the government. Now, the Ministry of Home Affairs, Government of India tells them that India is not their country, and they would be identified and sent back. Where will they go? Most of them do not know about laws. Every country is kicking them around. From one country to another, people are playing with them. They simply would like the world to make a decision about them. They want the world to give them back their land that they can call their home. But in reality, they are being pushed to 'oblivion of rightlessness'.[29] This book is about their torment.

Notes

1 E. Brennan, 'Southeast Asia is reliving its boat people crisis', www.huffingtonpost. com/elliot-brennan-/southeast-asia-boat-people-crisis_b_7437498.html?ir= India&adsSiteOverride=in, accessed on 26 July 2015.

2 'Bangladeshi migrants' mass grave in Thailand', www.thedailystar.net/country/ mass-grave-bangladeshi-myanmar-migrants-found-thailand-80115, accessed on 26 July 2014.

3 'Myanmar army denies ethnic cleansing of Rohingyas in Rakhine state', www. abc.net.au/news/2017-03-01/myanmar-army-defends-operation-against-rohingya/8316654, accessed on 9 March 2017.

4 *Ibid.*

5 N. Kumar, 'Reprisals, rape, and children burnt alive: Burma's Rohingya speak of genocidal terror', http://time.com/4596937/burma-myanmar-rohingya-bangladesh-refugees-crimes-against-humanity/, accessed on 2 March 2017.

6   R. Tripathi, 'Rise in number of Rohingya Muslims settling in India set alarm bells among security agencies', http://articles.economictimes.indiatimes.com/2015-07-21/news/64682996_1_security-agencies-jammu-and-kashmir-myanmar, accessed on 10 October 2015.

7   Indo Asian News Service, 'Over 5,000 Rohingya Muslims settled in Jammu: Sayeed', https://in.news.yahoo.com/over-5-000-rohingya-muslims-settled-jammu-sayeed-154403590.html, accessed on 11 October 2015.

8   S. Shafi, 'Rohingya refugees find safe haven in Kashmir', www.aljazeera.com/indepth/inpictures/2014/12/rohingya-refugees-find-safe-h-20141223163741968194.html, accessed on 11 October 2015.

9   *Ibid.*

10   T. Yeoh, 'Egalitaria–Rohingya refugee rights', www.thesundaily.my/node/414481, accessed on 6 March 2017.

11   *Ibid.*

12   *Ibid.*

13   Interview conducted by SucharitaSengupta on behalf of CRG at Cox's Bazar on 3 July 2015.

14   For details, please see G.E. Harvey, *History of Burma: From the Earliest Times to 10 March 1824 The Beginning of the English Conquest*, New Delhi: Asian educational Services, 2000, first published from Calcutta: Longmans, Green and Co., 1925; Nijarranjan Ray, *An Introduction to the Study of Theravāda Buddhism in Burma: A Study in Indo-Burmese Historical and Cultural Relations from the Earliest Times to the British Conquest*, Calcutta, University of Calcutta, 1946, cited in Parimal Ghosh, *Brave Men of the Hills: Resistance and Rebellion in Burma 1825-1932*, C. Hurst & Co., 2000, p. 64.

15   C. J. Christie, *A Modern History of Southeast Asia: Decolonization, Nationalism and Separation*, New York: Tauris Academic Studies, and Singapore: Institute of Southeast Asian Studies, 1996, p. 164.

16   List of Districts, Townships, Cities/Towns, Wards, Village Groups and Villages in Union of Myanmar, Ministry of Home Affairs, Government of Union of Myanmar, 2001.

17   T. Kean, 'Kyaukphyu-Yunnan oil pipeline to be completed by end of 2015', *Myanmar Times*, 30 November 2009.

18   J. S. Gaung, 'Massive loan from China to fund gas investment', *Myanmar Times*, 13 December 2010.

19   For details, see M. Smith, *Burma: Insurgency and the Politics of Ethnicity*, London: Zed Books, 1991.

20   For details, please see V. Choudhury, 'The Arakani governors of Chittagong and their coins', *Journal of the Asiatic Society of Bangladesh*, Dhaka, 42(2): 145–62.

21   For further details, please see M. Yegar, 'The Muslims of Burma', in R. Israeli (ed.), *The Crescent in the East: Islam in Asia Major*, London: Curzon Press, 1982, p. 102.

22   S.G. Grantham, Census of India 1921, Vol. X, Part I, Rangoon, 1923, cited in S. Bhattacharya, *India-Myanmar Relations, 1886–1948*, Kolkata: K. P. Bagchi and Co., 2007, p. 374.

23   Yegar, 'The Muslims of Burma', p. 103.

24   Chapter 2, 'The Rakhine state of Myanmar in the realm of South Asia', in Swapna Bhattacharya, *The Rakhine State (Arakan) of Myanmar: Interrogating*

History, Culture and Conflict, New Delhi: Manohar Publishers, and Kolkata: MAKAIS, 2015, pp. 44–64.

25 Cho Thwin, 'Mindful Communication and Media Training', in Kalinga Seneviratne (ed.), *Mindful Communication for Sustainable Development: Perspectives From Asia*, New Delhi: Sage, 2018, p. 119.

26 Convention Relating to the Status of Stateless Persons, 1954, Article 1(1).

27 Nicholas Van Hear, New Diasporas: The Mass Exodus, Dispersal and Regrouping of Migrant Communities, London: UCL Press Limited, 1998, p. 229.

28 Chris Lewa, "North Arakan: An Open Prison for the Rohingya in Burma", Forced Migration Review, No. 32, p. 11.

29 H. Arendt, *The Origins of Totalitarianism*, New York: Schocken Books, 2004, pp. 353–5.

1

STATELESS, FLOATING PEOPLE

The Rohingya at sea

Sucharita Sengupta

> Here in this deep and boundless waste where shore is none to meet the eye/
> Thy utmost strivings are in vain; – here in mid-ocean thou must die.[1]

Deaths have been more rampant and normal than survival among migrants who have crossed raging high seas amidst dire uncertainties. The chapter epigraph is from a fable based on the Bay of Bengal, denoting how furious is the *kalapani*, that is the water of the bay. Most would not dare to cross it, but one who does cross it is bold enough, as goes the myth. The old Buddhist *jataka* stories tell us how in one of his previous births in the fourth century, Prince Polajanaka had attempted to cross the sea to reach 'Suvarnabhumi – the land of gold' in order to fight to win back the throne of his father from his brother. The book sketching this story is beautifully written by Sunil S. Amrith. It captures the Bay of Bengal through many such stories – in both its tranquillity and fury. In fact, not only on the bay, but also deaths in the seas have been as consistent as the voyages itself. Exploring the interconnectivity of the South Asia and the Southeast Asia, the bay was once 'at the heart of global history'. With formation of nation states and rigid land boundaries, the strategic importance of the bay lessened a bit in the twentieth century only to regain its lost glory in the twenty-first century. It now remains as the epitome of the 'largest movements of people in modern history'. Migration has remained consistent despite high risk. Although crossings had reduced in the mid-twentieth century, mobility of the sea marked by large-scale migration continued and reached its zenith in the twenty-first century. In this age, once again the bay has attained paramount importance in international politics. Politically, culturally and in trade and commerce the sea plays a crucial role in boosting interconnectivity and mobility in Asia, binding South and Southeast Asia into an integrated whole. The entire region has grown economically, promoting the economy of states like Malaysia and Thailand, resulting in a massive flow of labour and capital. Illegal migration has also increased simultaneously in precarious conditions. This chapter explores one such context when the sea holds promise of a sacrosanct destination just across it, almost similar to the 'land of gold' that the prince in Amrith's book is tempted to reach even if it means death.[2] Is then the illusion so extreme that migrants, despite risks, often willingly undertake these journeys? In other words, what is it in the sea that allures, and why is journey in boats most dreaded yet acceptable, are two of the questions this piece is plagued with and inquires about.

Instances

News report one: ' "Why Do We Have to Do This Death Trip?" Migrant Crisis Continues as Boat Capsizes Off Libya' reads one headline. The news is published in the *New Statesman* on 5 August 2015.[3] It says: 'As rescuers search the Mediterranean for hundreds of migrants after a boat capsized off the Libyan, Syrian refugees in the most popular Greek arrival point tell us death is unavoidable without any safe routes.'

News report two: 'Migrant Deaths in the Mediterranean Continue as 40 Bodies Found in Hull of Smugglers' Boat'. The news, published on 7 September 2015 in *The Independent*, talks of the deaths of 40 migrants in the Mediterranean due to suffocation on board. 'The Italian navy announced the deaths this afternoon as the rescue operation continued for around 300 other passengers off the coast of Libya.'[4]

News report three: From *New Internationalist* magazine, people, ideas and action for Global Justice publishes news on how search and rescue operations (SAR) have led to causing more death in the high seas, especially the Mediterranean. In 2014, the report says, approximately 3,000 migrants have died in the Mediterranean and in 2015, 1,700 deaths have been reported. On 19 April 2015, 700 deaths were reported after a boat capsized on the sea. Italy had initiated Operation Triton in order to SAR the migrants in the boats.[5]

These three news reports are among hundreds of such reports daily coming out in the media on migrant deaths in the high seas, validating the introductory lines from the fable. The present chapter would also discuss a particular context and migration across the Bay of Bengal, although in this case mobility has hardly led to forging a connection between the recipient countries and the community seeking asylum – the Rohingya.

The prelude

Since the Indian subcontinent was partitioned in 1947, it has witnessed continuous transborder and internal migration caused by ethnic violence, economic compulsions and other factors. The borders dividing India, Bangladesh and Myanmar in the post-colonial period, for instance, are porous, defying their governments to control population flows. Illegal migration has inevitably increased.

This chapter attempts to trace the seaborne migration of the Rohingya of Myanmar, the uncertain conditions they exist in and the precariousness of their destinies and destinations. A Muslim minority ethnic group from the Arakan province of Myanmar, the Rohingya have been in such a state of flux that they have been in no position to negotiate with a particular nation state to secure a home for themselves. Having been denied citizenship in Myanmar, they constitute one of the world's largest deracinated communities in existence. Their identity is, however, difficult to pin down and, in context, it is difficult to categorise the community as stateless, refugee or asylum-seeker. Following massive persecution in Myanmar, the Rohingya have been forced from the 1970s to flee to neighbouring countries like Bangladesh, separated from the Arakan only by the Naf River, to seek asylum. Since then, they have been living for a protracted period as refugees, mostly in the Cox's Bazar area of Bangladesh's Chittagong Hill Tracts in two camps, whose residents are not allowed to interact with the local population. They are supported by the Government of Bangladesh and the United Nations High Commissioner for Refugees (UNHCR), along with other organizations. After a new government came to power in Bangladesh in January 2009, followed by fresh violence in Myanmar in 2012, it has adopted strict measures to stop the inflow.

An attempt has been made here to trace the Rohingya journey not from Myanmar itself, but from Bangladesh to Southeast Asian countries across the Bay of Bengal and Strait of Malacca and investigate the circumstances that prompt the 'Bangladeshi Rohingya' to flee overland to India and across the seas to Thailand and Malaysia. Several questions crop up: Do they remain asylum-seekers or become economic migrants? What is it that compels them to take to the sea on perilous journeys, usually in fishing trawlers, to cross to Malaysia, and why is the role of Bangladesh crucial? What are the conditions that reduce the Rohingya to being a community of 'boatpeople', compelled to risk their lives in their search for settlement and livelihood? The transformation of the Rohingya into a boat people will be the main focus of this chapter. Mapping this maritime and terrestrial journey through various legal regimes, this piece argues that the outcomes faced by the community have been historically inevitable.

My fieldwork in Bangladesh shows that it is generally members of the second and third generations of Rohingya, between the ages of 18 and 21, who are trying to leave Bangladesh mainly for Southeast Asia.[6] In this chapter I examine why this is so, for which understanding the history of the region, especially Bangladesh, is important. Already settled in the two refugee camps or in makeshift settlements in Cox's Bazar, these young men and women are taking to the sea to seek jobs in the Southeast Asia countries. Despite the risks, greater access to sea routes, in comparison to those across land, makes migrating, or often being trafficked, to Southeast Asia and Australia easier, even though they end up all too often in border-detention camps where they either die or become bonded labourers. The 'pull' factors which draw them into the smuggling-trafficking nexus, involving many regional and international actors, will be analysed. The three primary themes that will be discussed are: the evolution of Rohingya as boat people; the legal regimes to protect them; and their lives in camps in Bangladesh and the reasons for which they want to leave that country.

There are two broad sections in the chapter: one deals with the overall history of the region, of crossing the sea, the coinage of the term 'boat people' and the subsequent mixed flow of Rohingya and Bangladeshis over the seas; the other deals with the lives of Rohingya in the camps and explores the reasons behind Bangladesh producing the largest number of migrants in the world. The first section is based mainly on news chapters housed in Bangladeshi archives and online media resources. The second section is based on primary material and interviews with residents of the camps in the Teknaf area of Noyapara and the Kutupalong area of Ukhiya in Cox's Bazar and also people living in makeshift settlements, where unregistered Rohingya have been living without any formal acknowledgement or permission from the government. Because we did not have formal access to the camps, we mainly interviewed both registered and unregistered Rohingya in the makeshift camps, commonly known as *leda*. These settlements are scattered just outside the formal camp areas. We talked to approximately forty people about their lives in Bangladesh and why members of their families or people from the neighbourhood have been leaving for other destinations. Some of these narratives also describe their sea voyages. Information was also gathered from officials of various non-governmental organizations (NGO) and human rights organizations of Bangladesh.

The context

Since May 2015, the international and Bangladesh media have been abuzz with news reports and video clips of boats full of migrants from Bangladesh and Myanmar that were adrift. Countries in Southeast Asia were expected to help rescue the migrants and provide asylum. What was unveiled, however, was a petrifying picture of death, a smuggling-trafficking nexus and torture on the high seas and border-detention camps. It was after thirty-two shallow graves were discovered on a remote and rugged mountain in the border district of Sadao in Songkhla, Thailand, in 2015 that the enormity of the problem was exposed by media activism.[7] The migrants were a mix of Rohingya and Bangladeshis. Bangladesh was first in a state of denial, then shocked over claims that the boats were carrying Bangladeshi nationals. They finally came up with the response that the Bangladeshi nationals had been kidnapped whereas the Rohingya had willingly embarked on these precarious journeys. Dainik Janakantha, a local Bengali daily published from Bangladesh, reported on 8 May 2015 that many Bangladeshis had gone missing from the regions of Cox's Bazar, Pekua, Maheshkhali, Ramu and Shatkania, Lohagara and Bandarban of Chittagong.[8] Most of these men had been victims of trafficking. They had been lured with the promise of prosperity in Malaysia, but before they could reach there, they were kidnapped and imprisoned in Thai border-detention camps. Investigations indicated that 200,000 Bangladeshis and Rohingya had attempted to cross the sea in order to reach Malaysia. Most of them had been forced to do so. According to another report on 14 May 2015, the UNHCR has claimed that around 87,000 people have been trafficked across the Bay of Bengal since 2013–14.[9] Several syndicates operate in these four countries targeting poor Bangladeshis for ransom. The Rohingya, however, migrate because the UNHCR issues Rohingya refugee cards in Malaysia and they are not arrested there. This, coupled with the image of Malaysia being a dream destination, increasingly prompts Rohingya to migrate there.

A senior *Daily Star* reporter, S. Ashraf, visited the Thai border and interviewed migrants there.[10] He was also present at a meeting of states concerned in Bangkok on 29 May 2015.[11] Ashraf stressed the fact that Bangladeshis found in boats crossing the sea had been kidnapped, so their reasons to be in the boats clearly were different from those of the Rohingya found on board. There are two ways of illegally trafficking Bangladeshis. Either they are kidnapped or children below 18 are promised tours of Malaysia and then imprisoned in detention camps. He talked of a particular case in which a group of young boys, who had never seen the sea before and hailed from a very poor region of Bangladesh, was tempted to cross the sea. Once the boys boarded the ship, they were kept hungry and finally locked in a room at one of the transit points. So while Bangladeshis were being trafficked, Rohingya genuinely wanted to leave Bangladesh for better opportunities, usually work in rubber plantations. Women were hardly ever found on these boats, and the few found were always Rohingya. Ashraf claimed no Bangladeshi woman has yet been found to have taken to the sea.

The *New York Times* had reported that 6,000 to 20,000 people had been found in 'rickety flotillas' in the Andaman Sea and the Strait of Malacca.[12] After the graves were discovered in Thailand, the Thai government took strict measures to crack down on the traffickers.[13] Initially, after the Rohingya and Bangladeshis were abandoned at sea by traffickers, Malaysia had turned away two boats with more than 800 persons on board, and Thailand had also 'kept at bay a third boat with hundreds more'.[14] A Malaysian deputy minister had stated that Rohingya would not be welcomed anymore after they illegally entered Malaysia in boats. The Thai prime minister had also claimed that they lacked resources to host these refugees. Another boat was spotted on the maritime border between Thailand and Malaysia.[15] On receipt of news that Malaysia, Indonesia and Thailand had denied assistance to migrants, Zeid Ra'ad al-Hussein, the UN human rights chief, issued a statement saying:

> I am appalled at reports that Thailand, Indonesia and Malaysia have been pushing boats full of vulnerable migrants back out to sea, which will inevitably lead to many avoidable deaths. The focus should be on saving lives, not further endangering them.[16]

A UNHCR report on illegal maritime migration between April and June 2015 said 6,000 refugees had been abandoned by smugglers in the Bay of Bengal and Andaman Sea in May 2015. Since 2014, approximately 94,000 migrants had attempted to cross the seas. In the first three months of 2015, the figure was 25,000, which between April and August 2015 increased to 31,000 with 370 deaths in 2015 alone. This UNHCR report gave a day-to-day account of what unfolded between May and July 2015 after the migrants had been abandoned at sea. The UNHCR report is titled 'South-East Asia: Mixed Maritime Movements'.[17] This, in brief, is the backdrop to the present crisis.

History and the current scenario of the boat people in Southeast Asia

There is an uncanny resemblance of the Rohingya exodus with that of the Vietnamese boat people in the mid-1970s. The Vietnamese had also sought refuge in Southeast Asian countries like Indonesia and Malaysia before being accepted by Europe, North America and Australia.[18] The term 'boat people' was coined at this time while describing the escape of Vietnamese people from communist rule following the Vietnam War. The Vietnamese also fled in small boats, most often wooden fishing boats, after the Chinese invasion of Vietnam in 1979. Before the latter exodus, no other incident of people fleeing in boats to seek asylum had drawn worldwide attention. More than a million people fled Indochina after the war, and many perished either by drowning or at the hands of pirates. The survivors were accepted as refugees in the United States, Canada and Southeast Asian countries in the late 1970s and 1980s.[19]

The 'Boat for Vietnam' Committee was formed on 27 November 1978, when more than 160 prominent Parisians signed an appeal to stop the exodus. The crisis was alarming, because with each passing day more and more boats were reaching Malaysia, the Philippines, Indonesia and Hong Kong. Refugee camps were already full when suddenly the Malaysian vice president announced his country would not accept any more refugees and pushed 76,000 boat people back to the sea.[20] To ensure greater and more binding protection, and more resettlement commitments worldwide, in particular from Western countries like the United States, an international convention was organized in Geneva after the first phase of the Vietnamese crisis aiming to solve the crisis.[21]

There has been always a tendency to perceive boat people as a threat – countless incidents of pushing vessels back into the high seas testify to this. For instance, Australia has time and again expressed intolerance towards boat people arriving there. It flouted maritime rules by ordering the MV *Tampa* to return to sea in dangerous weather conditions.[22] This was a landmark event in the history of the boat people's migration that made Australia review its policy regarding disembarkation of boats and providing asylum to the people on board.[23] This policy was known as the 'Pacific strategy' with countries like New Zealand, Nauru, Papua New Guinea and Indonesia being parties to it. On 26 August 2001, MV *Tampa*, a Norwegian container ship, rescued 433 asylum-seekers from a boat (the *Palapa*) which was sinking between Indonesia and Christmas Island within Australian maritime jurisdiction. The captain of the *Tampa* was informed by the Australian Maritime Safety Authority about the *Palapa*. However, the *Tampa* was not allowed to dock at an Australian port and was redirected towards the island of Nauru. Over the next few months, New Zealand accepted 150 people from the *Tampa*. Despite being a party to several maritime conventions, and under obligation to provide asylum to refugees as per the 1951 Refugee Convention, Australia had violated several rules in regard to the *Tampa*.[24]

In the wake of the present crisis, the Australian government took a similar stance. Then Australian Prime Minister Tony Abbott went on record to say that allowing the refugees – in this case a mixed group of Rohingya and Bangladeshis – to enter Australia would encourage more such illegal sea voyages.[25] Historically, maritime migrants have always been more vulnerable than their terrestrial counterparts, especially because they can be tracked more easily or identified as pirates, or they can simply drown. Activists have even called the Mediterranean Sea a 'maritime cemetery'.

Search to rescue or to kill?

Search and rescue operations have, paradoxically, increased fatalities. Often migrants jump into the sea in desperation, failing to comprehend the reasons for interception. The question is whether interception of migrant boats is a rescue measure or one to tighten security. Interception is defined as the process of preventing a boat's onward movement after locating it. The state can either carry passengers on an intercepted vessel in one of its own vessels or force the former to alter course. This might occur in both jurisdictional and international waters.[26] Interception can also be used by a state to prevent the arrival of a ship into its jurisdiction.[27] Rescue, however, 'is the practice of assisting seaborne persons in some form of trouble or distress'. But in the guise of rescue boats have actually been intercepted, leading to more casualties. So the question is whether rescue operations are humanitarian and achieve the intended objectives. In fact, rescue operations begin with intercepting boats. Italy, for instance, had initiated a search and rescue operation after a boat wreck in Lampedusa. Daniele Esibini, the captain of one of the coastguard ships, revealed the danger of such rescue operations. The first problem is overloaded boats which 'leads to them capsizing – frequently exactly at the point of rescue. He has never come across a boat that was not overloaded and therefore dangerous.' He further states, 'The most dangerous part of a search-and-rescue operation is the moment of rescue. As rescuers approach, the very human reaction is to stand up and wave to guide your rescuers. If the [passengers] stand up, the boat capsizes.' The operation was abandoned after criticism from the European Union.[28]

While rescue operations are important, there is also a need to examine the situation after a boat is rescued by humanitarian agencies.[29] The human rights of migrants become crucial at this juncture, and it is important to ensure that the rescued ships are docked at a safe location. If a shipwreck occurs within the jurisdiction of a state,[30] or if boat people manage to reach the shore, the responsibility of the recipient state is to help in safe disembarkation. But ambiguity shrouds these procedures and relevant laws,[31] which usually work against the boat people and put them in a disadvantageous position. It should be borne in mind that in most cases, boat people are actually asylum-seekers in need of refuge. Although a substantial number of them are also economic migrants, the line between volition and coercion, searching for a safe place following threats to life and being compelled to move for economic reasons is very thin – the Rohingya provide a compelling example.

In 1975, the Executive Committee (EXCOM) of the UNHCR identified the need to address problems when asylum-seekers reached the maritime jurisdiction of a country, which led to the adoption of a series of mechanisms by the UNHCR. The first concern of asylum-seekers is to identify a safe destination, even if it means escaping in overcrowded vessels which are often at risk of sinking; many do, in fact, sink. A state has twin responsibilities to render assistance and help in search and rescue operations. The need for effective search and rescue operations, therefore, is a prerequisite. Article 98(1) of the United Nations Convention on the Law of the Sea(UNCLOS) lays down that 'if any vessel is in trouble at sea, the crews of all other ships are under an obligation to rescue those in distress.' It says:

> Every state shall require the master of a ship flying its flag, in so far as he can do [so] without serious danger to the ship, the crew or the passengers: (a) to render assistance to any person found at sea in danger of being lost; (b) to proceed with all possible speed to the rescue of persons in distress, if informed of their need for assistance, in so far as such action may reasonably be expected of him. This rescue is one form of humanitarianism.

Article 98(2) states that:

> Every coastal state shall promote the establishment, operation and maintenance of an adequate and effective search and rescue service regarding safety on and over the sea and where circumstances so require, by way

of mutual regional arrangements co-operate with neighbouring States for this purpose.[32]

Legal regimes and their complexities

The Rohingya are now the world's most persecuted minority without citizenship. Currently numbering around 33,788,[33] Rohingya registered with the UNHCR in Bangladesh live in two camps (Kutupalong camp and Nayapara camp) in Cox's Bazar – a tourist spot in Bangladesh with the world's largest unbroken beach. Unofficially, however, around 300,000 to 500,000 unregistered refugees live in abject poverty just outside the formal camps. They do not have access to food and shelter provided by the government or work permits. In order to seek a better life, they are now being compelled to take to the sea in perilous journeys to Southeast Asian countries like Malaysia, with Thailand being the main transit country. Labelled Asia's new boat people and compared to the Vietnamese,[34] thousands of Rohingya depend on countries willing to provide shelter and freedom. Malaysia and Thailand have been receiving Rohingya for a decade without any specific policy in this regard.

In 2007 a trawler carrying Rohingya was being smuggled to Malaysia, but it sank in the Bay of Bengal. Only eighty boarders survived. A week later, another boat sank, killing another 150 migrants. On 3 March 2008, twenty-two persons, most of whom were Rohingya, were saved by the Sri Lankan navy from a boat that had drifted into the Indian Ocean. According to a survey conducted under the Arakan Project, more than 8,000 boat people had departed from the coast of Bangladesh to Malaysia, through Thailand, between October 2006 and March 2008. So migration or trafficking of Rohingya from Bangladesh through sea routes is not a new phenomenon.[35] However, following the discovery of mass graves, and with international organizations like the United Nations (UN) and International Organization for Migration (IOM) urging Myanmar to take responsibility and appealing to Southeast Asian countries to act on humanitarian grounds, these countries first denied refuge but began accepting migrants after the meeting in Bangkok on 29 May.

Bangladeshi nationals have only recently joined Rohingya in taking to the sea. This complicates matters: asylum-seekers cannot be termed illegal, but the issue is clouded because boats carrying Rohingya now also carry Bangladeshis who are neither 'stateless' nor 'asylum-seekers'. The problem is that Rohingya are known in Myanmar and to the world as 'Bengalis' because of linguistic similarities. Their dialect matches that of the people of Chittagong, especially those Rohingya who have been living in Bangladesh for years or who have been born and brought up there, so it is very difficult to distinguish between them. Although legally the Rohingya residing within the camps are not allowed to interact with the locals, they do, working in the informal sector, for instance, pulling rickshaws – this interaction has deepened the similarity of language/dialect and habits. Therefore, the issue of rendering aid to this mixed group of migrants from Bangladesh and Myanmar has become problematic, especially because Bangladeshis often claim to be Rohingya.

A. Munier, the IOM protection officer in Cox's Bazar, who is also in charge of working with unregistered refugees in the makeshift camps in Teknaf, says:

> The process of carrying Bangladeshi nationals along with the Rohingyas in boats have been going on since the last ten to twelve years. There were police reports of young boys going missing in the adjourning areas of Cox's Bazaar, but the reasons were unknown till now. It is only due to the media reports in May and June 2015 that we could fathom the exact figures and amount of boat migration that has been going on. Historically, labour migration from Bangladesh to Malaysia was allowed by both the governments in 2010 and even long before it, Rohingyas have been going to Malaysia primarily because it is a Muslim country and there is an active labour market with a demand for cheap labour. After labour migration from Bangladesh to Malaysia was allowed, a boom in the trafficking racket also followed. The traffickers are well aware of the areas from where they can lure Bangladeshi nationals along with the Rohingyas . . . and they are targeted because they are likely to pay bigger ransoms that what the Rohingyas can afford.[36]

The IOM is in charge of providing health facilities, sanitation and capacity building facilities to unregistered Rohingya since 2009–10. In collaboration with the Bangladesh government, it also organizes medical facilities near the camps.

Over the last year, the Bangladesh government has decided to resettle the 32,000 registered Rohingya to a different region because Cox's Bazar is primarily a tourist area and the smuggling-trafficking nexus in the region has led to a lot of anti-social activities, including drug smuggling. The place where the registered camps might shift is a barren island in the Bay of Bengal called Thengar Char. It is Prime Minister Sheikh Hasina's desire that the Rohingya people be relocated, says the police chief of Hatiya, Mohammad Nazrul Huda.[37] The government, however, is silent about the fate of the unregistered refugees. Hence, despite being recognized as stateless or refugees by the UNHCR, the Rohingya have been living in extreme adversity, sometimes even being denied proper shelter. Some of them have received temporary refugee cards from the UNHCR but have still been subjected to violations of basic human rights. While the registered Rohingya in Bangladesh are comparatively better off in terms of receiving food and shelter from the UNHCR, sanctioned by the government, they still live in appalling conditions, denied freedom of movement or access to sufficient food, water and sanitation till recently. The government has now taken the initiative to distribute cards to families of registered refugees, with which they can buy the necessary quantity of food. This has been a positive development because previously only a fixed amount of food was distributed by the authorities per family. While the camp refugees we spoke to are happy with this step, it is not enough because there is a limit on the quantity a family can buy with the food cards.

There were reports prior to August 2017 that thousands of Rohingya children have been barred by the Bangladeshi authorities from attending public schools, as they are not officially registered. Instead they receive a religious education where they mainly memorize the Quran in the Islamic classrooms called maktabs. In contrast, the children of refugees living in the UN-registered camps were able to go to school. In fact, the number of such unregistered refugees has increased manifold since the fresh influx of refugees since August 2017.[38]

After the Awami League was voted into power, the influx of the Rohingya was combated with harsh measures. Sources in Bangladesh, not willing to be identified, told us that adopting strict measures to combat illegal migration from Myanmar was on the Awami League agenda before the national elections. Keeping its promise, vigilance was increased at the shores in the Naf area. Following a fresh Rohingya exodus in 2012, it is alleged that the Border Guard Bangladesh (BGB) had pushed back several boats carrying Rohingya to Myanmar, as a result of which they were forced to turn to countries like Thailand and Malaysia. A sharp rise of sea voyages from Bangladesh was also recorded in 2012.

It was obvious that none of them wanted to return to Myanmar. Some of them were arrested by the BGB on grounds of illegal entry. In India, too, Rohingya have been indiscriminately incarcerated for illegal infiltration. Although India and Bangladesh are not parties to the 1951 Refugee Convention, they have agreed to a number of international legal instruments, including the Universal Declaration of Human Rights (UDHR). Article 14 of the UDHR states: 'Everyone has the right to seek asylum and to enjoy in other countries asylum from persecution.' Paragraph one of Article 3 of the Convention Against Torture, of which Bangladesh is a signatory, also says: 'No State Party shall expel, return ["refouler"] or extradite a person to another State where there are substantial grounds for believing that he would be in danger of being subjected to torture.' Hence, Bangladesh and India cannot, on humanitarian grounds, violate the principle of non-refoulement, despite not being signatories to the 1951 convention or the 1967 Additional Protocol, and cannot term Rohingya infiltrators or illegal migrants because they are asylum-seekers. The strategy of refoulement has followed when they have embarked upon the sea as well, either from their homeland of Myanmar, where they are living under continuous persecution, or from other states like Bangladesh, where they are living in a limbo. It has been clearly stated by the UNHCR that the two international conventions on refugees will be applicable to maritime migrants as well if they are found to be refugees or asylum-seekers. Here again is the complication of intermixing, because Bangladeshis are not asylum-seekers and the conventions are not applicable to them.

According to the guidelines on rescue at sea jointly prepared by the UNHCR and IOM,

> If people rescued at sea claim to be refugees or asylum-seekers, or indicate in any way that they fear persecution or ill-treatment if disembarked at a particular place, key principles prescribed by international refugee law need to be upheld. The Master is not responsible for determining the status of rescued persons.[39]

Article 33[1] of the 1951 Refugee Convention also clearly states that refugees or asylum-seekers cannot be returned to the territory where their lives are under threat. This refers not only to the country of origin from where they are fleeing, but also includes the territory where they might face a threat to security. Even

> [r]escued persons who do not meet the criteria of the 1951 Refugee Convention definition of a 'refugee', but who fear torture or other serious human rights abuses or who are fleeing armed conflict may also be protected from return to a particular place ('refoulement') by other international or regional human rights or refugee law instruments.[40]

This is applicable even for maritime migrants if they are asylum-seekers. Clearly a violation of rules repeatedly took place with the Rohingya, particularly when some of them were found stranded at sea. No state was willing to allow disembarkation within its maritime jurisdiction. Although the rescue at sea guidelines further states that governments and rescue coordination centres have the responsibility to ensure a 'place of safety' to ships in distress,[41] governments have been found playing insensitively with the lives of thousands crammed in rickety boats, neither rescued nor allowed to land, blaming each other and debating whose responsibility it is to provide protection and asylum.

States concerned feign ignorance of the plight of the Rohingya. Pushing back Rohingya travelling either over land or sea has been the policy followed by most governments. As a result many Rohingya have either perished in the seas or have been living in detention camps as bonded labourers along the Thai-Malaysian border. On the other hand, when it comes to employing people in the most labour-intensive industries, it is the Rohingya who are chosen. Thus the expansion of a well-knit trafficking network connecting Myanmar, Thailand, Indonesia, Malaysia and Bangladesh to take innocents on perilous journeys was with the bait of providing work opportunities. The sea is the most accessible route because Rohingya settlements in Bangladesh are mainly in Cox's Bazar, which is a coastal area. While young men are trafficked to Thailand, Philippines and Malaysia and robbed, women and children are increasingly being trafficked for sexual exploitation to these countries and India. Economic considerations are major pull factors for young boys, because they are not allowed to work in Bangladesh, even if they are registered with the UNHCR.

Maritime migration has increased exponentially from 2006, when Malaysia started registering Rohingya for residence or work permits. The process was soon suspended due to allegations of fraud and trafficking. Around USD 300 was charged for a sea passage to southern Thailand and USD700–1,000 for one to Malaysia. A big network of officials, brokers and agencies is involved in this process and operates in these countries. Till March 2007, arrested boat people on the southern coast of Thailand were deported to a cease-fire zone in Myanmar, close to Mae Sot. They were released after paying USD700 and taken back to Thailand or Malaysia. In the initial years, many managed to reach their destination and find jobs. Many have settled in Malaysia, which has encouraged others to follow suit, taking the same risks. But with more and more migrants reaching these countries, the authorities have become more cautious about allowing them in. Still, instead of a reduction in the number of migrants, figures have increased. While traffickers continue to lure people to make these journeys, very few make it to their destinations and find work. In most cases, even after ransoms had

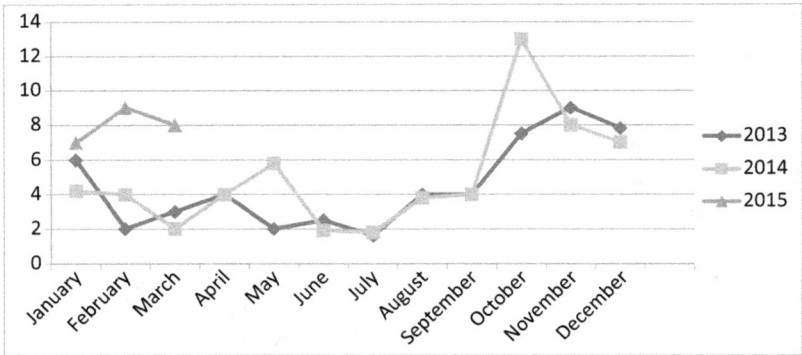

FIGURE 1.1 Estimated number of people making irregular departures by sea from Bangladesh/Myanmar border (in thousands)

Source: www.economist.com/news/asia/21651877-poverty-politics-and-despair-are-forcing-thousands-rohingyas-flee-myanmar-authorities, accessed on 27 July 2015

been paid, migrants were not released. Many are killed or simply die from hunger, resulting in mass graves – some of which, as mentioned, were discovered in 2015. It was believed that the Thai authorities had been handing them over to the brokers along the Thai-Malaysia borders. Those who were unable to pay ransoms were sold to plantation owners or fishing boats as bonded labour. The problem with the authorities in these countries is that instead of viewing the Rohingya as asylum-seekers, they are considered economic migrants and security threats.[42] Figure 1.1 shows that the maritime movement of Rohingya in the years 2013–15 has been very irregular.

Narratives from the two camps in Bangladesh

Women from among the Rohingya have mainly attempted to cross the sea attracted by promises of marriage, work and a better future. Tahera Bibi, age 17, who is registered and lives in the Kutupalong camp in Ukhiya of Bangladesh, has studied in the camp till class 7. We met her outside the camp, in the house of a local NGO worker, introduced to us by a research organization based in Dhaka. Our driver, Mohiuddin, who took us to the camps, and the person associated with the NGO were our interpreters. Tahera was one among thirteen women, all of them from the registered Kutupalong camp, surrounded by ten men. We wanted to know whether any of them had ever attempted to go to Malaysia over the seas, but we were greeted by silence. We were later told that camp-dwellers had been avoiding this subject because of increased surveillance by the government following the recent crisis. After much persuasion, an elder woman persuaded Tahera to narrate her story. After completing her formal studies, she worked on an initiative started by BRAC (formerly known as the Bangladesh Rehabilitation Assistance Committee), an international NGO based in Dhaka, known as 'Save the Children'. Although there was no official permit for it, she worked there for three years and got BDT1,000 a month. At this time, she heard of Malaysia from a friend. 'As you know, our society does not give us freedom to work but I heard there was scope for work in Malaysia even for girls,' she told us. She also got a proposal of marriage from a person of her community settled in Malaysia. (Tahera was reluctant to divulge details of how she met this person or whether she had met him before landing in Malaysia, or who the middleman was facilitating the connection. She confessed, however, to having spoken to this man over the phone a few times before meeting him in person.) With dreams of a better life and the hope of freedom, Tahera decided to leave for Malaysia. The agent who had helped Tahera was also a Rohingya from Teknaf. The money for her travel was arranged by her would-be husband, who was working as a labourer in Malaysia. The total amount paid was BDT 150,000.

> We were first taken to a small boat which was carrying around eighty persons. From there we were taken to a ship where the number of persons rose to 160. The journey from the small boat to the ship took around fourteen hours. The ship first took us to the Thailand border, which took around twelve days, where we were kept in a cave for five days. From there we were taken to Malaysia, first in a small boat and then in a car. We were taken to the Thai-Malaysia border – Badamosha – where we were caught by the police and taken into custody. I spent four months in the prisons of Malaysia.

Her husband tried to help her by contacting the UNHCR office, which could not help because she had been booked for entering Malaysia illegally and did not have a UNHCR registration card. As a last resort, therefore, she paid a hefty sum as bail and fled back to Bangladesh. Tahera, clearly uncomfortable, remained silent on being asked whether she was sexually harassed in the vessel; several UNHCR reports say almost all women who have embarked upon migration by sea have been sexually assaulted either on ships or in border-detention camps.

Hatis Sultan Mohammad, another resident of the Kutupalong Camp, talked about his son who has been missing since 2012. He was studying in class 7 and had not informed his family before leaving. It was from other sources and friends that Mohammad came to know that his son had left for

Malaysia. Since then they know nothing about his whereabouts, or whether he is even alive. Sanoara Begum, his wife, said they had been living in this camp from 2000. Because they were extremely poor, they did not have enough food and had no work opportunities. Her son had attempted to cross the sea for employment. She said they were generally helped by middlemen who were either Rohingya or Bangladeshis.[43]

Zahida Begum, age 28, has been living outside the camp area for nine years. She and her family are unregistered. She came to Bangladesh with her husband and two children after being attacked in Myanmar, crossing the Naf river in a boat. They had to pay MMK 6,000. Her husband was working as a daily labourer clandestinely, but his earnings were not enough for daily sustenance. Zahida said that they also wanted to leave for Malaysia because they had heard of lots of job opportunities in Malaysia. 'But do you still want to go, when so many have died or abducted?' I asked them.

> There are risks, yes, but if once we can reach there we will have a better life. Is it possible to live here, in this way? During monsoon we face the toughest time. We can't work, have to live constantly hiding our identity, or else would be imprisoned. Whereas in Malaysia there is ample work opportunity couple with security of life.[44]

On the next day, we visited the settlement areas outside the Teknaf camp. We were introduced to 60-year-old Abdul Mafalat. He has been living with his family outside the camp for thirteen years after leaving the Mungdow district of Myanmar. Mafalat is the informal representative of their settlement area. It was decided he would talk on behalf of the entire camp. Most of the residents of this settlement area came to Bangladesh after the violence of 2012 in Myanmar. They were registered and work as daily labourers, receiving BDT 200–500 for their work. We were amazed to see small shops within the settlement area. There was no clear answer about how they collected the capital necessary to start these shops. Mafalat crossed over to Bangladesh with his wife and two children; his eldest son left for Malaysia long ago. Although they are not in regular contact, he knows his son is earning well over there. The work is precarious, but being in Malaysia is better than living in Myanmar or in Bangladeshi camps. It is unfortunate, however, Mafalat said, that many in his neighbourhood have lost their sons to sea voyages. They are either dead or missing or detained in border camps.

From these accounts and interviews taken in both the camps and with various UNHCR officials and respondents at the US embassy in Dhaka, it is clear that there is a strong desire among the Rohingya to leave their camp lives and move to a 'free space' in search of job and livelihood. It is also evident that despite strict measures taken by the Bangladesh government to restrict the movement of the Rohingya – both registered and unregistered – interaction between those living in the camps and the settlements, and the local population continues. The Rohingya have many Bangladeshi friends who help them buy food and work outside their restricted space.

Pushed and pulled

As noted earlier, officials we spoke to opined that while the Rohingya had crossed the sea voluntarily in overcrowded boats, Bangladeshis had usually been abducted. On the contrary, Mohiuddin and some Bangladeshis we were introduced to by him told us that they wanted to leave the country. We were surprised and asked them the reason. 'Didi, we have heard India has more job opportunities. Can you make arrangements for us to go to India, somehow? Our job security is tenuous here and most of us are unemployed. Surely India can offer us jobs.' The allure of India seemed to be a better quality of life.

The Rohingya and Bangladeshis in Bangladesh, thus, have increasingly become victims of trafficking rackets operating by offering often chimerical safe refuges or economic opportunities, once in West Asia, but increasingly in Southeast Asian countries. They are ferried in small boats, mainly fishing trawlers, to a large ship where they are grouped with more persons from other boats. This ship then carries them first to the Thai coast and then to the final destination, Malaysia, through the Bay of Bengal, Andaman Sea and the Strait of Malacca.

According to a report, the transnational human traffickers have kept around 250,000 Bangladeshis captive in Thailand, extracting huge amounts as ransom. First, local brokers get BDT 5,000–10,000 for each person and their bosses anything in the range of BDT 15,000–30,000. They are not released till a sum of BDT 200,000–350,000 is paid. Often, even after this amount is paid, families are unable to trace the victims. Most of the transactions are carried out through various mobile banking services. In 2014, according to a UNHCR report, 53,000 persons went to Thailand and Malaysia from Bangladesh.[45] According to the UNHCR, between January and March 2015, 25,000 persons (40–60 per cent of them Rohingya) have departed across the Bay of Bengal and around 300 are estimated to have died. Around 5,400 are languishing in detention centres in either Thailand or Malaysia. The figures have doubled from what was reported in the first quarters of 2013 and 2014.

Migration of women has also increased. Like Tahera, many are said to have been lured with the promise of marriage or abducted. The money is paid by their 'prospective husbands'. Usually, however, they are sold into the sex trade. Most 'migrants', both men and women, are under below the age of 18. Since October 2014, boats departing from Sittwe (in Myanmar) have carried 30 to 100 passengers, with arrangements usually handled by friends or associates. These passengers are allowed to carry their own food on board. But even these boats have either fallen in the hands of smugglers or have been attacked during disembarkation in Thailand. The conditions during the journey across the Bay of Bengal and Andaman Sea continue to be dire. Women passengers, who have been interviewed by the UNHCR, have also talked about sexual abuses and rapes on board.

Contextualizing Bangladesh: a migrants' nation

This section is crucial to comprehending why Bangladeshis, mostly from Chittagong (and specifically Cox's Bazar), have also been found on the boats along with the Rohingya. India, Bangladesh and Myanmar have the same colonial past and the countries, despite today's boundaries, have remained tied with one another socially, culturally, politically, geographically and economically. The Awami League government has, on the one hand, adopted strict measures to stop the influx of Rohingya into Bangladesh; on the other hand, it has made it clear that Bangladesh needs Myanmar for its own economic benefits. Myanmar is the only country with which it shares a boundary in Southeast Asia. With Myanmar's increasing role in both the Association of Southeast Asian Nations (ASEAN) and Bay of Bengal Initiative for Multi-Sectoral Technical and Economic Cooperation, Bangladesh cannot suspend diplomatic ties with the country on the Rohingya issue.[46] Hence it has addressed the issue cautiously, particularly in the context of mixed maritime population flows.

Historically, one should also note that Bangladesh is one of the highest-ranking countries in migration, especially for work. According to the IOM, around five million Bangladeshis are currently working overseas in various countries. Migration has been recognized as an important livelihood option for Bangladeshi nationals. Remittances sent by migrants officially amounted to USD 11 billion in 2010. It is the seventh highest remittance-receiving country. In 2014 it received USD 14.94 billion as remittance, 5.3 per cent higher than the previous year. Of the annual remittance, 30–40 per cent flows through informal channels, according to an International Labour Organization report. But the remittances received are generally not used for directly productive purposes,[47] with families that already have members working abroad trying to send more members using these remittances.

Against this backdrop, it is easy to understand why migration from Bangladesh – both legal and illegal – is so high. Bangladeshis have been migrating across the Bengal-Bangladesh border for several decades. It is, therefore, unsurprising that Rohingya refugees, registered and unregistered, who have been living for a decade in Bangladesh also feel the need to migrate, surviving as they do in the most adverse of circumstances. In 2011, the total number of migrants was 568,062, which rose to 607,798 in 2012. In 2013, the number dropped to 409,253, but in 2014 it rose again to 425,684.[48] The year 2012 was a significant year for Bangladesh in terms of labour migration. Ironically, it was also in 2012 that there was a fresh exodus out of Myanmar, with people fleeing in boats to either Bangladesh or other neighbouring countries. And again, it was from that year that the government of Bangladesh decided not to entertain more migrants from Myanmar, who turned to other destinations – mainly in Southeast Asia.

On 26 November 2012, an understanding was signed by the Malaysian and Bangladeshi governments, according to which Malaysia would formally receive workers from Bangladesh in the plantation, agriculture, manufacturing, construction and service sectors. Thirty thousand male workers were to get jobs in the first phase. However, this effort was difficult to activate in practice due to structural and other complexities. Very few migrated under this system. In 2012, only about a thousand could make it and in 2013, the number recorded was 5,191. Plantations in Malaysia require hard work and Malaysia is in need of recruiting labourers in the sector, especially in rubber plantations. So although there is need of labour from Bangladesh, very few are going. This step also generated among the youth in Bangladesh the idea that Malaysia could provide assured work opportunities, resulting in the steady growth of trafficking as shown above. The idea was that if one could not go there legally, one could do so illegally by sea, paying one's way.

Conclusion

The chapter began with a number of questions on why the Rohingya, especially those in Bangladesh, sail in rickety boats for new destinations. On the one hand, we have Rohingya leaving Myanmar, stateless and helpless; on the other hand, we have Bangladesh becoming a major country of transit, giving rise to complex issues. Many factors produce the migration patterns described above. Chittagong's access to the sea, the economic prosperity of some Southeast Asian countries, the success stories of some camp-dwellers in Malaysia, the initial acceptance of the Rohingya in rubber plantations in Malaysia, and the mobility that Rohingya in Myanmar, Bangladesh, India, Southeast Asia, Australia and West Asia has acquired over time, having had no particular state to negotiate with while seeking settlement, have sent them on these perilous journeys. The need to leave, even if there is no particular destination, has been of utmost urgency.

Given the variation in contexts I have encountered, it would be unwise to generalise too readily. However, there is no denying the fact that the conditions that create boat people generally stem from crises – war, ethnic clashes and continual persecution being most identifiable. Thus deaths or accidents do not act as deterrents for migrants crossing the seas, whether Vietnamese, Rohingya or now the Syrians leaving for Europe. The distinct feature of Rohingya migration is the mixed character it has acquired, which states concerned have increasingly found difficult to address. On 5 May 2015, representatives of Bangladesh and the Southeast Asian countries concerned, along with human rights organizations in these countries, assembled to untangle the issues. The assembled countries consented to provide refuge when a boat was located instead of turning it back, following widespread international criticism of the earlier policy. While Bangladesh is bringing back her people from these boats and the detention camps, for the Rohingya the wait is endless. Arrests of agents and middlemen involved in trafficking have followed. But the problems of illegal migration and statelessness are unlikely to be solved with arrests or the destruction of existing trafficking nexuses. What is also clear is that there is a need for more broad-based dialogue and policy advocacy.

Notes

1 E. B. Cowell and W.H.D. Rouse (eds), *The Jataka, or Stories of the Buddha's Former Births*, Cambridge: Cambridge University Press, 1895–1913, cited in S. S. Amrith, *Crossing the Bay of Bengal: The Furies and the Fortunes of Migrants*, Cambridge, MA: Harvard University Press, 2013, p. 24.

2 *Ibid.*, pp. 1–25.

3 *New Statesman*, www.newstatesman.com/world-affairs/2015/08/why-do-we-have-do-death-trip-migrant-crisis-continues-boat-capsizes-libya, accessed on 30 April 2018.

4 *Independent*, www.independent.co.uk/news/world/europe/migrant-deaths-in-the-mediterranean-continue-as-40-bodies-found-in-hull-of-smugglers-boat-10457049.html, accessed on 30 April 2018.

5 'Death in the Mediterranean' in https://newint.org/features/webexclusive/2015/05/27/mediterranean-refugee-crisis, accessed on 30 April 2018.

6 Interview taken by the author at Teknaf on June 28, 2015.

7 'Bangladeshi migrants' mass grave in Thailand!: Bangladeshi survivor undergoing treatment at hospital is now stable' in *The Daily Star*, Dhaka, 2 May 2015, www.thedailystar.net/country/mass-grave-bangladeshi-myanmar-migrants-found-thailand-80115, accessed on 26 July 2015.

8 'Thailand er Jangal e aro 30 Ganakabarer Shandhan', *Dainik Janakantha*, 8 May 2015, p. 1.

9 H. M. Ershad, '*Sagar e bhashche hajar abhibashi*', Moyajjemul Haque, *Dainik Janakantha*, 14 May 2015.

10 Interview taken at the office of the *Daily Star*, 30 June 2015.

11 'Southeast Asia nations agree on anti-trafficking task force', *Asia Pacific*, 29 May 2015, www.channelnewsasia.com/news/asiapacific/southeast-asia-nations/1880868. html, accessed on 30 July 2015.

12 Thomas Fuller, 'Boat Carrying Hundreds of Migrants Moves Farther From Land, and Safety' in *The New York Times*, 16 may 2015, New York, p. A8, www.nytimes.com/2015/05/16/world/asia/migrant-boat-myanmar-thailand. html?module=ArrowsNav&contentCollection=Asia%20Pacific&action= keypress&region=FixedLeft&pgtype=article, accessed on 5 September 2015.

13 Thanyarat Doksone, 'Thailand cracks down on human trafficking syndicates, targeting corrupt police, officials,' http://www.680news.com/2015/05/08/thailands-crackdown-on-human-trafficking-syndicates-targets-corrupt-police-local-officials/, accessed on 30 April 2018.

14 'Malaysia and Thailand turn away hundreds on migrant boats', *Guardian*, 14 May 2015, www.theguardian.com/world/2015/may/14/malaysia-turns-back-migrant-boat-with-more-than-500-aboard, accessed on 31 July 2015.

15 *Ibid.*

16 *Ibid.*

17 Mixed Maritime Movements in South-East Asia in 2015, Bangkok: UNHCR Regional Office for South-East Asia, February 2016, UNHCR, April–June 2015.

18 Elliott Brennan, 'Southeast Asia Is Reliving Its Boat People Crisis', *Huffington Post* blog in https://www.huffingtonpost.com/elliot-brennan-/southeast-asia-boat-people-crisis_b_7437498.html accessed on 30 April 2018.

19 Corey Kilgannon, 'Vietnamese Refugees Find Their Rescuers', *The New York Times*, New York, 8 November 2017, p. A20, www.infoplease.com/encyclopedia/ history/boat-people.html, accessed on 1 September 2015.

20 'Faced with more than 76,000 people camping out along the Malaysian coast, and other boats arriving daily, Deputy Premier Datuk Mahathir had announced to the international community that his country would start shipping refugees out to sea, and shoot on sight those who tried to land. "If they sink their boats, they will not be rescued," he said. "They will drown."' cited in Erin Anderssen and Marina Jiménez, 'Summer of Love', 3 July 2004 in https://www.theglo beandmail.com/news/world/summer-of-love/article25679395/ accessed on 30 April 2018.

21 C. Parsons and P.-L. Vezina, 'Migrant networks and trade: The Vietnamese boat people as a natural experiment', working paper submitted to the Department of International Development and Department of Economics, Oxford University, 17 September, 2013, pp. 3–4, www.economics.ox.ac.uk/materials/ events/12846/VEZINA_vietnam.pdf, accessed on 30 July 2015.

22 M. Pugh, 'Drowning not waving: Boat people and humanitarianism at sea', *Journal of Refugee Studies*,17(1), 2004: 50–69.

23 S. van Joanne and B. Cooper, *The New 'Boat People': Ensuring Safety and Determining Status*, Washington, DC: Migration Policy Institute, pp. 23, 24.

24 *Ibid.*

25 'Lost voices of the world's refugees', *New York Times*, 13 June 2015, www. nytimes.com/2015/06/14/opinion/lost-voices-of-the-worlds-refugees.html, accessed on 7 July 2015.

26 Joanne and Cooper, *The New 'Boat People'*, p. 5.

27 *Ibid.*

28 'Death in the Mediterranean', *New International Magazine: People, Ideas and Action for Global Justice*, 27 May 2015 in https://newint.org/features/web-exclu sive/2015/05/27/mediterranean-refugee-crisis, accessed on 30 April 2018.

29 *Ibid.*

30 M. Pallis, 'Obligations of states towards asylum seekers at sea: Interactions and conflicts between legal regimes', *International Journal of Refugee Law*, 14(2/3), 2002.

31 Pugh, 'Drowning not waving', p. 50.

32 *Ibid.*

33 https://data2.unhcr.org/en/situations/myanmar_refugees accessed on 2 May 2018.

34 J. Pearlma, 'Who are the Rohingya boat people?', *Telegraph*, Sydney, 21 May 2015, www.telegraph.co.uk/news/worldnews/asia/burmamyanmar/11620933/Who-are-the-Rohingya-boat-people.html, accessed on 30 July 2015.

35 C. Lewa, 'Asia's new boat people in Burma's displaced people', *Forced Migration Review*, (30): 40–1.

36 The interview was taken in Cox's Bazar, at the office of the International Organization of Migration on 3 July 2015.

37 Interview with the author on 28 May 2015, www.economist.com/news/asia/21659769-oppressed-myanmar-muslim-rohingyas-are-unwelcome-bangladesh-too-exile-island?frsc=dg%7Cd, accessed on 28 August 2015.

38 https://www.rfa.org/english/news/myanmar/rohingya-education-02072017 171233.html accessed on 30 April 2018.

39 https://www.westpandi.com/globalassets/loss-prevention/loss-prevention-safety-alerts/imo.ics.unhcr.rescue-at-sea.2015-version.pdf, accessed on 30 April 2018.

40 https://www.westpandi.com/globalassets/loss-prevention/loss-prevention-safety-alerts/imo.ics.unhcr.rescue-at-sea.2015-version.pdf, accessed on 30 April 2018.

41 'Rescue at sea: A guide to principles and practice as applied to migrants and refugees', IMO and UNHCR, https://www.westpandi.com/globalassets/loss-pre vention/loss-prevention-safety-alerts/imo.ics.unhcr.rescue-at-sea.2015-version.pdf, accessed on 30 April 2018.

42 *Ibid.*

43 *Ibid.*

44 Interview taken on 3 July 2015.

45 'Slave trade blooms in dark triangle', *Daily Star*, www.thedailystar.net/front page/slave-trade-booms-dark-triangle-80354, accessed on 28 July 2015.

46 S. Bhattacharya, 'Exodus of Rohingyas from Myanmar to Bangladesh: Concern for India', in *The Rakhine State (Arakan) of Myanmar: Interrogating History, Culture and Conflict*, New Delhi: MAKAIAS-Manohar, 2015, p. 142.

47 *Ibid.*

48 Tasneem Siddiqui, Md. Ansar Uddin Anas and Marina Sultana, Labour Migration from Bangladesh: Achievements and Challenges, Refugee and Migratory Movements Research Unit, Dhaka, 2013, 2014 and 2015.

2

WHERE DO #IBELONG?

The stateless Rohingya in India

Sahana Basavapatna

In India, the image of the Rohingya is unenviable: foreigner, Muslim, stateless, suspected Bangladeshi national, illiterate, impoverished and dispersed across the length and breadth of the country. This makes the Rohingya illegal, undesirable, the other, a threat, and a nuisance.

The law and institutions have responded multi-dimensionally. At the level of policy, the Office of the United Nations High Commissioner for Refugees (UNHCR) carries out Refugee Status Determination (RSD) and recognizes them as *refugees*. Since the end of 2011, the Government of India has ostensibly established an RSD system that will scrutinise asylum claims and issue long-term visas (LTV). In law, this entitles refugees to legalized stay, employment in the private sector and access to education, like other foreigners. Legal protection also technically opens access to protection measures of the UNCHR through its implementing partners.

Rohingya experiences, however, tell a different tale. Unlike most other refugee groups, a large number have been and continue to be arrested for violation of the Foreigners Act, 1946, and the Passports (Entry into India) Act, 1929, among other legislation. Unknown numbers remain in detention, some despite serving out sentences. Those in Assam and West Bengal, for instance, are unable to register with the UNHCR and join the queue for RDS. A majority lives in deplorable conditions in slums or unauthorized colonies.

In Jammu, there is a conscious awareness of the growing number of Rohingya settling there. The 'fear of demographic change' is a view that, it is argued, cannot be discounted. Perhaps because of the politics of Jammu and Kashmir, enforcement agencies such as the Foreigners Regional Office

(FRO) view them with circumspection. There is suspicion that Rohingya men marry local people. However, those working closely with the Rohingya community, such as the Sakhawat Centre, argue that the fact that Rohingya have not migrated to Kashmir, which has a Muslim majority, is evidence enough that the community is not taking to violent activities. In Jaipur, there appears to be little awareness of Rohingya because of their relatively small numbers. The FRO in Jaipur says there are no Rohingya in the city. In Mewat, there is a heightened sense of caution, given that Rohingya settlements are considered the hub of links to terror organizations. Recent reports in *Daily Excelsior*, a newspaper circulated in Jammu, and the *Business Standard*, a national daily, say that the government is concerned about the large number of Rohingya migrating to India – a clear indicator that Rohingya are not considered benign.[1]

Unlike other mandate refugees, Rohingya are spoken of in the same breath as Bangladeshi nationals. For the Indian state, Bangladeshi immigration has remained a constant source of worry, with even the higher judiciary agreeing that their migration constitutes 'aggression', as interpreted under Article 355 of the Constitution. Rohingya are linked to terror groups and alleged to be members of or participants in activities of the Rohingya Solidarity Organization.[2] Lastly, their proximity to or collaboration with some Muslim organizations may have provided them material needs but not the credibility needed by a community seeking asylum from persecution.

A note on the structure of the chapter and methodology

Against this background, this chapter approaches the Rohingya migration into India from a legal perspective. The primary focus is the ways in which laws view Rohingya in India, and in doing so I provide a fragmentary account of Rohingya lives in Delhi, Jaipur, Jammu and Mewat. It is foregrounded in refugee experiences, analysing the plenary powers of the government of India vis-à-vis foreigners, the place of the new legal developments in the broader context of 'refugee law' and the extent to which being recognized as a refugee has secured rights for Rohingya. It also seeks to analyse developments in refugee law, one in which a state-led status determination mechanism appears implicit.

A fragmentary account from North India: seeking refuge, eking out a living

The introduction began by advancing the view that Rohingya migration to India has been characterized by a vocabulary that articulates diverse and conflicting concerns and assumptions. The impression that Rohingya are 'vulnerable to radicalization',[3] Bangladeshis and illegal migrants, coupled with the fact that they are poor and seek refuge, has resulted in atypical reactions from several quarters, some of which amount to a discursive and policy break. The increase in the number of Rohingya – said to be more than 100,000, according to Government of India estimates[4] – has put the government on alert. Implicit in this view is that Bangladesh is now the originary point of not only its citizens illegally migrating to India but also Rohingya. Thus, distinguishing a Bangladeshi passport holder from a Rohingya becomes necessary in ensuring that no illegal unlawful activities are carried out on its soil. In the public domain, however, the Rohingya migration has centred more on the context of refugee law than on statelessness. This decentring of statelessness has been effortless because the legal category of the 'refugee' appears to provide sufficient basis for protection. As stateless people, Rohingya present a situation which has not been explored adequately in law. This leads to the questions: Are Rohingya experiences of eking out a living any different from other refugees because they are dejurestateless? Is statelessness manifested in a way different from other legal categories in the Indian context, which would then require a reconsideration of the analytical lens? And conversely, would the recognition of Rohingya as *stateless* make a difference to the way in which one may comprehend the state of Rohingya refugees?

Introducing the Rohingya in India

Rohingya are known to have migrated to India since the late 1970s[5] in a trickle and until a few years ago remained unknown. Protests in May 2012, when an estimated 3,000–4,000 Rohingya squatted in Delhi, caused much alarm and made this stateless community visible. Demanding legal protection and aid, the group stated that the 'asylum-seeker cards' issued to them did not amount to legal protection. They demanded UNHCR documentation that would recognize them as refugees. In the Rajya Sabha, Sumitra Mahajan, a member of parliament (MP) from the Bharatiya Janata Party (BJP), remarked that the journey of such a huge number of people travelling 2,500–3,000 km to reach Delhi raised concerns of the safety of local people and of Delhi. She also raised concerns of terrorism. In pointing to lacunae in the law, she asked how in the absence of a refugee law protestors were asking for refugee cards, and the government had announced it would give LTVs.[6]

Because India does not have borders with Arakan, Rohingya usually migrate to Bangladesh before travelling northwest into India. Some Rohingya that I spoke with said they had lived in Bangladesh for a few years to about a decade before travelling to India. The decision was made on the basis of what their compatriots had to say about the conditions in India and the levels of insecurity faced there.[7] Karim, age 24, fled to Bangladesh around 1995 with two aunts, Ruksana and Shazia, and his cousins. He left behind his mother, Fatima, and younger sister, and had lived in Bangladesh for thirteen to fourteen years. None in the family, I was informed, had registered with the UNHCR in Bangladesh. Karim's life revolved around catching fish and scrap-dealing to supplement the meagre family income. They migrated to India around five years ago and registered with the UNHCR. Karim has little recollection of his parents or contact with his younger sister. I was also told that his father died when his sister was about a year old and he was taken from his mother's custody because she suffered from a 'mental illness'. Karim's life for the last fifteen-odd years has been one of dire poverty coupled with no legal existence. For the state, Karim is an illegal migrant who can be proceeded against not only for illegal entry but also failure to possess valid identity documents of Myanmar. His mother apparently followed this route and is currently lodged in a jail in Balurghat, West Bengal, having been arrested en route to Jaipur. Another respondent was a young man of about 25 who grew up in Bangladesh. He said his mother had spent about twenty-five years there. His father left for Malaysia and now wants his family to move in with him.[8]

Hanifa came to India about ten years ago around 2009 after having lived for about three years in Bangladesh. She says she was about five when she left Arakan, with her mother and two sisters. Her father was already in Saudi Arabia and her mother was preparing to leave to join him. She told me her brother died at that time and due to the shock of losing his son, her father also passed away. Her family felt unsafe in Bangladesh and left for Jammu via Dhaka with the help of a trafficker.

In the early years after arriving in India, Rohingya seemed to have waited before approaching the UNHCR. Mehrana, one of the earliest arrivals in India with whom I was able to speak, registered with UNHCR only in 2009 although she came to Jaipur in 2005.[9] When asked why she waited for so many years, she said she did not know there was an avenue in the form of the UNHCR. Rohingya are extremely poor, and may often migrate internally for better prospects or safety. The caution is also the result of strong reliance on informal and invisible information networks, a hedge against insecurities and threats that span many countries. With the availability of technology, these networks have been strengthened and information flow has been made easier.

Rohingya across the four cities began to be recognized by UNHCR after the protests in 2012. In several interviews it was noted that the UNHCR began issuing 'asylum-seeker cards' in 2011.[10] Registration prior to this period did not start the RSD process. An under-consideration certificate was given and an interview fixed for a date about a year to a year and a half away.[11] There was a mandatory period of six months before which asylum-seekers were not to contact the UNHCR enquiring about results.[12] In 2012, following protests, some policy announcements were made. It was stated:

> following discussions with the Government of India, UNHCR has been informed that the Government will give them long stay visas that will allow them to legally remain in India, based on their UNHCR asylum-seeker cards. For this purpose, they need to return to their places of residence in India and approach the local Foreigner's Registration Officers (FRO).[13]

The nature of refuge

The Rohingya, a highly mobile group,[14] have found refuge and shelter in the literal and figurative margins. In Jammu,[15] Mewat,[16] Delhi[17] and Jaipur,[18] they show a remarkable similarity in living conditions in that a majority live in slums, slum-like settlements or unauthorized colonies. Some reports describe the slums or slum-like settlements as 'camps', although officially neither the Indian government nor the UNHCR considers them as such. A report in the *Times of India* dated 20 November 2014 described the settlement in Jammu as the only officially recognized 'camp'. The article said,

> While an official camp for Rohingyas, under the United Nations High Commissioner for Refugees (UNHCR) is located in Jammu, members of the community are spread across India, including some parts of Kolkata. There are nearly 20–25,000 Rohingyas [*sic*] living in India, most of them in Jammu.[19]

The term 'camp' in its classical sense denotes some organization and management of the refugee population. It would be more appropriate to understand these spaces as they are officially described, that is slums or slum-like settlements. Employing official labels reveals not only the reasons for the lack of basic facilities but also allows us to understand the limits of the law that is invoked in support of refugee rights.

These habitations are defined by open sewerage systems, lack of sanitation, and absence of water or electricity. Excepting Mewat, Rohingya settlements are located in urban areas. Slums/unauthorized colonies occupy densely populated government or private land that is central to the imagination of the city. The master plans of cities view slums as an aberration that ought to be improved, while slum-dwellers should be 'resettled'[20] so that 'world-class' cities can emerge as new locales for growth and industry. Slums, however, host more than half of the country's urban population. From the perspective of refugee protection policy, it is relevant to ask how scholarship on slums may inform refugee management and care. How would an indeterminate body of refugee law, inherently capable of being withdrawn, speak to demands for shelter, health care, education and food? In what ways can these fundamental rights be invoked by Rohingya as slum-dwellers?

In this typology of housing, the best-case scenario of being a refugee, which formally provides legal status, does not always assure safety, security or economic mobility. In situations of unsuccessful claim-making or when claims are under consideration by the UNHCR, arrest, harassment or other hazards can follow. In these four cities, evictions and the non-renewal of informal lease agreements are common.[21] Settlements with a concentration of Rohingya may not attract such risks in Jammu, but they do in Mewat and Jaipur. A group of about fifty families living on a government plot a few kilometres from Chandeni near the district headquarters Nuh (Mewat) was asked to shift in around the third week of February 2015.[22]

Further, slums are contested spaces where its dwellers are caught in the crossroads of legal interpretation of slums as 'nuisance' and governmental policy of 'improvements' and 'resettlement' – a euphemism for evictions, homelessness and marginalization.[23] Existing scholarship[24] reminds us in no uncertain terms that slums or illegal settlements have only further marginalized its dwellers.[25] These are due to the inherent risks of the urban environment (unhygienic housing conditions, absence of sanitation, etc.) as well as the result of how such settlements are viewed in law and governmental policy. Ghertner, who analyses cases from 1980 to 2000, concludes how laws have been interpreted to eventually view slums as a problem of overpopulation. Courts, she argues, devised dual categories of citizenship where taxpaying citizens living in formal colonies were considered the rightful owners of the city while slum-dwellers were identified as 'illegals', 'aliens', 'anti-social', 'criminal' and 'people of Bangladeshi origin', and demolition was the solution.[26]

Under the slum rehabilitation and resettlement policies, demolitions are carried out in the 'public interest': dwellers are relocated or transferred to resettlement plots. Resettlement programmes, however, also exclude families either because of the eligibility criteria or conditions of the programme implementation. The eligibility of any resettlement programme rests on a certain cut-off date which a family has to qualify for. Further, documents such as the voter's identity card or the ration card is also an important prerequisite to determine whether the family is eligible. In addition, there are financial implications of such resettlement programs to gain access to a resettlement plot. Financial constrains have often excluded poor families from such programmes, which has impoverished them even further.[27] Research shows that evictions have routinely been undertaken without resettlement. And further, resettlement has less to do with improvement of conditions and services in the settlement but is based on the real estate entrepreneurs' need for the land.[28] And lastly, scholarship has also explained how a household's livelihood,

> incorporating 'capital' of different types – human, financial, physical and social – whose paucity or deprivation makes access to certain resources and meeting basic needs more difficult, thereby contributing to poverty and reversely, whose strengthening contributes to the improvement of the households' living conditions.[29]

The politics of slums and the further complexities of their 'improvement' and 'rehabilitation' helps in attempting a nuanced understanding of Rohingya in India. Research on slums also points out to the various ways in which slum-dwellers are rendered 'illegal'; it is also known that various kinds of documentation of slum-dwellers are made a prerequisite for their emergence as *citizens*. Rohingya, on the other hand, are viewed as suspect before they can claim a piece of land in a slum dwelling. The lack of address and the risk of mobility are factors that inherently give rise to suspicion. In this typology of housing, even the best-case scenario of a refugee, which formally provides legal status, does not always assure safety, security or economic mobility. In case of an unsuccessful claim making or claims under consideration by UNHCR, these risks can prove expensive and open up risk of arrest, harassment or exposure to hazards. Even when not evicted, families move in search of employment, to be in close proximity to UNHCR, to escape harassment or to look for cheaper accommodation. In turn, these have a bearing on the individual/family's ability to seek employment and so forth, or to build ties in the neighbourhood.

In the four cities, evictions and the non-renewal of informal agreement to rent places are common.[30] Settlements which have a concentration of Rohingya may not pose such risks in Jammu, but this is not a factor in Mewat and Jaipur. A group of about 50 families, living on a government plot a few kilometres from Chandeni near the district headquarters Nuh, was asked to shift around the third week of February 2015.[31] The risks of eviction and the structure of slums also impact the ability of Rohingya to acquire basic documents such as proof of residence, which in turn affects their ability to secure other documents, such as LTVs (Long-Term Visas). It is not uncommon in such conditions for Rohingya to acquire the Aadhar or the voter's identity card and be labelled as criminals for violating laws.

Building social, economic and political capital

The last few years have seen an engagement between non-governmental organizations (NGO) and the community. Provision of household needs and improving conditions in slums with respect to water supply, sanitation and health, and education have been among the main issues addressed.

The Socio-Legal Information Centre, a UNHCR implementing partner, has intervened in the Supreme Court highlighting sanitation and health. Fact-finding teams[32] sent to settlements to access the situation formed the basis for a writ petition. In the petition filed in 2013 through two Rohingya refugees,[33] a number of directions were sought against the Governments of India, Delhi and Haryana praying for access to basic facilities. The petition argued that this class of people, which has suffered persecution, violence and displacement in Burma is subject to further 'serious violation' of the right to life, maternal health and basic human dignity. It noted that Rohingya live in deplorable conditions in 'makeshift camps'[34] in Delhi and Mewat where basic medical care, education and a conducive atmosphere for a life of dignity is violated.

The petition made it clear that it 'does not seek changes to the official refugee status of this community', that only humanitarian assistance is prayed for to ensure their survival and wellbeing.[35] This effort was aimed at compelling state authorities to implement schemes and programmes on the strength of the argument that even as non-citizens, Rohingya are entitled to a minimum amount of charity and protection under the Constitution and statutory enactments. The matter was last listed before the Court in February 2015 with no date for further listing noted in the case status. Despite the urgency evident in the petition, no efforts have been made to expedite a decision.

As the instances below suggest, influencing local authorities and humanitarian efforts have been marginally more successful than seeking the assistance of courts.

Jamaat-e-Islami Hind and Jamait Ulema-I-Hind have intervened on behalf of the Rohingya in a number of ways. In a letter dated 20 April 2012 from Mahmood A. Madani, a former member of the Rajya Sabha, to P. Chidambaram, the former home minister, the abject living conditions of

Rohingya were explained. Madani requested UNHCR to intervene 'to solve the entangle issue of the grant of refugee status [*sic*]' and take 'urgent steps for providing relief and shelter on humanitarian grounds'.[36] This was just prior to the protests of May 2012, which proved a turning point in the Rohingya asylum matter in the country. Parallel to the lobbying and advocacy efforts, Jamaat's work, like many others, involved a multi-pronged approach. Zakat was collected on behalf of the community, recognized refugees were allowed free access to medical facilities at Al-Shifa Hospital near Jamia University (Delhi), programs were initiated to facilitate employment in the Kalindi Kunj settlement, legal assistance was provided where necessary and the organization reached out to the local Member of Legislative Assembly (MLA) bringing the situation in the settlement to his notice.[37] Mohammad Nayyar argues that as a policy they assist only those who hold refugee certificates.

The Sakhawat Centre (Jammu), Zakat Foundation (Delhi) and Tayyab Trust (Deoband) have also provided humanitarian assistance in times of crisis, but appear to be engaging with the Rohingya from a long-term perspective. In Delhi, the Zakat Foundation's property (about 1,100 yards) in Madanpur Khadar, a resettlement colony, has been permanently let out to about 54 families.[38] Efforts are being made to provide water facility, including tanks and laying of pipelines. Discussions continue on how housing conditions may be improved and whether over time Rohingya may shift from slum-like settlements to concrete houses.[39]

While provision of essentials is easier, health has proved to be a difficult area in which to intervene. Birth takes place within the settlements with few women, if at all, getting admitted to hospital despite guarantee of free treatment.[40] This view was echoed in Jammu too, with some stating that the fear of authorities, and the inability to explain the validity of refugee cards and thus risks of arrest, were some of the reasons for home births.

Registration of births is one of the most important advocacy initiatives of the statelessness campaign worldwide. Under the Indian Registration of Births and Deaths Act, 1969,[41] it is mandatory for every child born in the country to be registered. Although no concrete census has been carried out in case of the Rohingya, few reportedly register with the local authorities for reasons noted above.[42] However, birth registration is fraught with many shortcomings.

A study carried out by National Law University titled *India and the Challenge of Statelessness, A Review of the Legal Framework Relating to Nationality*[43] notes that there is 'no mention in the Act about ascertaining the nationality of parents of a child, or even about the effect of nationality of parent(s) on registration of birth of a child'.[44] This is true in case of Rajasthan, Haryana, and Jammu and Kashmir, where residential address of the parents at the time of the birth is among the only details asked.[45]

In case of Delhi[46] foreign 'nationals', registering births are required to provide details. So is the case in Maharashtra, for instance, where the

> registration authority may register the nationality of non-Indian parents as entered in their passports. If doubt arises, this can be ascertained from the police authority where he or she is registered and issued with residential permit. As regards, the foreigners who pretend to be Indian nationals and the doubt is raised by the local registrar, the only alternative is to get the matter enquired by the police of the area concerned.[47]

It is evident from the foregoing that states may differ in what information is sought while registering births. While the study rightly points out that there is nothing in the statute about ascertaining the nationality of the parents of the child or the effect on the nationality of the parents on the birth registration of the child, as a first step a birth certificate assures documentation attesting to residence in India, and in case of Delhi, in the least, it amounts to an indication that the parents of the children are foreigners from Myanmar. Birth certificates are valid documentary proof for school enrolment. The failure of Rohingya to register births has a visible impact on their identity and education. For children with no birth certificates, the procedure under the Registration of Births and Deaths Act, 1969, is long drawn, involving paperwork and an order from the magistrate.

Like health care, the outcome of the intervention with respect to education have been uneven. Development and Justice Initiative (DAJI), a UNHCR implementing partner, focuses on enrolling children in government schools.[48] Their efforts have resulted in the district education officers in the Education Department issuing instructions to enrol children in Jaipur, Jammu and Mewat.[49] Even so, in the absence of a policy, one of the recurring concerns with respect to education is the failure to enrol children in grades that match their age. Schools in Jammu, for instance, insist on all children, irrespective of their age, being enrolled in Grade/Standard 1. As a result, DAJI focuses on the age group of 6- to 8-year-olds.[50] Enrolments involve a great amount of documentation with no clear guidelines on whether UNHCR documentation is universally accepted. Even when this hurdle is crossed, as in the case of Jaipur and Mewat, birth certificate and a rent agreement as proof of residence is mandatory. For children with no birth certificates, acquiring one years after birth is a long drawn procedure. Even in a best-case scenario, and in the absence of monetary assistance, a number of children are likely to be left out of formal schooling. Informal literacy classes, while exploring other avenues such as open schools, have been initiated but are not a substitute for formal schooling.[51]

Considerations of livelihood and personal security, among others,[52] have led Rohingya to forge relationship with the *thekedars* or middlemen, humanitarian organizations and landlords. As noted in the foregoing paragraphs, for a variety of reasons Rohingya do not always approach UNHCR as soon as they arrive in India. These include lack of knowledge of the presence of UNHCR, extreme poverty or continuous migration for better prospects. Further, as UNHCR itself admits, RSD is a slow process, leaving many with an 'under-consideration certificate' that may not be recognized as a valid document systemically.[53] While practically families may be able to lead quiet lives outside the bounds of law, these decisions also have an underside. At any given point of time, Rohingya can be identified without documentation that is accepted by authorities. These have overall impact on the negotiating powers of the stateless in the form of exploitation at work, inability to access government health or educational opportunities and the fear of arrests and deportation on the completion of sentence.

In this context, ties with the locals have proved an effective informal means to ensure security. It is not uncommon for 'leaders' to mediate in case of labour disputes or skirmishes in the locality. It is reported that often the local police in Jammu asks one of the male members of the concerned slum to mediate.[54] These are some of the reasons why the loss of home has an adverse impact on employment, the ability to build social ties, the impossibility of proving residence and acquiring documentation such as LTVs.

Rohingya migration and the law

The management of refugees

This section begins with an analysis of recent legal developments in India that have a direct bearing on the legal status of Rohingya while they remain in India. In order to comprehend these developments, the expanse of the legal framework is pertinent, at times, retracing the constitutional law supporting and reiterating refugee rights.

A legal analysis of the law on refugees and the stateless in India

In India, stateless Rohingya are foreigners as defined under the Foreigners Act, 1946, and are permitted to register with UNHCR and seek asylum.

Thus they are 'mandate' refugees because they fall within the UNHCR mandate. UNHCR's mandate is traceable to the Statute of the Office of the United Nations High Commissioner for Refugees (UNHCR Statute), adopted following the General Assembly Resolution in 1950. The statute demarcates the role for the high commissioner. The 'competence' of the high commissioner has been recognized to have expanded since the adoption of the resolution. It is noted,

> [i]n addition to refugees as defined in the Statute, other categories of persons finding themselves in refugee-like situations, have in the course of the years come within the concern of the High Commissioner in accordance with the subsequent General Assembly and ECOSOC Resolutions.[55]

Article 6B of the UNHCR Statute considers the asylum claim of a stateless individual, that is 'if he has no nationality, the country of his former habitual residence'.

In its India operations, UNHCR carries out RSD but does not recognize Rohingya as stateless. UNHCR's stance may be explained by the fact that in India it is allowed no role in the protection of stateless individuals irrespective of nationality. A statelessness determination system does not exist within the UNHCR mechanism. Officially, successful RSD makes Rohingya 'refugees'[56] although in registering individuals, their legal status is marked as 'stateless'.[57] In the Indian context, however, where a large number of Rohingya may find it extremely difficult or even impossible to access UNHCR, the failure to officially recognize refugees as stateless has serious implications.

UNHCR argues that the absence of a mandate to address the legal and protection concerns of the stateless is immaterial because asylum-seekers who are able to prove that they are Rohingya and originally belonged to Arakan State are recognized as refugees. A rejection in case of a Rohingya then is only indicative of suspect ethnicity. It is stated that 'almost all' Rohingya registering with UNHCR are recognized as refugees. The fact that some may have lived in Bangladesh before making an onward movement to India is not a barrier for their qualification under the 1951 Convention/ UNHCR Statute.

Thus, the international refugee agency would not, under its status determination mechanism, officially recognize a Rohingya or alleged stateless person as stateless while assessing an asylum claim. This argument appears convincing except that it goes against the very basis of the Convention on the Status of Stateless Persons, 1954. In its Preamble, the 1954 Stateless Persons Convention is conscious of the fact that the 1951 Convention covers only those stateless persons who are also refugees and 'that there are many stateless persons who are not covered by that Convention'.[58] This background is useful in understanding the Government of India's recalibrated policy towards persons from Myanmar, and in particular, the Rohingya.

A recalibrated refugee policy

Rohingya began to be interviewed under the UNHCR RSD mechanism after the protests[59] in 2012. Prior to this period, they were only issued 'asylum-seeker cards'.[60] Registration in this period thus did not kick-start the RSD process. An 'under-consideration certificate' was given and a date for interview fixed at a date about a year or a year and a half away.[61] Further, there was a mandatory period of six months before which asylum-seekers were not to contact UNHCR enquiring about their results; this practice continues for applicants to this day.[62]

In 2012, following protests, a policy announcement was also made, a discursive break for refugee policy governing mandate refugees in India. UNHCR stated:

> following discussions with the Government of India, UNHCR has been informed that the Government will give them long stay visas that will allow them to legally remain in India, based on their UNHCR asylum-seeker cards. For this purpose, they need to return to their places of residence in India and approach the local Foreigner's Registration Officers (FRO).[63]

Note that the LTV, a mechanism to regulate and legalize the stay of foreigners in India, is applicable to Hindus from Pakistan and Bangladesh too. To that extent, the aforementioned announcement is not novel and yet, it is a modification of refugee policy as it applies to mandate refugees. For mandate refugees, the residence permit issued by the Indian government was a decision arbitrarily made; some such as the Chins from Myanmar/Burma were entitled to apply while others were not.

Mandate and non-mandate refugees

To better appreciate the LTV policy, relevant to note are two distinct approaches of the Government of India towards refugee management. Unofficially, there are 'mandate' and 'non-mandate' refugees.

'Mandate refugees' is a term referring to the category of nationals who do not migrate from India's immediate neighbourhood (excepting Burma).[64] UNHCR, under the aegis of the United Nations Development Programme (UNDP), discharges its functions by conducting RSD and outsourcing protection functions to various local NGOs that work with the agency as implementing and operational partners. Under this policy, refugees from the African continent (Congo, Sudan, Somalia, Eritrea), Middle East (Afghanistan, Syria, Palestine, Iran, Iraq) and Burma (Chins, Kachins, Burmans, Rakhines and most recently, the Rohingya) have sought asylum. Successfully seeking asylum in the case of these nationalities means three possibilities: resettlement, repatriation or integration in India.

Some categories of mandate refugees have been issued with residence permits (Chins, Kachins, Burmans and Rakhines from Burma/Myanmar, ethnic Afghans (i.e. Muslims), signifying the right to residence. Chins, Afghans and those from some of the countries in the African continent have been resettled over a period of time. Overall, the Government of India has formally allowed access to government schools and hospitals, reiterating its tacit acceptance of refugees on its soil. The aspiration for citizenship has however never been articulated in most of the discussion on mandate refugees.[65] Mandate refugees have primarily aspired for resettlement.

In case of non-mandate refugees, UNHCR has no or little role to play (e.g. repatriation of Sri Lankan Tamils). Their arrival, assistance and overall management is in the exclusive domain of the Government of India, discharged through its Ministry of Home Affairs and the concerned department in the states/union territories. These include asylum-seekers from Sri Lanka (Tamils only), the Tibetans, Chakmas from Chittagong Hill Tracts in Bangladesh, and the minority communities from Bangladesh and Pakistan (Hindus, Christians, Buddhists and Sikhs).

The Burmese[66] and Afghan refugees[67] have been granted residence permits; the Tibetans have been issued with registration certificates, identity certificates and special entry permits.[68] The Indian government's policy towards the Bangladeshi and Pakistani Hindus has been to issue them with LTVs until their application for citizenship is processed.

India's refugee policy

The presence of UNHCR in India, the unofficial categories of mandate and non-mandate refugees and the practices of refugee management are founded on the exercise of wide sovereign power of the state. India's refugee policy has thus been rightly characterized as ad hoc and provides the flexibility to respond to situations as they arise. The wide plenary powers have a constitutional and statutory basis, as noted below.

Foundation of India's refugee law

Constitutional basis for law making in India

Articles 245 and 246 read with Entries 17 to 19 and 97, List I of the Seventh Schedule of the Constitution give the powers and authority to the central government to frame laws with respect to matters that broadly fall under the subjects, foreigners, aliens and immigration. Articles 245 and 246 speak of distribution of legislative power of the parliament and the state legislatures. Read together, these two articles empower the parliament to make laws with respect to matters enumerated in List I in the Seventh Schedule, the Union List of the Constitution.

Further, under Articles 73(1)(a) and (b), the executive power of the union extends to 'all matters with respect to which Parliament has power to make laws' and to 'the exercise of such rights, authority and jurisdiction as are exercisable by the Government of India by virtue of any treaty or agreement'. The executive power is co-extensive with the legislative competence of the union. The case of *Ram Jawaya v State of Punjab*[69] interpreted Articles 73 and 162[70] and held that these provisions do not define 'executive function', nor do they define what activities would legitimately come within its scope. Article 73 implies that the power of the central government extends to matters upon which the parliament is competent to legislate. They are not confined to matters over which legislation has been passed already. The Indian Constitution does not strictly follow the doctrine of separation of powers; it can exercise the powers of subordinate legislation when such powers are delegated to it by the legislature. It can also exercise judicial functions in a limited way but not go against the provision of the Constitution or any other law.[71]

The foregoing speaks of three ways in which a valid law may be made. One is in the form of a bill passed by the parliament; another, in the form of a delegated/subordinate legislation under an existing and valid statute; and a third, through the exercise of executive functions under Article 73.

It is under this constitutional scheme that an indeterminate[72] body of judge-made law and delegated legislation constitutes 'refugee law'. Several academics and lawyers have analysed the import of precedents, the nature of refugee law and the various subjects that it covers.[73] Refugee status determination, the principle of non-refoulement and access to basic rights to education, among others, have been recognized as being integral parts of Articles 14 and 21, the right to equality and life, respectively. Other provisions under Parts III and IV of the Constitution directly protect refugees, including the right to religion (Article 25), rights in respect of arrest, detention and criminal prosecution (Articles 20 and 22) and the right to legal and constitutional remedies (Article 32 and Article 39-A).

At the end of 2011, India's refugee policy was further developed. Until 2011, reference to a specific order spelling out the basis for legal recognition of rights of refugees falling under the mandate of UNHCR was absent. It is only on the strength of the decisions of the higher judiciary and constitutional principles that advocates of refugees rights spoke of valid refugee law. The sections below note these developments chronologically.

Standard Operating Procedures, December 2011

In December 2011, the Ministry of Home Affairs (MHA) drew up guidelines in the form of Standard Operating Procedures[74,75] to deal 'with foreign nationals who claim to be refugees'. These guidelines

> stipulate that cases, which are prima facie justified on the grounds of a well-founded fear of persecution on account of race, religion, sex, nationality, ethnic identity, membership of a particular social group or political opinion, can be recommended by the State Government/ Union Territory Administration to the Ministry of Home Affairs for grant of Long Term Visa (LTV) after due security verification.

In December 2014, the MHA made yet another announcement,[76] keeping in view the context of Hindus from Pakistan. The validity of the LTV was increased to five years at a time based on the recommendation of the state government/union territory (UT) administration. The LTV processing by the FRRO/FRO was to be a time-bound exercise: one month for FRRO/FRO and 21 days for the state government/ UT administration. State governments/UT administrations were also empowered to grant a

> maximum of two additional places at any given point of time in addition to the place of stay, grant of Return Visa for a maximum period of 90 days at a time and permission for change in mode of travel and port of exit in respect of minority nationals from neighbouring countries living in India on LTV or whose LTV proposal is under consideration.

In May 2015,[77] yet another Press Information Bureau release reproduced the Question Hour proceeding in the Lok Sabha, reiterating that Standard Operating Procedures deal with those who claim to be refugees in India. What is of interest is its title. Under the heading 'Refugee Determination System', the Minister of Home Affairs was asked questions pertaining to India's legal framework and 'determination system for refugees', the number of refugees and asylum-seekers in the country at present, country-wise, the facilities being provided to the refugees and asylum-seekers in the country and the views of the government regarding the refugee determination system followed by the UNHCR.[78] In addition to stating that Standard Operating Procedures apply to those who claim asylum in India, the minister's answer with respect to the query about UNHCR's RSD stated:

> Refugees are registered under the mandate of the United Nations High Commissioner for Refugees [UNHCR] who meets regularly with all refugees and their representatives to discuss their concerns and jointly look for solutions to their problems as much as possible. In very exceptional circumstances, UNHCR provides individual assistance that may include monthly stipends or resettlement to a third country. India is not a signatory to the 1951 United Nations Convention on the Status of Refugees.[79]

It is easy to get distracted by the title, but it would be wise not to conjecture a policy on the basis of a title given by a team in the Lok Sabha Secretariat who are charged with the task of organizing the proceedings of the parliament. Additionally, an answer with respect to the status determination mechanism was never sufficiently provided. Nevertheless, the Press Information Bureau press release, as well as the Corrigenda document, arouse enough curiosity and beg questions. The language used in the title is similar to the one used in international refugee law, of a procedure that is central to the functioning of the international refugee agency.

Refugee claims of Myanmar nationals, June 2012

In June 2012, the Foreigners Division of the MHA issued an order in the form of Executive Instructions relating to the grant of LTV for refugees from 'Myanmar' (Executive Instructions). The instructions were directed at FRRO/FROs to aid them in gathering information with respect to the application made for LTV. The recommendations of these authorities are the basis on which the MHA decides to grant or refuse LTV. The report is to contain:

1   Complete details of the reasons for leaving the originating country and the version of the foreign national making such claim;
2   Manner in which entered – border checkpoint, etc.;
3   Documents possessed by the foreigner – issued by anybody either in India or abroad;
4   Full justification for claiming status as refugee (i.e. whether on the grounds of well-founded fear or persecution on account of race, religion, sex, nationality, ethnic identity, membership of a particular social group or political opinion);
5   Explicit/clear cut views/opinion of the concerned FRRO/FRO, whether LTV in respect of the particular foreigner is to be considered or not.[80]

It was also stated that the

> Long Term Visas are granted to refugees based on existing guidelines after due security verification etc. which permits them to access facilities at par with other foreigners such as – employment in the private sector and undertake studies in any academic institution.[81]

The LTV is valid initially for one year and 'can be renewed every year on case to case basis on merit'.[82]

In a reply to the Right to Information (RTI) application filed in this regard, the Executive Instructions are further explained by MHA as a system to guard against 'possibilities of misuse of law by illegal economic migrant by way of wrongful representation of facts [*sic*]'.

It was added that '[t]here are also reports of foreign nationals having entered the country without documents. As entry of such foreign nations [*sic*] into India is clandestine and surreptitious.'[83] What follows is an analysis of the June 2012 order at the backdrop of constitutional law, the law of foreigners and the UNHCR mandate.

The import of the June 2012 MHA order

The significance of the June 2012 order becomes clear on revisiting the history of the refugee law debate. In 2003, Rajeev Dhavan, a senior Supreme Court lawyer and at that time the head of PILSARC, UNHCR's Operational Partner, was asked by the National Human Rights Commission to respond to the Model Law on Refugees. Because the terms of reference for the query were left vague, Dhavan set out 'to examine broader issues and controversies relating to the Convention of 1951 and the constitutional and legal regime on the protection of foreigners in general and refugees in particular'.[84] He critiqued the Model Law on Refugees, offered his legal opinion on all its substantive and procedural aspects and advised,

> [g]enerally, the Model law is based on a judicialised model, which needs to be discussed further. . . . But this can be done during the parliamentary process. In other words, it is not necessary to refine the Bill further. It should be introduced in Parliament critique and refinement through the Select Committee procedure.

In his conclusion, he noted that, short of a parliamentary legislation, 'immediate and interim reliefs' can be provided by 'enacting rules through the Foreigner Act 1946 which (a) defines refugee according to the model law (b) sets up a process of refugee determination (e) enshrines the principle of non-refoulment and (d) provides basic protections'.[85]

In 2006, in an opinion titled 'Refugee Protection by Executive Action',[86] Dhavan argued that a refugee protection system can be drawn up by executive action or under the Foreigners Act, 1946. He analysed the entire body of law on foreigners in India and the constitutional scheme including the powers of the executive under Article 73 (the wider executive powers) and exercise of its narrower executive power to give to powers, responsibility and discretions under the existing legislation. He stated:

> [c]onsistent with its exercise of its wider executive power, the Union has made arrangements with the UNHCR . . . to effect refugee determination for 'foreigner-refugees' who enter India – albeit illegally – from areas other than South Asia. Any certification by the UNHCR is respected as a matter of practice. It must be assumed that the Union's arrangement with the UNHCR is in addition to, and not in derogation of, statutory provisions.[87]

Thereafter, the discussion on the exercise of the wider executive powers under Article 73 ensued, that is, the exercise of executive powers 'not emanating from legislation and which cannot be exercised in a manner contrary to any legislation'.[88] He proceeded to analyse the exercise of the executive powers in the light of the Foreigners Act, 1946, the Foreigners Order, 1948, and the Registration of Foreigners Act, 1939, and opined that the wider executive powers can be used to provide a refugee regime. Alternatively, even in the face of the Foreigners Act, 1946, and the Registration of Foreigners Act, 1939, recourse may be had to the exception clauses of these acts to setup such a regime.[89] And lastly, the separate treatment of refugees as a special class of foreigners requiring special treatment is a valid reasonable classification permissible by the Constitution.[90]

He concluded that a system for refugee care and protection can be created by executive action or under the Foreigners Act, 1946.In general, a case relating to foreigners and deportation would be subject to a limited judicial review. Lastly, he argued, inter alia, that the Foreigners Act, 1946, contains ample provisions to create a class of foreigners called refugees, permits examination of such persons for refugee determination, sets up places of refugee determination under the Foreigners Order, 1948, ensures that persons are not subject to refoulement – both as a general principle in all deportations and especially in relation to refugees – and lastly, provides a measure of socio-economic support.[91]

The MHA reply to the RTI application states that the order of June 2012 has been passed under the Foreigners Act, 1946.[92] Thus one obvious conclusion that may be made is that the government has chosen to exercise its wide executive powers to deal with refugees. It has explicitly adopted the definition of refugee as per the 1951 Convention on the Status of Refugees, overtly recognized a class of foreigners as refugees and normatively guaranteed the most basic protection by issuing a document legalizing stay. Implicit in the June 2012 order – unless proved to the contrary – is the retention of the RSD mechanism implemented through the aegis of UNHCR.

The FRRO/FRO are mandated to make a recommendation on the basis of the following: 'justification for claiming his status of refugee', 'complete details of reasons for leaving the originating country and the version of the foreign national making such claim'. Technically, foreigners may make an application for an LTV without taking recourse to the UNHCR system. However, arriving at such a conclusion would amount to ignoring the existing and valid arrangement between the Government of India and the UNHCR. On this ground alone, the order changes the existing status quo and is a welcome development.

Three issues are germane in this discussion. First, in itself, the order provides merely specific instructions to the FRRO/FROs to send their recommendations on the basis of which a decision to grant or refuse refugee status is made by the Ministry of Home Affairs. This is thus similar to the procedure in force with respect to the Hindus from Pakistan and Bangladesh. However, there is no clarity in scrutiny procedure that is central to determination of refugee status and issuance of LTV.

The second concerns the stated goal of the order and the approach of the Ministry of Home Affairs. The foregoing paragraphs reproduced the rationale of the Ministry of Home Affairs in issuing the order. While on the one hand, the order connotes the recognition of asylum claims of a class of foreigners, on the other hand, the absurdity of its intentions is laid bare when the Ministry articulates its unease over the possible 'misuse of law by illegal economic migrants by way of wrongful representation of facts'. It elaborates on the government's fears of illegal migration by stating that foreigners enter the country with documents clandestinely.[93] This is a clear indication of the government's conflation of the Rohingya migration from Bangladeshi migration. It also amounts to a contradiction: the law of immigration is a broader category, one that subsumes within itself a distinct class of foreigners. Given that only recognized refugees who would have registered with UNHCR will make an application for LTV, it is unclear how the order, in its current form, would assist in detection of illegal migration.

Lastly, the order of 2012 is a lost opportunity in terms of addressing statelessness.[94] A move that is unprecedented in the legal history of forced migration in India, by not addressing statelessness this executive decision also fails to address its own fears of distinguishing the Bangladeshi migrant from the Rohingya, and thereby it fails to respond to one of the most important fallouts of the conflict in its neighbourhood. The LTV in relation to the Rohingya applies, unlike in case of the Hindus from Pakistan or Bangladesh, to afford temporary protection only. With the heightened sense of fear of radicalization that undergirds the growing influx of Rohingya on its soil, the issuance of the order does not indicate a long-term measure of refuge for the Rohingya.

To conclude this section, two points that allude to bottlenecks in the LTV implementation may be also be made. Few Rohingya have received LTVs. It was reported that since December 2014,[95] the Government of India stopped issuing the document. One interviewee explained that initially there was not much by way of scrutiny, that the police verification was slack and Rohingya did get the visa for a short duration. Some others remarked that they have made an application for LTV but have not heard about the fate of their applications for about two years. None of the Rohingya refugees has applied for LTV in the recent past.

Second, typically, applicants make an online or physical application at the local FRO/FRRO. Documentary proof includes the 'refugee card', a UNHCR letter stating that the individual is a refugee as recognized by it with details of the family and lastly, proof of residence. It appears from applications made so far that the LTV procedures are akin to the residence permit procedure.[96] Although the FRRO itself mistakes the LTV for a residence permit,[97] the Ministry of Home Affairs states that this is not so.[98]

UNHCR also states[99] that some refugees have received a Stay Visa, one that Afghan refugees have been issued.[100]

Conclusion

This chapter is concerned with an examination of statelessness in the Indian context. It began by asking whether Rohingya experiences of eking out a living are any different from other refugees because they are dejurestateless. It was also considered relevant to question whether statelessness is manifested in a way different from other legal categories in the Indian social, political and economic context, which would then require a reconsideration of the analytical lens. Lastly, I posed the question whether the recognition of Rohingya as stateless makes a difference to the way in which one may comprehend the state of Rohingya refugees.

To the extent that like millions of other refugees and stateless, Rohingya are subject to the same conditions of deprivation, their experiences of finding refuge, security and protection may not be very different from others similarly placed. But this conclusion is an oversimplification.

In order to able to push the argument forward, it is worth reiterating that India's stand on refugees has moved in a positive direction; it now needs to be clarified so as to bring it within the constitutional framework and implemented in keeping with the clear intentions that lie at the heart of the policy. The fact that the policy has not been allowed to take on a life outside of the written word clearly indicates that Rohingya have been treated unlike other refugee groups. The ongoing detention of a large number, even where some are holders of refugee certificates from UNHCR, confirms such an inference.

To note is also the apparent tectonic shifts in the refugee and citizenship questions over the course of the last few years, in the form of amendments to the Citizenship Act, 1955. This amendment is reportedly a direct response to the persecution of minorities in the neighbouring states. In the light of these developments, India needs to align its aims and purpose to a refugee policy that is even, uniform and non-discriminatory.

To be able to move ahead, it also needs to be acknowledged that the Rohingya crisis is a parallel fallout of the phenomenon of partition and state building. To speak only of guarding borders instead of focusing on those already within would not amount to prudence. To begin with, legal documentation that is not part of the law of the land should become a reality as a first step in discharging India's responsibilities internally as well as on the international sphere. Highlighting concerns of terrorism and so forth (as the media reports suggest) without finding ways to resolve them would only lead to an impasse, and would fuel and sustain a singular argument that Rohingya are a threat.

Postscript

This chapter was written and completed in 2015 and was researched from 2014 to 2015. The postscript (dated August 2017) notes a few developments since then to highlight how the Rohingya story is likely to unfold. Around February 2017, the Panther's Party in Jammu began demanding that Rohingya, along with Bangladeshis in Jammu, be evicted. A public interest petition praying for the same relief also followed in the Jammu and Kashmir High Court. The crux of the petition is that Rohingya and the Bangladeshis in Jammu are spoiling the social fabric of the state and will result in anti-national activities.

In August 2017, Minister of State for Home Affairs Kiren Rijiju stated that all Rohingya in India, irrespective of whether they were recognized as refugees or not, would be deported. With the Chin refugees in Mizoram, such calls for deportation were regular but could never be achieved. In 2016, MPs Rabindra Jena, Varun Gandhi and Shashi Tharoor each tabled a private member's bill on refugee law. This was also the time that the Citizenship Act, 1955, was sought to be amended by way of Citizenship (Amendment) Bill, 2016. If the amendments to the Citizenship Act, 1955, were to be adopted, citizens from Afghanistan, Bangladesh and Pakistan entering the territory of India who are either Hindus, Sikhs, Buddhists, Jains, Parsis or Christians without a valid passport or travel document would not be treated as illegal migrants.

Across borders, the Advisory Commission on the Rakhine State, headed by former UN Secretary-General Mr Kofi Annan, presented an interim report. What the commission proposes to do is to 'address institutional and structural issues which undermine the prospects for peace, justice and development in Rakhine, and to propose concrete steps that may contribute to improving the well-being of all communities in the state'. The interim report submitted in March 2017 considered several aspects such as inter-community dialogue, closure of internally displaced person (IDP) camps, set up since 2012, the question of citizenship and so forth. The commission report in August 2017 is awaited.

Given the ground realities that refugees in general and Rohingya in particular face, both in India and in Burma, these developments are important markers in the narrative of Rohingya refugeehood in India. Because it is unlikely that Rohingya inflow into India would stop or decrease in the foreseeable future, what one ought to understand is the ways in which the Indian government's stand is likely to impact them. Because the refugee bills are not likely to be tabled in the parliament anytime soon, are there more local level changes that one might see in the way Rohingya face the legal and political system? And given the real possibility of institutions like UNHCR being made irrelevant, as is indicated by Rijiju's statement, in what ways can the international institution be assisted in carrying out its mandate?

Acknowledgements

I acknowledge the assistance of the following individuals: Ishita Dey, a PhD scholar at Delhi University, gave valuable inputs at the initial stages of my research and asked pertinent questions about the framework that I have employed. Tarangini Sriraman, Assistant Professor at Delhi University, directed me to some fascinating work on identity documentation work among the urban poor and shared some of her own work. Ashok Agrawal, lawyer and colleague, helped during the preliminary stages of this work, without which this chapter would not have taken shape.

Notes

1 'Government calls meet on Rohingya Muslims', *Daily Excelsior*, 7 July 2015, www.dailyexcelsior.com/govt-calls-meet-on-rohingya-muslims/, accessed on 2 August 2015.
2 B. Jain, 'India alerts Bangladesh about Rohingya terror training camps in Chittagong Hill Tracts', *Times of India*, 25 July 2013, http://timesofindia.indiatimes. com/india/India-alerts-Bangladesh-about-Rohingya-terror-training-camps-in-Chittagong-Hill-Tracts/articleshow/21320102.cms, accessed on 19 July 2015; S. Gupta, 'Lashkar Radicalises Rohingyas to wage war against India', *Hindustan Times*, 2 August 2013, www.hindustantimes.com/newdelhi/lashkar-radicalises-rohingyas-to-wage-war-against-india/article1-1102056.aspx, accessed on 19 July 2015; T. Biswas, 'Top Taskher terrorist Abdul Karim Tunda arrested by Delhi Police', *New Delhi Television*, 17 August 2013, www.ndtv.com/india-news/top-lashkar-terrorist-abdul-karim-tunda-arrested-by-delhi-police-531895, accessed on 19 July 2015; V. Nanjappa, 'Rohingya Muslims: Worry ahead for India', *One India News*, 4 June 2015, www.oneindia.com/feature/rohingya-muslims-worry-ahead-for-india-1767313.html, accessed on 29 June 2015; J. Gupta, 'Khalid's arrest sparks off debate on Rohingyas in India', *Times of India*, 20 November 2014, http://timesofindia.indiatimes.com/india/Khalids-arrest-sparks-off-debate-on-Rohingyas-in-India/articleshow/45220794.cms, accessed on 19 July 2015.
3 'Govt calls meet on Rohingya Muslims', *Daily Excelsior*, 7 July 2015, www. dailyexcelsior.com/govt-calls-meet-on-rohingya-muslims/, accessed on 2 August 2015.

4 *Ibid.*

5 J. P. Anand, 'Refugees from Burma', *Economic and Political Weekly*, 8 July 1978, p. 1110.

6 Lok Sabha debates, 'Situation arising due to the arrival of refugees from Myanmar in Delhi', *Sumitra Mahajan*, http://164.100.47.132/LssNew/psearch/Result15. aspx?dbsl=7319, accessed on 2 August 2015. Translation from Hindi by the author.

7 Interviews with Shazia, Jammu, 9 July 2015; Noor Mohammad, Jaipur, 16 July 2015; and Mohammad Salim, Jammu, 7 July 2015.

8 Interview with Abdul, Jaipur, 16 July 2015.

9 Interview with Mehrana and Anwar (son), 18 July 2015, Jaipur. Similar was the case of Mohd. Tariq who arrived in India in around 2009 and was recognized as a refugee only in 2013. Interview with Mohd. Tariq, 16 July 2015, Jaipur.

10 Interview with Mehrana and Anwar (son), 18 July 2015, Jaipur. Interview with Mohammad Amir, 16 July 2015, Jaipur.

11 Same interviews. In Mehrana's case, an asylum-seeker card was issued in August 2011 and refugee cards given in February 2014.

12 Several of the interviewees currently awaiting results showed a slip of paper issued by UNHCR which stated that the agency would contact the application within six months, and clearly indicating that the office should not be contacted before the expiry of the six-month period.

13 See 'Summary conclusions of meeting with representatives of asylum-seekers from northern Rakhine State, Myanmar, 2012', UNHCR, www.unhcr.org.in/pages/ showmainstory/10, accessed 11 August 2012. For reports about the protests, see Z. Mann, 'Rohingya protesters in Delhi urged to leave', *Irrawaddy*, 16 May 2012, www.irrawaddy.org/refugees/rohingya-protesters-in-delhi-urged-to-leave.html, accessed on 24 February 2015; S. Bhattacharya, 'India Myanmar refugees get visas after month of protests in Delhi', *National*, 17 May 2012, www.thenational. ae/news/world/south-asia/indias-myanmar-refugees-get-visas-after-month-of- protests-in-delhi, accessed on 12 August 2012.

14 See, for instance, B. S. Perappadan, 'Rohingya asylum seekers back in Delhi', *Hindu*, 18 May 2012, www.thehindu.com/news/national/rohingya-asylum- seekers-back-in-delhi/article3433267.ece, accessed on 22 February 2015.

15 Twenty-two localities spread across the city and its suburbs. A significant major- ity of the families live in squatter settlements. Typically, a group of families rents a small piece of land from a private owner. Jammu settlements appear like camps but are not officially designated as such; people live in close proximity in each *basti* but have spread out because of lack of space and the competition with respect to employment. This city has seen the largest population of Rohingya. For a preliminary account of Rohingya in Jammu, see 'National Consultation on the Right to Survival, Protection and Education of Children of refugees, migrants and stateless persons in India', Development and Justice Initiative, 2012, unpublished.

16 Six plots of land most concentrated in Nuh *tehsil*, about three hours' drive from New Delhi. See also 'Rohingya refugees and asylum seekers in India: A situ- ational analysis', UNHCR India, February 2014.

17 Rohingya are scattered in Delhi. Delhi has a mixed settlement type. There are slum-like settlements such as in Madanpur Khadar, a resettlement colony, adjoining Shaheen Bagh and Khajuri Khas in northeast Delhi as well as scattered families over various unauthorized colonies living in Jahangirpuri, Vikaspuri and Uttam Nagar.

In Madanpur Khadar, a slum housing about seventy families is on land owned by a non-governmental organization, Zakat Foundation, 'which collects and utilizes "zakat" or charity for socially beneficial projects in a transparent and organized manner'. The organization has been providing assistance to the Rohingya since 2012; www.zakatindia.org/AboutUs.html, accessed on 2 March 2015.

18 Around 100 families live in and around Hatwara, a predominantly Muslim-populated locality near the railway station. This comprises a few slum hutments running parallel to an open sewerage at the edge of the unauthorized colony.

19 Gupta, 'Khalid's arrest sparks off debate on Rohingyas in India'.

20 While scholarship on slums and slum policies are far too many to cite, I would like to note some that have focused on Delhi. See the set of research papers on the website of the Centre for Policy Research under their 'Cities of Delhi' project (http://citiesofdelhi.cprindia.org/about/, accessed on February 2015). See also D. A. Ghertner, 'Analysis of new legal discourse behind Delhi's slum demo-litions', *Economic and Political Weekly*, 43(20), 2008: 57–66, T. Sriraman, 'Enu-meration as pedagogic process: Gendered encounters with identity documents in Delhi's urban poor spaces', *South Asia Multidisciplinary Academic Journal*, 8, 2013, http://samaj.revues.org/3655, accessed on 21 January 2015.

21 Interviews with Abdul Salam, 16 July 2015; Mohammad Amir, 16 July 2015; and Mohd. Tariq, 16 July 2015.

22 Interviews with Mohammad Najeeb, Abdul, Sikander and Ali, Mewat, 12 Febru-ary 2015.

23 See Slum Areas (Improvement and Clearance) Act, 1956. Under this law, slums are spaces 'in any respect unfit for human habitation' or places that 'are by reason of dilapidation, overcrowding, faulty arrangement and design of such buildings, narrowness or faulty arrangement of streets, lack of ventilation, light or sanitation facilities, or any combination of these factors, are detrimental to safety, health or morals'. Under the law, the local authorities are to ensure that necessary repairs and structural alterations are carried out, there are provisions made for light points and water taps, drains are constructed, latrines are provided, additional or improved fixtures or fittings are ensured, courtyards are opened up or paved and rubbish removed. See also S. Sheikh and S. Banda, 'The Delhi Urban Shel-ter Improvement Board (DUSIB): The challenges facing a strong, progressive agency', *Centre for Policy Research*, May 2014, p. 6.

24 D. Asher Ghertner, 'Analysis of New Legal Discourse behind Delhi's Slum Demo-litions', *Economic and Political Weekly*, Vol. 43, No. 20, 17 May 2008, pp. 57–66.

25 See for instance Ghertner, 'Analysis of new legal discourse behind Delhi's slum demolitions,' LSE Research Online. Ghertner analyzes High Court and Supreme Court cases between 1980 and 2000 (which involved the interpretation of the nuisance provision under Section 133, Cr.P.C) and concludes that the courts have been responsible, in no small measure, for slum demolitions. In 1980s and 1990s, the courts interpreted the law in a manner where municipal bodies had a duty 'to provide clean and safe environment for city residents'. In the year 2000 and thereafter, beginning with the decision in *Almitra Patel v Union of India* (2000 (2) SCC 679), slums and not the municipal authorities were viewed as being respon-sible for solid waste mismanagement. In effect slums were now the nuisance, contrary to the import of Section 133, Cr.P.C.

26 *Ibid.*, pp. 10–12.

27 V. Dupont and D. Vaquier, 'Slum demolition, impact on the affected families and coping strategies', in M.-C. Saglio-Yatzimirsky and F. Landy, *Megacity*

Slums: Social Exclusion, Space and Urban Policies in Brazil and India, London: Imperial College Press, 2013, pp. 307–61. Unpublished draft. On file.

28 Sheikh and Banda, 'The Delhi Urban Shelter Improvement Board (DUSIB),' p. 12. For a critical analysis of the in-situ rehabilitation of Kathputli colony, one of the famous localities in Delhi for its artisans, see S. Banda, Y. Vaidya and D. Alder, 'The case of Kathputli colony: Mapping India's first in-situ slum rehabilitation project', *Centre for Policy Research*, June 2013. On file.

29 *Ibid.*

30 Interviews with Abdul Salam, 16 July 2015; Mohammad Amir, 16 July 2015; Mohd. Tariq, 16 July 2015.

31 Interviews with Mohammad Najeeb, Abdul, Sikander and Ali, Mewat, 16 July 2015.

32 Fact-finding on access to contraception, Rohingya refugee camp, Mewat dated April 2013; Rohingya refugee camp, fact-finding, Kalindi Kunj, New Delhi dated November 2012; Rohingya Delhi camp, fact-finding dated July 2013.

33 Jaffar Ullah and Anr v Union of India, W.P.(C) No. 859 of 2013, Supreme Court, pending. Copy of the writ petition was accessed on the website of Human Rights and Law Network.

34 *Ibid.*, para. 1.

35 *Ibid.*

36 Letter dated 20 April 2012 from Mahmood A. Madani to P. Chidambaram. On file.

37 Interview with Mr Mohammad Nayyar, Production Manager, MMI Publishers, 16 February 2015.

38 Contrary to reports of eviction, Rohingya continue to live on the site. Interview with Mr Imtiaz Siddiqui, Director, Zakat Foundation, New Delhi, 1 July 2015. Zakat Foundation's website can be accessed at www.zakatindia.org.

39 Meeting with Mr AsimQasmi, Chairman, Tayyab Trust, Jammu, 9 July 2015. Tayyab Trust's website can be accessed at www.thetrustofindia.org/about-us. html.

40 Interview with Mr Mohammad Nayyar, Production Manager, MMI Publishers, 16 February 2015.

41 The Registration of Births and Deaths Act, 1969, is a central law that falls within the domain of List III of Seventh Schedule of the Constitution of India. Therefore, each state, as is provided under Section 30, is required to pass rules, with the approval of the central government, for the implementation of this act.

42 Interview with Mr Ravi Hemadri, executive director, Development and Justice Initiative, New Delhi, 2 July 2015 (interview in Jammu).

43 S. Karkala, *India and the Challenge of Statelessness: A Review of the Legal Framework Relating to Nationality*, New Delhi: National Law University, Delhi Press, 2012. On file.

44 *Ibid.*, p. ix.

45 See the Birth Reporting Form in the State of Rajasthan, http://statistics. rajasthan.gov.in/Details/FORM_1.pdf, Birth Reporting Form in the State of Haryana, p. 44, http://haryanahealth.nic.in/userfiles/file/pdf/Manual%20 on%20Civil%20Registration%20System.pdf, last accessed on 1 August 2015.

46 Application for Obtaining Birth Registration, Municipal Corporation of Delhi, Health Department, drawn up under Delhi Registration of Births & Deaths Rules, 1999, http://111.93.47.72/rbd/content/birth.pdf, accessed on 1 August 2015.

47 FAQs on Registration of Births & Deaths, https://arogya.maharashtra.gov.in/ Site/Uploads/GR/FAQs-on-Registration-of-Births-and-Deaths.pdf, accessed on 1 August 2015.

48 Booklet of Development and Justice Initiative, undated. On file.

49 Meeting with Mr Vishnu Swamy, District Education Office, Education Department, Jaipur, 17 July 2015, Jaipur.

50 Interview with Ms. Rena Sanyal, programme manager, Jammu, Development and Justice Initiative, 6 July 2015.

51 Interview with Prof. Abdul Rashid, administrator, Sakhawat Centre, J&K, Jammu, 10 July 2015.

52 For instance, walnut crushing (Jammu) and scrap collection and sale, construction work, janitors in malls, domestic work, health and education assistants working with implementing partners in Jammu and other cities covered in this research.

53 UNHCR states that several factors delay RSD, including inadequate country of origin information, lack of staff and office space, and pilot practice of writing reasoned notification letters specifying reasons for rejection has also absorbed staff time and slowed RSD. In India, the inadequate country of origin information is cited specifically as a factor delaying RSD. See M. Morand et al., *The Implementation of UNHCR's Policy on Refugee Protection and Solution in Urban Areas, Global Survey – 2012*, UNHCR.

54 Interview with Mohd. Hamid, 7 July 2015, Jammu.

55 Footnote 1 to Article 6, Statute of the Office of the United Nations High Commissioner for Refugees.

56 Interview with Ms. Ragini Trakroo Zutshi, senior protection officer, UNHCR India, 23 February 2015.

57 Interview with Mr Ravi Hemadri, executive director, Development and Justice Initiative, New Delhi, 2 July 2015.

58 Preamble to the Convention Relating to the Status of Stateless Persons, 1954, p. 85, Basic International Legal Documents on Refugees, Eighth Edition, December, 2011, UNHCR.

59 For reports about the protests, see Z. Mann, 'Rohingya protesters in Delhi urged to leave', *Irrawaddy*, 16 May 2012, www.irrawaddy.org/refugees/rohingya-protesters-in-delhi-urged-to-leave.html, accessed on 24 July 2015; S. Bhattacharya, 'India's Myanmar refugees get visas after month of protests in Delhi', *National*, 2012, www.thenational.ae/news/world/south-asia/indias-myanmar-refugees-get-visas-after-month-of-protests-in-delhi, accessed on 12 August 2012.

60 Interviews with Mehrana and Anwar (son), 18 July 2015, Jaipur; Mohammad Amir, 16 July 2015, Jaipur.

61 *Ibid*. In Mehrana's case, asylum-seeker cards were issued in August 2011 and refugee cards given in February 2014.

62 Several of the interviewees currently awaiting results showed a slip stating that UNCHR would contact the application within six months, and clearly indicating that the office should not be contacted before the expiry of the six-month period. Copy of the UNHCR slip on file.

63 Undated note titled 'Summary conclusions of meeting with representatives of asylum-seekers from northern Rakhine State, Myanmar', issued by UNHCR at the time the announcement was made. On file. Also see UNHCR, www.unhcr.org.in/index.php?option=com_content&view=article&id=18&Itemid=103, where UNHCR reiterates that recognized refugees will be entitled to an LTV, accessed on 9 August 2015.

64 See UNHCR, 'Figures at a glance', www.unhcr.org.in/index.php?option= com_content&view=article&id=3&Itemid=125, accessed on 18 July 2015.

65 Most literature on mandate refugees has not considered the possibility of citizenship. On the other hand, a discussion on mandate refugees has often opened up the most vexed question of refugee law for India. It may not be incorrect to also state that no mandate refugees have themselves sought citizenship in India; their aspirations have always been to be settled in a third country.

66 Sahana Basavapatna, Counting the Migrant in India: Forced Migration and the Identification Project, in Ashish Rajadhyaksha (ed.), *In the wake of Aadhar: The digital ecosystem of governance in India, Centre for the Study of Culture and Society,* 2013, pp. 446–7.

67 *Abandoned and Betrayed: Afghan refugees under UNHCR protection in New Delhi, South Asia Human Rights Documentation Centre,* November 1999, pp. 30–3.

68 Tibet Justice Centre, 'Tibet's stateless nationals II: Tibetan Refugees in India, a report', September 2011, pp. 44–50, www.tibetjustice.org/reports/stateless-nationals-ii/stateless-nationals-ii.pdf, accessed on 3 August 2015.

69 AIR 1955 SC 549.

70 Extent of executive power of the state.

71 Infra note 93, para. 7 at p. 554 and para. 12 at p. 556.

72 See also Rajeev Dhavan, Refugee Law and Policy in India, PILSARC, 2004, for a composite account of refugee policy, the legal framework and its evolution. Although more than a decade old, this and other accounts of India's refugee policy provide a historical and legal account that remains relevant. Other references include Ragini Trakroo Zutshi (ed.), *Refugees and the Law,* HRLN, 2007.

73 *Ibid.* See also R. Samaddar (ed.), *Refugees and the State: Practices of Asylum and Care, 1997–2000,* New Delhi: Sage, 2003.

74 Press Information Bureau, Government of India, Ministry of Home Affairs, Law for Refugees in India, 6 August 2015, http://pib.nic.in/newsite/PrintRelease. aspx?relid=108152, accessed on 30 August 2015.

75 Lok Sabha, Corrigenda to the List of Questions for Written Answers on July 15, 2014/Ashadha 24, 1936 (Saka), Question No. 739 by Kodikunnil Suresh, p. 219, http://164.100.47.132/questionslist/MyFolder/15072014.pdf. For the reply, see Press Information Bureau, Ministry of Home Affairs, Government of India, dated 15 July 2014, www.pib.nic.in/newsite/erelease.aspx?relid=113535. This was reiterated in both the Lok Sabha and Rajya Sabha subsequently. See Press Information Bureau, Ministry of Home Affairs, *Asylum to Foreigners Fleeing Religious Persecution,*17 December 2014. This was in response to a question asked by Dr Chandan Mitra in the Rajya Sabha, www.pib.nic.in/newsite/erelease. aspx?relid=113535; Question No. 4650 titled *Rehabilitation of Pakistani Migrants,* by Udit Raj, Ashwini Kumar and Col. Sonaram Chaudhary, Lok Sabha, List of Questions for Written Answers Tuesday, August 12, 2014/Shravana 21, 1936 (Saka), http://164.100.47.132/questionslist/MyFolder/12082014.pdf. The minister noted in his reply that the Ministry had issued instructions on 7 March 2012 to all states/UT administrations to consider requests from Pakistani nationals for grant of LTV on the basis of the guidelines already issued. On 5 September 2014, the Ministry set up a task force to monitor and expedite processing of citizenship/LTV applications. See Press Information Bureau Release titled *Task Force on Citizenship/Long Term Visa (LTV) to Visit Lucknow on October 16,* Ministry of Home Affairs, Government of India, 9 October 2014, www.pib.nic.in/newsite/ erelease.aspx. Subsequently, reportedly a decision was taken that the MHA team

would visit 24 districts in India and take grievances from applicants. These districts were Indore and Bhopal (Madhya Pradesh); Mumbai, Pune and Nagpur (Maharashtra); Ahmedabad and Gandhi Nagar (Gujarat); Jodhpur, Jaisalmer and Barmer (Rajasthan); Lucknow (Uttar Pradesh); and Bangalore, Krishna and Karwar (Karnataka). It was noted that

> MHA had received representations from time to time citing hardships and difficulties in grant of LTV/Citizenship applicants, especially of minorities from neighbouring countries who are often of poor economic standing. Reviewing the procedure, the Union Home Minister had directed senior officials in the MHA to expedite the entire process.

See Press Information Bureau Release titled *MHA to expedite LTV/Citizenship issues of minority nationals from neighbouring countries*, Ministry of Home Affairs, Government of India, 15 December 2014, www.pib.nic.in/newsite/erelease.aspx and Press Information Bureau Release titled *Teams to visit identified districts to expedite LTV/Citizenship issues*, Ministry of Home Affairs, Government of India, 23 December 2014, www.pib.nic.in/newsite/erelease.aspx. All links accessed on 28 July 2015.

76 Press Information Bureau Release titled, *Facilities to minority nationals from neighbouring countries to stay in India on Long Term Visa*, Ministry of Home Affairs, Government of India, 16 December 2014, http://pib.nic.in/newsite/PrintRelease.aspx?relid=113490, last accessed 30 August 2015. On the basis of the LTV, children could now seek admission in schools, colleges, universities, technical/professional institutions and so forth without any specific permission from the state government/UT administration; the concerned FRRO/FRO were only to be intimated in this regard. The state governments/UT administrations were also empowered to grant permission to 'minority nationals from neighbouring countries' staying on LTV to work only in the private sector.

77 Press Information Bureau release titled *Refugee Determination System*, Minister of State for Home Affairs, Government of India, 5 May 2015, http://pib.nic.in/newsite/mbErel.aspx?relid=121170. See also Question No. 6307, Lok Sabha Corrigenda to the List of Questions for Written Answers on May 5, 2015/Vaisakha 15, 1937 (Saka), p. 1911, http://164.100.47.132/questionslist/MyFolder/05052015.pdf, both documents accessed on 1 August 2015.

78 See also Question No. 6307, Lok Sabha Corrigenda to the List of Questions for Written Answers on May 5, 2015/Vaisakha 15, 1937 (Saka), p. 1911, http://164.100.47.132/questionslist/MyFolder/05052015.pdf, both documents accessed on 1 August 2015.

79 'Refugee Determination System', *Press Information Bureau*, Government of India, Ministry of Home Affairs, Press Release made on 5 May 2015.

80 'Case of registration in respect of Myanmar nationals Claims to be refugees – reg.' No. 18029/23/2012-F-IV, dated 11 July 2012.

81 *Ibid.*

82 Reply dated 12 March 2015 to RTI application by the author dated 15 January 2015 by Foreigners Division, Ministry of Home Affairs, Government of India. On file.

83 *Ibid.*

84 R. Dhavan, On the Model Law for Refugees: A Response to the National Human Rights Commission (NHRC), 2003, Para 1.4. On file.

85 *Ibid.*, paras. 7.12 and 7.13.

86 R. Dhavan, Refugee protection by executive action, PILSARC, 2006. Unpublished article. On file.
87 *Ibid.*, clause 2.3, p. 2.
88 *Ibid.*, clause 2.4, p. 3.
89 Section 3A, Foreigners Act, 1946 empowers the parliament to exempt all or any particular provision of the Act in relation to citizens of any specified commonwealth country or any 'other individual foreigner or class or description of foreigner'. Section 6 of the Registration of Foreigners Act, 1939, provides that the central government may declare, by order, that any or all provisions of the rules made under the act shall not apply, or apply with modifications, or be subject to specified conditions, to or in relation to an individual foreigner or any class or description of foreigner.
90 Rajeev Dhawan, 'The Refugee in India', *The Hindu*, 28 June 2003 in http://www.thehindu.com/2003/06/28/stories/2003062800811000.htm, accessed on 30 April 2018.
91 *Ibid.*
92 Reply dated 12 March 2015 to RTI application by the author dated 15 January 2015 by Foreigners Division, Ministry of Home Affairs, Government of India. On file.
93 *Ibid.*
94 For an analysis of nationality laws in India under the Convention Relating to the Status of Stateless Persons, 1954 and the Convention on the Reduction of Statelessness, 1961, see Sitharamam Karkala, India and the Challenge of S.
95 Interview with Abdul, New Delhi, 5 May 2015.
96 According to information available from the Ministry of Home Affairs and the FRRO, the LTVs and stay visas/residential permits are issued by the FRRO. This process involves, in case of refugees, an application to the FRRO, a letter from the UNHCR confirming that the applicant is a recognized refugee, utility documents as proof of residence and a letter from the house owner confirming the same. Media reports have quoted the Ministry of Home Affairs to state that on the basis of the verification conducted by the FRRO or FRO (as the case may be), the Ministry will further verify whether the refugee is an economic migrant or a refugee fleeing persecution and issue a 'long term visa' only to the latter. See P. Raina, 'Thousands of Myanmar Rohingyas struggle for refugee status in India', *New York Times*, India Edition, 18 May 2012, http://india.blogs.nytimes.com/2012/05/18/thousands-of-myanmar-rohingyas-struggle-for-refugee-status-in-india/, accessed on 7 September 2012.
97 Interview with Mr Harbhajan, Assistant FRRO, New Delhi, dated 9 February 2015 by the author.
98 Supra note 97.
99 Interview with Ms. Ragini Trakroo Zutshi, Senior Protection Officer, UNHCR Delhi, dated 5 August 2015.
100 See Item 53, Powers delegated to State Governments/UT Administrations/FRROs/FROs for various visa-related services, updated as on 16 September 2014, Foreigners Division, Ministry of Home Affairs, http://mha1.nic.in/pdfs/ForeigD-PwrdlgtFRROs.pdf, last accessed on 8 August 2015.

3

THE STATELESS PEOPLE

Rohingya in Hyderabad

Priyanca Mathur Velath and Kriti Chopra

'Boat people' and 'nowhere people' are terms that have become synonymous with one of the most persecuted minorities in the world, the Rohingya. Unable to claim citizenship in Myanmar, where about 1.1 million of them live in the Rakhine province, or in any other country, these 'stateless' people have been living with the curse of having no nationality to claim as their own.[1]

The world witnessed one of its gravest humanitarian challenges in recent times when images started flooding the media of people fleeing religious persecution in Myanmar and economic misery in Bangladesh, left to die in traffickers' boats in the Andaman Sea and Indian Ocean – people who could not turn back to the countries they had run away from and those the Southeast Asian countries that lay on their horizon were refusing to let in. Where could the Rohingya go?

The Myanmar government's peace process makes no provision for dealing with the ongoing sectarian violence. The country refuses to even recognise the term 'Rohingya', let alone recognizing that the community exists. If the situation does not change, it may soon have its wish. Since 2012, 153,300 Rohingya, well over 10 per cent of the population in Myanmar, have boarded boats operated by human traffickers in an attempt to reach Malaysia, according to data released by a human rights organization, Arakan Project.[2]

The Rohingya claim to citizenship rests on their assertion that they constitute an ethnic indigenous group of Myanmar which can trace its lineage to the old Arakan kingdom, and that they are not merely Bengalis. The word 'Rohingya' could originally just have meant inhabitant 'of Rohang', the early Muslim name for the independent kingdom of Arakan (now Rakhine).

But the Myanmar government continues to deprive the Rohingya citizenship, marking a policy of exclusion that was implemented since anti-Muslim violence started in 2012, with hundreds of thousands of Rohingya fleeing the country and another 150,000 winding up in camps within the country. They continue to flee to Indonesia, Malaysia, Thailand and the Philippines. Some have even come to India.

This chapter looks at the Rohingya refugees living in Hyderabad city from an ethnographic, anthropological and human rights perspective, particularly through the lens of their crisis of assimilation.

Statelessness and Rohingya

Statelessness refers to a legal condition in which a person is deprived of the nationality or citizenship of any country. While numerous causes lie behind this phenomenon of statelessness, one of the primary reasons is the conflict which exists in the laws determining nationality or citizenship in a given nation state.

The international legal definition of a stateless person, as set out in Article 1 of the 1954 Convention Relating to the Status of Stateless Persons, is one 'who is not considered as a national by any State under the operation of its law'. A prominent example of this kind of statelessness is found in the Palestinian territories. Rohingya are a similar group of people that has been rendered stateless as they are not recognized under any country's legal framework.[3]

The name 'Rohingya' has been a matter of debate for a long time now. To some, the Rohingya are a group of people who originally belonged to Bengal but subsequently migrated to Burma during colonial times. Another viewpoint is that the Rohingya hailed from Arakan in Myanmar. Many historians are of the belief that there were no people called the Rohingya before the 1950s; it was only after that decade that a group of Bengali Muslims migrating to Burma started calling themselves Rohingya. Whatever their origin might be, the stateless Rohingya have been facing a number of challenges not only in Myanmar but also in the countries they have been migrating to. This chapter specifically looks into the kind of challenges the Rohingya face in India, particularly in south India, in Hyderabad.

Legal refugee protection framework in India

India's laxity in framing proper refugee laws seems to have escalated the problem. Despite being asked to sign the Refugee Convention of 1951 and the Additional Protocol of 1967, and promulgate a legal framework for refugees, the Indian government has been lackadaisical. The United Nations High Commissioner for Refugees (UNHCR), however, hails India for its record in supporting refugees. It says in a report, 'Overall, India offers safe asylum to refugees and asylum seekers. Even in the absence of a national legal framework for refugees, India has traditionally been hospitable towards refugees.'[4]

Meanwhile, judicial intervention has done some good for the refugees. With respect to Articles 21 and 14 of the Constitution, the Supreme Court has declared that these (apart from other constitutional rights) are applicable to everyone residing in India, that is, not merely to citizens of the country.

Rohingya in Hyderabad

Rohingya refugees have been crossing the international border and coming into India for a long time now. In 2013, when the conflict between the Rohingya Muslims and the Buddhists in Myanmar intensified, several thousand Rohingya Muslims fled Myanmar and took shelter in India. It has been estimated that around 25,000 Rohingya Muslims have taken shelter in India, but not all of them are in government refugee camps.[5]

Minister of State for Home Affairs Kiren Rijiju (in a written reply to a question by Shri Adhalrao Patil Shivaji Rao in the Lok Sabha) recently stated that there are upwards of 10,500 Rohingya Muslims who have taken shelter in India. Of them, 6,684 are in Jammu and Kashmir, 1,755 in Andhra Pradesh (mainly Hyderabad), 760 in Delhi, 677 in Haryana, 351 in West Bengal, 162 in Rajasthan, 111 in Uttar Pradesh, 50 in Punjab, 12 in Maharashtra and 3 in the Andaman and Nicobar Islands.[6]

'More than 1,500 Rohingyas who were displaced from Myanmar have been camping in the city of Hyderabad for more than a year, but basic amenities such as food, clean water, medicine and clothes still elude them,' writes Nanjappa.[7] According to police records, 1,679 Rohingya refugees live in ten different parts of Hyderabad: Camp 1 in Balapur (298); Camp 2 Balapur (150); Camp 3 Balapur, Pahadishareef (87); Shaheen Nagar, Pahadishareef (127); near Fatima Masjid, Balapur (258); Royal Colony (160); Baba Nagar, Kanchanbagh (412); Barkas, Chandrayangutta (51); Shastripuram, Mailardevpally (29); and Kishanbagh, Bahadurpura (153).[8] That the state's knowledge and documentation of Rohingya is far from perfect is clear: the number provided by the police doesn't tally with the sum of the numbers provided.

The Rohingya arrived in India after being attacked by the ethnic Rakhine Buddhists, while Myanmar's government forces did little to stop the violent assaults. Mohammed Shaker was one of those who reached the Muslim-friendly city of Hyderabad:

> [He took] a circuitous route travelling the first three days on foot through rough mountain terrain in the dead of the night to reach the Myanmar border. Then he boarded a boat run by smugglers to reach the Bangladesh border. Hours later, he was stowed in a truck to be finally dropped near the West Bengal border. All in all, it took him nine days to finally land in Hyderabad.[9]

Delhi, being the national capital and the seat of the UNHCR office, is naturally the place they get pulled to. The Rohingya migrants also believe that Hyderabad, on account of its substantial Muslim population, will welcome them. In fact, the Hyderabad-based Confederation of Voluntary Organisations (COVA), a non-governmental organization (NGO) at the forefront of Rohingya rehabilitation, says many more are likely to come. The influx of Rohingya Muslims into Hyderabad has been taking place over the past five to six years, explains Mazher Hussain, executive director of COVA, implementation partner of the UNHCR in Hyderabad. According to Hussain, Hyderabad received around 100 refugees in 2010.[10] According to COVA data, from about 150 settlers in early 2011, the number of Rohingya Muslims currently residing in the city stands between 1,400 and 2,000. It also says 1,200 asylum-seekers have registered with them so far and many more are likely to come.[11]'Most of the refugees live in groups, with the highest number of them concentrated in Balapur,' says Kiran Kumar, programme officer at COVA, who looks after the welfare of these asylum-seekers.[12]

According to UN estimates, around 11,000 Rohingya have moved to various parts of India in the aftermath of communal violence since June 2012.[13] According to Malla Reddy, joint commissioner of police, Special Branch, Hyderabad, many Rohingya end up in Hyderabad while others move to Delhi, Aligarh, Mathura, Kolkata and other places.[14]

We visited the Kiskanabagh area in Hyderabad where we met Rohingya families living in rented houses. The first family we spoke to was of Rahman, his wife, Iffat, and son, Arfat, who had come to Hyderabad in 2012 fleeing riots in Myanmar. Initially they lived in a camp in Myanmar but decided to migrate to Hyderabad because living conditions there were bad.

They took boats and travelled for days to reach the city. Having arrived, they were confronted with greater problems of shelter, food and water. This family had come to Hyderabad with a group of other refugees. Lack of money forced them to stay on the footpaths and streets. Later on, having found jobs, they collected money to rent the room they were staying in. When we asked them what were the problems they faced, they said the people in the area were cold and shop owners were often rude because they were poor. Apart from this, surviving each day without proper food was a major challenge given the lack of employment opportunities.

Fatima and her son Farzan also live in Kiskanabagh. She fled with her son to Hyderabad after her husband was killed in riots. They were hesitant to tell us much about what they went through due to the callous response of the Myanmar authorities. She said that her husband was beaten to death in front of her; the trauma of that horrific incident was evidently still with her. It compounded her feeling of helplessness. She migrated to Hyderabad because all other families who got on to the ferry did the same. She began to look for jobs but found it difficult to find one for a year. Finding shelter, too, was a problem. Now she works as domestic help near where she lives, but she can't afford an education for her son.[15]

UNHCR refugee status: identity crisis

Recognition, Malik says, is the most important thing: 'Our cries are heard but not acted upon. We were born to see bloodletting. Now, we have resigned ourselves to torture and persecution.'[16]

The survival of Rohingya refugees in Hyderabad depends on their getting UNHCR refugee cards. The inability to get refugee cards compounds the hindrances of their daily activities. The prospective refugee has to undergo gruelling interviews to establish his or her identity and the purpose of migration. If the UNHCR is convinced, it can take three to six months to process the application and give the asylum-seeker a temporary card. A Rohingya can only get a refugee card once he passes the temporary card stage. That takes two more years; the refugee card has to be renewed every five years. Under the 1951 Refugee Convention, a refugee applying for asylum has to prove that he or she underwent persecution in his or her home country. If a migrant is from the eastern part of Myanmar where there is no disturbance, the UNHCR may reject his request for asylum and send him back to his country. But the refugee is also given a chance for second appeal. Abdul Majeed Madani and Mohammad Jawad are now living in Hyderabad as refugees holding identity cards jointly issued by the Indian government and UNHCR. Madani recalled:

'The attack and killing of Muslims in Myanmar have become a norm. One night about six months ago, a Buddhist mob attacked and torched the madrasa founded by my father Jalaluddin Usmani and killed him.'[17]

Community and international support

Rohingya migrants survive on community support and the networks they have created amongst themselves. With little money and no aid from the government, most of them struggle to meet their day-to-day expenses. COVA and the Civil Liberties Monitoring Committee (CLMC), an NGO in Hyderabad, seek donations from local people to support the migrants. 'Last year, during Ramadan, donations poured in. It was more like a Ramzan fad. Scores of people made donations to help them survive,' says Kiran, adding that donations have gone down this year (2015). Lateef Mohammad Khan, the convenor of the CLMC, stated that some locals have decided to help them as a goodwill gesture.[18] Nazimuddin Farooqui, chairman of the Salamah Trust, said his organization planned to help Rohingya by providing basic education to their children by enrolling them in schools and providing hostel facilities, besides taking up issues including refugee status.[19]

Iran had offered cash assistance to a group of Rohingya migrants in Hyderabad who had fled the ethnic violence in Rakhine State. The Iranian consul general in Hyderabad, Mahmoud Safari, handed over a cheque of INR 65,000 to the COVA, trying to help them get official status for the Rohingya from the UNHCR in 2012. Qaderi, trustee of the Dargah, thanked the Iranian consulate for extending assistance and said Iran was the first country which came forward to help the Myanmar refugees in Hyderabad. He added, 'Iran's spiritual and material support has been a ray of hope among the victims of the ethnic clashes in Myanmar.'[20]

A delegation from *Siasat Daily* had visited the refugee camp at Shaheen Nagar and interacted with all forty-two families.[21] A programme of distribution of foodgrains among the refugees was conducted on Tuesday, 2 July 2013. In the meantime, efforts are also on to donate rickshaws and *bandi* for vegetables to the male members who could thereby earn a livelihood. Ahmed Al Saadi, a businessman, was among those who donated land for the refugees. 'What I am doing is a kind of charity but they need a lot more help and support from individuals and organisations. They left everything back home,' he said.

But local residents sometimes fear differences cropping up in the larger community due to the presence of these refugees. Thus the Rohingya live in constant distress and fear of being attacked.

Language and cultural barriers

Language is another barrier for the community in India, especially in Hyderabad. This restricts employment opportunities because most do not know either Urdu or Telugu. Some who do speak Urdu help others to communicate. In addition, their food habits and culture are completely different. All this creates problems of assimilation and makes the Rohingya feel insecure, alienated and discriminated against. The feeling of alienation is the major reason behind conflicts, which cause disharmony and turmoil.

Search for livelihood

Often met with suspicion, the Rohingya search for livelihood becomes even more difficult. To make a living they work as daily wage labourers and seek odd jobs as security guards and helpers in small shops, says Lateef Mohammed Khan of CLMC. As Dudu Miyan, another migrant, says, around 150 men went to the local 'labourer adda' in Babanagar one day, but only fifty found work. This happens every day. 'A man who is busy looking for work every day has no time to even think about causing trouble,' he said, countering allegations that Rohingya were involved in violent incidents.[22]

At the Balapur camp, we asked the Rohingya living there a number of questions: How long they had been there? What kind of work did they do? How much did they earn? Why had they come to Hyderabad? What was it like living in Hyderabad? What were the problems they faced? Did they want to return to Myanmar? Did staying in Hyderabad satisfy their needs?

Abu Hussain, who has been living in the camp from the past two years, said he came to the camp in 2012. He said there was no fixed work and went to a nearby place where they were given daily jobs. There were days when they did not get any work, but when they did they earned around INR 400 a day. The reason why he came to Hyderabad was that he thought that if he stayed in Myanmar any longer, his family would be killed.

Living conditions

The hundreds of Rohingya settled in makeshift camps in Hyderabad struggle for survival every day. The living conditions in the camps are pathetic: they live in unsanitary conditions and have no water to drink most of the time. Many have been camping in the city for more than a year, but basic amenities such as food, clean water, medicine and clothes still elude them.[23] Instead, tarpaulin sheets and open sewerage drains greet visitors. At the

Balapur camp, however, the Rohingya said they had faced water problems in the past, but thanks to the efforts of the Salamah Centre a borewell had been installed to solve the problem.

Women and children

A number of widows and pregnant women live in precarious conditions in the Rohingya camps, but children are the worst affected, with many falling sick due to the lack of proper food and medicine.[24] The UNHCR says many children work to support their families instead of attending school. 'Sanitation and health issues are of concern, especially in the makeshift settlements, including maternal and child health,' a spokesperson of the agency said.[25]

We conducted a focused group discussion at the Balapur camp, speaking to eleven women in a group: Kaushala, Zoharhati, Mariam, Alwar, Umahato, Arafa, Jamila Behen, Sanam, Swamina, Anawar Begum and Noor Fatima. All of them have been staying in the camp for the past two years except Jamila Behen and Zoharhati. During our discussion it was revealed that these two women had been living in the camp for the past ten years. Although we had got the impression that the Rohingya refugees had been migrating to Hyderabad in recent times, we realized that migration could be traced further back. Jamila Behen's and Zoharhati's responses were similar to those of more recent refugees, which showed that their issues had remained largely unaddressed for so many years. Most of them believed that unemployment and health care were the biggest challenges they faced; due to lack of money they went hungry for days, or sometimes ate on alternate days; the children in the camp lived in unhealthy conditions, with no proper sanitation and nutrition. Language was a major problem for them, hampering negotiations for jobs. Nonetheless, the women felt they were much safer in Hyderabad as compared to Myanmar, where many women have been raped and abused frequently. The education of the children was also an issue: the money they earned was not sufficient to provide for it.

The Salamah Centre, administered by Mansoor Ahmed, takes in migrants, including Rohingya, and gives children an education along with accommodation. Field visits to Rohingya camps in Hyderabad revealed that education can make a big difference. This was evident when we met the children at the centre who were better read, better spoken and more motivated to do something in life compared to the children we met in the Balapur camp.

On 7 January 2015, I visited the head office of the Salamah Centre in Char Minar.[26] It was basically a relief and rehabilitation committee run by Mansoor

Ahmed. I spoke with some children: Sheikh Alkama, Farhana, Asama, Nazima, Farzan and Sheikh. All these students loved staying in the hostel and going to school every day. When I asked them whether they missed home, they said they did a little but enjoyed being in Hyderabad. I asked them their favourite subjects: they ranged from mathematics to English and the social sciences. A feature of this school, beginning with lower kindergarten and going up to class 10, was that it was not an Islamic institution. It gave equal weight to all subjects. I went to see the school and the hostel the girls were living in; it was neat and clean, and the kitchen was hygienic and the space adequate. The students were happy and did not experience the difficulties their parents faced. Talking to Mansoor Ahmed, I gathered that the Salamah Centre was a place for children from the disadvantaged and backward sections of society. The fees were nominal: INR 300 per month. The school was only for girls.

Health facilities and issues

Rohingya face acute healthcare problems. The physical infirmities suffered by the Rohingya in the Balapur camp are exacerbated by their inability to afford a doctor. There have been instances of Rohingya collecting money for months just to afford medical tests and buy prescribed medicines. Field interviews also showed that there were some clinics and doctors who exploited their vulnerability, charging for repeated and unnecessary check-ups and tests.

During an interview, Abu Hussein at the Balapur camp reiterated that the major issue was healthcare. He had taken his son Zia to a local hospital called St Martha's where the doctor asked him to undergo a number of cumulatively expensive blood tests. Not having enough money, he could not get all the tests done, so he started saving money for the tests. When he went to the doctor the second time, after the tests were done, he gave him a list of other tests to be carried out. This attitude of doctors towards the Rohingya was a matter of deep concern for them.[27]

Police persecution

The Rohingya in Hyderabad are wary of needless police interrogation every time a Hindu or Buddhist structure comes under attack, as the needle of suspicion invariably points to them. Although hundreds of Rohingya refugees have made the city their own, they are still apprehensive about policemen knocking on their doors, as they did after the serial blasts in Bodh Gaya,

Bihar, in July 2013. Says Abdullah, a Rohingya who came to Hyderabad in 2012: 'The local people told us about the blasts. The police frequently ask us to produce documents and such harassment has become part of our lives.'[28]

Then in November 2014, Khalid Mohammed, arrested by the National Investigation Agency from Hyderabad in connection with the Khagragarh blast in Bengal, turned out to be a Rohingya Muslim from Myanmar, who had allegedly spent considerable time in Myanmar training batches of militants along with members of the Lashkar-e-Toiba, before slipping into India in 2013.[29] This irreversibly cast the entire Rohingya community under a shadow of suspicion.

A government official told the news agency Press Trust of India that a meeting convened for state principal secretaries (home) was meant to take note of alarming reports of Rohingya marrying Indian girls, especially in Jammu and Kashmir (Rohingya Muslims get married to natives of Kishtwar and Baramulla),[30] and staying in Jammu and Kashmir, Delhi, Haryana, Maharashtra, Rajasthan, Uttar Pradesh, Andhra Pradesh and Manipur. An alert had been sounded across India after to keep an eye on Rohingya migrants. Nonetheless, as a senior police officer said,

> Since they are poor, uneducated and alien to the land here, they are likely to be exploited and used by hardliners. There is no hard evidence to suspect anyone and the police are maintaining total surveillance. Other than offences related to fake passport or Aadhar, they have not been involved in any act threatening the security of the nation.[31]

The police and security agencies however have been caught off guard by the presence of the Jamat-Ul-Mujahideen Bangladesh, connected to the Rohingya Solidarity Organisation, in their backyard. So they are keeping tabs through a host of measures like fingerprinting, keeping records of employment status, demographic details and photographs and stepping up vigilance.[32] Hyderabad police commissioner C. V. Anand has issued instructions for migrants to be registered in some way and wants long-term visas and UNHCR cards issued to them immediately so that the local police and intelligence agencies can monitor them. On 20 July 2015, the Indian government convened a meeting of principal secretaries (home) of seven states to discuss the arrival of more than 100,000 Rohingya Muslims who were settling in India and measures to monitor 'their activities given their vulnerability to radicalisation'.[33]

According to the COVA, 1,806 refugees from Myanmar have registered with them. Physical verification has shown that only 1,725 refugees were found staying in camps in Hyderabad. Only 461 refugees from Myanmar were issued refugee cards; these were being processed.[34] Till the UNHCR issues cards to all of them, COVA will help the local police station to get Rohingya staying in their area registered and get details of families, SIM cards/cell numbers, Aadhar cards, voter identification cards, ration cards, driving licences and other forms of documentation. A sub-inspector will maintain separate registers for the camps in relevant police stations. If they are moving in and out of settlements and travelling to Jammu and Kashmir or other states, they have to inform the local police station about their movements and report to relevant police stations on their return. Their sources of livelihood will also be enquired into and noted along with details of bank accounts. Police officials do not deny the vulnerability of Rohingya, who they believe can be easily persuaded by extremists to take to radical paths.

The criminalization of the Rohingya is thus a reality in India. As Arendt had foretold years ago:

> The stateless person, without right to residence and without the right to work, had of course constantly to transgress the law. He was liable to jail sentences without ever committing a crime. More than that, the entire hierarchy of values which pertain in civilized countries was reversed in his case. Since he was the anomaly for whom the general law did not provide, it was better for him to become an anomaly for which it did provide, that of the criminal.[35]

Humanitarian perspective

The challenges that Rohingya continue to face are grim reminders of a humanitarian crisis. Their daily struggle for existence persists not just in Myanmar, but as this chapter has illustrated, even in countries they have been migrating to. In Myanmar the Rohingya faced continuous discrimination, as was evident from the 2014 census which took place in Myanmar and from which the Rohingya were excluded.[36] Actions like these merely illustrate the unequal and unfair treatment meted out to Rohingya in the state of Myanmar. The Buddhist majority believes that the state belongs to them and not to the Rohingya. Ethnic violence has become an everyday part of the lives of people in Myanmar and created fear in the minority group.

The facilities given to the displaced Rohingya in the camps set up in Myanmar are inadequate. The quality of health care is poor, especially because most doctors treating the Rohingya are Buddhists and in many cases not very concerned about their patients. The deplorable conditions in the Rohingya camps in Myanmar highlight their terrible condition. The actions of the authorities have been described as a 'crime against humanity'.[37]

Legal perspective

The process of addressing any refugee issue has been hindered by the lack of an effective legal framework in India. The manner of dealing with issues has often been politically motivated; often actions have been taken mainly to improve diplomatic relations with a particular country. Existing laws in India like the Foreigners Act, 1946, are completely outdated. This law simply defines any person as a foreigner who is not a citizen of India; this includes refugees and stateless people. A similar provision was also introduced through an amendment of the act in 2003 which failed to make any distinction between refugees and their special circumstances and other foreigners and illegal immigrants.[38]

Under Section 3(2) of the Act, the Indian government has wide discretionary powers to regulate the entry and movement of foreigners within India. The Foreigners Order, 1948, also restricts the entry of foreigners into Indian territory without proper authorization at given entry points. Every foreigner should be in possession of a valid passport and visa while entering India, unless exempted. Most often, refugees are not in possession of these documents and thus are refused entry.[39]

India is not a party to the 1951 Refugee Convention, but it is bound by the international principle of non-refoulement, which prevents a country from repatriating refugees to countries where their life and liberty are under serious threat. The Foreigners Act lays down the principle that the Indian government can *repatriate* foreigners, including asylum-seekers, through deportation, and this is therefore in violation of international customary law. Here again we see a conflict between the existing laws.

Article 51(c) of the Constitution provides that India 'shall endeavour to foster respect for international law and treaty obligations in the dealings of organised peoples with one another'. Article 253 of the Constitution gives parliament the 'power to make any law for the whole or any part of the territory of India for implementing any treaty, agreement or convention with any other country or countries or any decision made at any international conference, association or other body'. India is in favour of formulation of an international and domestic law consistent with its fundamental rights.

A national model refugee law for granting statutory protection to refugees has long been considered in India but is yet to be implemented. The model law aims to harmonize norms and standards on refugee law, establish a procedure for granting refugee status and guarantee them their rights and fair treatment.

In India, refugees are placed under three broad categories. Category I refugees receive full protection from the Indian government (for example, Tamil refugees from Sri Lanka); category II refugees are those who are granted refugee status by the UNHCR and are protected under the principle of non-refoulement(for example, refugees from Myanmar and Afghanistan); and category III refugees, who are neither recognized by the Indian government nor the UNHCR but have entered India and have been assimilated into the local community (for example, Chin refugees from Burma living in the state of Mizoram). The question is whether India needs a proper and appropriate refugee law and what are the advantages of framing such a law. Till there is further clarity on the legal framework within which refugees and stateless persons stay on Indian soil, people like the Rohingya will always be living in a state of limbo.

Political dimensions

The challenge for the Rohingya is not just to deal with the ethnic conflict but also to deal with the government in Myanmar, which opposes the community due to perceived threats. One of the major reasons for the government of Myanmar not to recognise the Rohingya community is the fear of the other ethnic communities in Myanmar who are and can be in conflict with them in the future. Thus the Rohingya live in fear of the government eventually committing genocide against them. Therefore, there is a great need for international support to promote awareness about their plight. Although the international media played a crucial role in focusing attention on the grave plight of the Rohingya in 2012, it is seen to be generally skewed towards emphasizing the 'unsympathetic' role played by Bangladesh and Thailand in turning back genuine refugees, and criticizing their approach towards the accommodation of vulnerable individuals.

Myanmar President Thein Sein has been much applauded for implementing successful political and economic reforms in the country but at the same time has been criticized for discrimination against Rohingya by the government. The Rohingya were given voting rights in Myanmar's 2010 elections with the promise of citizenship if they voted for the military regime's representatives. But the Rohingya continued to remain deprived of citizenship, marking a policy of exclusion that was made official with the passing of the

1982 Citizenship Law that deemed them stateless. Then came the ethnic cleansing in Rakhine State in 2012, triggered by the rape and murder of a Rakhine woman by three Muslim men, which led to Rakhine mobs rampaging through Sittwe and other parts of Rakhine to drive out the Rohingya from their midst. The violence that ensued led to the deaths of hundreds and mass displacement of thousands of Rohingya.

Myanmar's policies continue to be discriminatory towards its minorities. President Thein Sein has recently signed a new law that requires women to wait at least thirty-six months between bearing two children. Activists allege that this law is to target the Muslim Rohingya community, in the context of the perception that their high rate of population growth will turn the Buddhists into a minority in Rakhine State.

More disturbing is the fact that even some pro-democracy dissidents belonging to Myanmar's ethnic majority refuse to acknowledge the Rohingya as compatriots. Pro-democracy organizations are of the view that the Rohingya do not constitute a Burmese ethnic group. The nationalists also say that countries criticizing Myanmar for its refusal to recognise the Rohingya should respect the country's sovereignty. They are not alone in taking this position.

When it comes to the Rohingya and the kind of atrocities they live under, one needs to question the political willingness of the governments of Myanmar and other countries to work towards a solution. The major countries to which the Rohingya have migrated are Bangladesh, Thailand, Malaysia and India. Bangladesh has been receiving Rohingya migrants for a long time now and this trend is not likely to stop in the near future. Although Bangladesh has been trying to accommodate the Rohingya, they have not been able to provide basic necessities. Efforts have been made by the Bangladesh government to resettle the Rohingya, but these have failed. This failure is partially due to political unwillingness and also because resettlement is not a viable option with regard to the Rohingya, who represent a stateless people.

The recent humanitarian crisis that was exposed with reports and images of thousands of Rohingya Muslims being trapped in rickety boats on the high seas, fleeing persecution at home, and not being admitted by Malaysia, Thailand and Indonesia, has turned the world's eyes towards 'the most persecuted people'.[40] Still, the Rohingya remain stateless and unwanted.

Notes

1 See P. M. Velath, 'The tragic case of the Rohingya Refugees', *Deccan Herald*, 25 July 2015, www.deccanherald.com/content/485583/tragic-case-rohingya-refugees.html, accessed on 7 September 2015.

2 *Ibid.*
3 See 'Ending statelessness', www.unhcr.org/pages/49c3646c155.html, accessed on 1 January 2015.
4 T. Pagadala, 'Seeking new homes in Hyderabad', *India Together,* Hyderabad, 2013, http://indiatogether.org/rohingya-human-rights, accessed on 1 January 2015.
5 See V. Najappa, 'Rohingya Muslims: Worry ahead for India', 4 June 2015, www.oneindia.com/feature/rohingya-muslims-worry-ahead-for-india-1767313.html, accessed on 1 August 2015.
6 *Ibid.*
7 *Ibid.* The Government of India says that as long as the Rohingya obtain a valid visa and a refugee card, there is no major problem. However, the issue is with those who are staying illegally. There is a dedicated refugee camp in Jammu and Kashmir, and all formalities need to be completed there. The problem, however, is that the Rohingya Muslims are found in several other places such as Delhi, Noida, Mewat, Saharanpur, Muzaffarnagar, Aligarh, Hyderabad and Mumbai. These places do not have certified camps and many are living illegally without a valid visa or refugee card.
8 See S. Janyala, 'Cyberabad police seek UNHCR help to keep tab on Rohingya refugees', 1 August 2015, www.indianexpress.com, accessed on 1 September 2015.
9 Interview held on 9 January 2015.
10 *Ibid.*
11 See S. Mohammed, 'Rohingyas in Hyderabad live in fear', *Times of India,*9 July 2013, http://timesofindia.indiatimes.com/city/hyderabad/Rohingyas-in-Hyderabad-live-in-fear/articleshow/20980972.cms, accessed on 1 January 2015.
12 *Ibid.*
13 Pagadala, 'Seeking new homes in Hyderabad'.
14 *Ibid.*
15 Narrated in interviews conducted by Kriti Chopra in Hyderabad on 10 January 2015.
16 Pagadala, 'Seeking new homes in Hyderabad'.
17 Interview with author in Hyderabad in June 2015, see 'Buddhist mob attacked madrasa at 02 midnight, killed over 200', *Ummid.com*, 10 July 2015.
18 See 'Around 1500 Rohingya Muslims take refuge in Hyderabad', 11 July 2013, www.rediff.com/news/report/around-1500-rohingya-muslims-take-refuge-in-hyderabad/20130711.htm, accessed on 10 August 2015.
19 See 'Hyderabad's Rohingya refugees fight language barriers', 30 June 2013, www.thehindu.com/news/cities/Hyderabad/hyderabads-rohingya-refugees-fight-language-barriers/article4866622.ece, accessed on 10 August 2015.
20 See 'Iran offers cash assistance to Rohingya refugees in Hyderabad', *Reliefweb,*3 August 2012, http://reliefweb.int/report/india/iran-offers-cash-assistance-rohingya-muslim-refugees-hyderabad, accessed on 10 September 2015.
21 The *Siasat Daily* is an Urdu-language daily published from Hyderabad.
22 Mohammed, 'Rohingyas in Hyderabad live in fear'.
23 M.A.R. Farheed, 'Rohingyas exile struggles in India', *Al Jazeera*, 6 January 2014, www.aljazeera.com/indepth/features/2014/01/rohingya-exiles-struggle-survive-india-201416143243337187.html, accessed on 23 November 2014.

24 *Ibid.*
25 *Ibid.*
26 First-person account of Kirti Chopra.
27 After interviews with the migrants, as the researcher was leaving the camp, a man called Rehman came by, desperately asking for help, asking for money to be given to him as the doctor had prescribed him a few medicines and a number of tests for which he did not have money. The researcher herself took the prescription and went along with him to St Martha's Hospital to look into the matter. On reaching there around late evening, she found that the doctors had left and the hospital was going to be closed soon. She tried to talk to the authorities, but they refused to talk to her about anything and they were rude in all their replies.
28 See 'Serial blasts rock Bodh Gaya temple', *Hindu*, 8 July 2013, www.the hindu.com/news/national/other-states/serial-blasts-rock-bodh-gaya-temple/article4891094.ece, accessed on 20 September 2015.
29 According to intelligence officials, Khalid mentioned receiving large funds from Rohingya based in Karachi and Saudi Arabia. After slipping into India in November last 2014, Khalid confessed having travelled extensively to meet Rohingya migrants in Delhi, Lucknow and Jammu before setting up a base in Hyderabad. It confirmed the suspicions of the Intelligence Bureau of India that terror groups like the Jamaat-ul-Mujahideen Bangladesh (JMB) and the Al-Qaeda had managed to infiltrate their men into Rohingya camps. See S. Datta, 'Arrested Rohingya trained Militants in Myanmar', *Hindustan Times*, 23 November 2014, www.hindustantimes.com/india-news/arrested-rohingya-trained-militants-in-myanmar/article1-1289131.aspx, accessed on 30 March 2015.
30 'Government calls meeting with 7 states to discuss activities of Rohingya Muslims in India', *Press Trust of India*, 6 July 2015, http://www.worldbulletin. net/haber/161896/india-calls-meet-with-7-states-on-rohingya-muslims, accessed on 30 April 2018.
31 See 'Terror threat in Hyderabad, Rohingya Muslims under scanner', *Siasat Daily*, 23 July 2015, https://archive.siasat.com/news/terror-threat-hyderabad-rohingyas-muslim-under-scanner-797988/, accessed on 30 April 2018.
32 See R. V. Pisharody, 'After terror threat in Hyderabad, cops step up vigil on Rohingyas', *New Indian Express*, 23 July 2015.
33 See, 'India calls meet with 7 states on Rohingya Muslims', 8 July 2015, www. worldbulletin.net/todays-news/161896/india-calls-meet-with-7-states-on-rohingya-muslims, accessed on 15 September 2015.
34 See Press Trust of India, 'Cops seek UNHCR help to monitor Rohingya refugees in Hyderabad', www.business-standard.com, accessed on 31 July 2015.
35 H. Arendt, *The Origins of Totalitarianism*, Cleveland and New York: Meridian Books, World Publishing Company, 1958, www.cscd.osaka-u.ac.jp/user/rosaldo/101010OTHA.htm, accessed on 1 June 2015.
36 See 'Burma Census is not counting Rohingya Muslims', www.theguardian.com/world/2014/apr/02/burma-census-rohingya-muslims-un-agency, accessed on 1 June 2015.
37 See J. Motlagh, 'These aren't refugee camps, they are concentration camps, people are dying in them', *Time*, 10 June 2014, http://time.com/2888864/rohingya-myanmar-burma-camps-sittwe/, accessed on 1 August 2015.

38 B. Acharya, 'The law, policy and practise of refugee protection in India', 2004, www.researchgate.net/publication/256016766_The_Law_Policy_and_Practice_of_Refugee_Protection_in_India, accessed on 1 August 2015.

39 *Ibid.*

40 See H.-Y. Lo, 'The plight of the Rohingya Muslims: The world turns a blind eye', *International Post*, 10 June 2015, http://theinternationalpostmagazine.com/10/06/2015/world/plight-rohingya-muslims-world-turns-blind-eye/, accessed on 1 September 2015.

4

THE JAILED ROHINGYA IN WEST BENGAL

Suchismita Majumder

Stateless in fact

Among Myanmar's ethnic minorities, the Rohingya, a stateless population, stand out for the severe repression they have suffered at the hands of the Burmese authorities for decades. The term 'Rohingya' refers to Muslims from northern Rakhine State (formerly Arakan) in Myanmar. They form an ethnic, linguistic and religious minority both in Buddhist-majority Myanmar and in their province Rakhine and have been subjected to repeated waves of persecution and forced displacement.

The Rohingya lack a nationality or 'status' in accordance with the liberal notions of citizenship. They became stateless in 1982 with the enactment of a revised citizenship law, which excluded the Rohingya from a list of 135 national ethnic groups. In law, statelessness is lack of nationality or the absence of a recognized link between an individual and any state. There is general agreement that a dejurestateless person is someone who is 'not considered as a national by any state under the operation of its law', says the Convention Relating to the Status of Stateless Persons. However, there are millions of people who have not been formally denied or deprived of nationality but who lack the ability to prove their nationality or, despite documentation, are denied access to many human rights that other citizens enjoy. These people may be de facto stateless – that is, stateless in practice, if not in law – or cannot rely on the state of which they are citizens for protection. Although individuals who have legal citizenship and its accompanying rights may take both for granted, what they enjoy is one extreme of a continuum between full, effective citizenship and de jure statelessness, in which individuals have neither legal citizenship nor any attendant rights. In between these extremes are millions of de facto stateless persons denied effective protection. Estimates of the current number of stateless persons in the world range from eleven million to fifteen million, who live without a nationality in legal limbo.[1]

Although Myanmar shares borders with five countries (Bangladesh, China, India, Laos and Thailand), Rohingya are found across the world. Many of them have crossed more than one international border in search of a secure life. They enter India through the northeast, say officials. Thousands of Rohingya Muslims have taken refuge in Delhi, Jammu, Noida, Mewat, Saharanpur, Muzaffarnagar, Aligarh, Hyderabad and Mumbai.[2] A steady influx of Rohingya into West Bengal via Bangladesh is causing concern. A senior intelligence official told the *Hindu* that 'more than one thousand' Rohingya refugees had been detained and sent to prisons in the state in the last six months. But the West Bengal government has no clear idea of the actual number of the undocumented immigrants who have entered the state in the past few years.[3]

This chapter is an attempt to depict briefly the life of Rohingya in their own country as well as in Bangladesh and India, where they have migrated to seek refuge. It explores the struggle of these people for survival, against all the discrimination, exploitation and difficulties they face, focusing on those who are detained in correctional homes in West Bengal.[4] It also tries to understand how Rohingya live amidst persecution, what they do, how they migrate and what they need at present to have a secure life. With these objectives, the author conducted interviews with 100 Rohingya in correctional homes. The data used in this study was gathered from February to July 2015. Discussions and interviews were also held with officers of the Department of Correctional Administration. At a meeting with the Relief and Charitable Foundation of India (RCFI), their services for Rohingya people in correctional homes were also discussed. The RCFI has signed a memorandum of understanding with the Global Rohingya Centre (GRC) to support and rehabilitate Rohingya in India. The RCFI will be the only partner of GRC in India.[5] Some information about Rohingya in Bangladesh was provided by the Ain o Salish Kendra (ASK), a human rights organization in Bangladesh. Apart from these, research chapters, articles and media reports were also consulted.

Driven out

Of the 100 Rohingya who were interviewed, sixty-nine were male and thirty-one female; ninety-nine of them were born in Arakan. Most of them were from Akyab, and a few were from Buthidaung. Most of those interviewed were between the ages of 18 and 30; six were older than 60. Most of them could speak only their mother tongue, Rohingya/Ansolik – Bengali mixed with Urdu, Arabic, English and Burmese. They knew little Bengali. Fifty-seven per cent of respondents were illiterate. Although the International Organization for Standardization (ISO) has recognized the Rohingya language, it does not have a script. The literate among them can read and write the Burmese language. Some Rohingya know Urdu and a few of them also learn Arabic to read the Quran.

In Myanmar, the respondents had mainly been agriculturists. A small percentage was engaged in fishing and trade and business. A few Rohingya were daily labourers and two were clerics. Women were mainly involved in household work. Fifty-five per cent of the respondents, mainly those between below age 24, were unmarried.

Table 4.1 Age- and sex-wise distribution of the select 100 Rohingya refugees interviewed by the author

	Sex		
Age	Male	Female	Total
Below 18	2	0	2
18–24	33	15	48
25–30	13	8	21
31–35	3	4	7
36–40	5	1	6
41–45	3	0	3
Above 45	6	1	7
Above 60	4	2	6
Total	69	31	100

Source: Analysis of field data

Table 4.2 Education levels of the select 100 Rohingya refugees interviewed by the author

	Rohingya		
Education	Male	Female	Total
Illiterate	32	25	57
Literate	26	5	31
Primary education	11	1	12
Total	69	31	100

Source: Analysis of field data

Table 4.3 Marital status of the select 100 Rohingya refugees interviewed by the author

	Rohingya		
Marital status	Male	Female	Total
Unmarried	30	5	35
Married	37	18	55
Widow/widower	1	6	7
Other	1	2	3
Total	69	31	100

Source: Analysis of field data

Violence against Rohingya has mainly been committed by the border police (the infamous Na Sa Ka) in recent times. The forms of violence as reported by respondents under the study were as follows:

Forced labour: All Rohingya men had experienced this, and the women confirmed it. At least a week every month, Rohingya had to work without payment for the military or the border police, when they were beaten indiscriminately or physically tortured in other ways. They have to provide for their own food. Forced labour was a huge burden, leaving them with insufficient time to earn a living. Protest could lead to death.

Restrictions on movement: Rohingya were virtually confined to their village tracts. They had to apply for permission to leave their village, even to visit another one nearby. Sometimes they had to pay for this permit as well. Those given permission to travel had to return home before 10 p.m. 'A Rohingya of my village was murdered by the Buddhists as he was travelling at night,' a respondent said. Although Rohingya were not allowed to have mobile phones, some did so secretly to maintain contact with family members in the other countries.

Restrictions on religious activities: Burning of mosques is very common in Arakan. In the Ramzan month, Buddhists lock the mosques. Rohingya cannot celebrate Eid and are not allowed to sacrifice animals. Sometimes Buddhists lock the doors of mosques and throw stones at the people inside at the time of *namaz*, killing many. The brother of Md. Kalu, a respondent, was attacked with a sword when he was returning from a mosque. His head was separated from his body. 'There is no place for the son of a Muslim. It is a curse to be a Muslim in Burma,' said a respondent. But none of the Rohingya mentioned forced conversions.

Restrictions on marriage: Since the creation of the border police in 1992, the authorities in northern Rakhine State have made it mandatory for Rohingya to seek permission to get married. In recent years, imposition of restrictions on marriage has further intensified. Both families have to pay a fee to get permission. The amount varies. The age of consent for girls is 18.

Restrictions on family size: Respondents said that from 2007, couples who wanted to marry had to sign a contract specifying they would not have more than two children. Non-compliance was punished with imprisonment. A Rohingya family had to pay MMK 7,000–8,000 to register a birth.

Land confiscation and burning the houses of Rohingya are regular incidents in Arakan. 'We had our own paddy field, vegetable garden, and a house. Our house was set on fire. Our land was taken away. We have lost everything,' said a respondent.

Since independence, Myanmar has been plagued by ethno-religious tensions and armed conflicts. While most conflicts have been between the central government and ethnic minorities on the question of autonomy, tensions also exist between ethnic groups, as with those between the Rakhine Buddhists and Rohingya Muslims in Rakhine State. On 28 May 2012, the tension between these two communities was sparked with the rape and murder of a Rakhine woman, which was followed by the retaliatory killing of ten Muslims by Rakhine Buddhists on 3 June. Following the two incidents, riots broke out between the two communities in three different townships: Sittwe, Maungdaw and Buthidaung. Rioters on both sides torched and destroyed homes, shops and guest houses and engaged in a killing spree.[6] Violence between Buddhists and Muslims in Arakan State has existed for several decades, leading, for example, to an exodus of Rohingya Muslims in 1978 during the Burma Socialist Programme Party (BSPP) military government and in 1991–2, at the time of Operation PyiThaya. Sixty-eight of those interviewed were affected by the 2012 riots. Abdul Kasim, age 19, was in Akyab, Arakan, at the time of the riot. The *madrasa* where he studied was burnt, as was his neighbour's house. He wandered in the hills for seven days, eating what he could gather. Returning to his village, he found it had been completely destroyed. He went from village to village in the mountains looking for his parents. While he was roaming, he met a group of Rohingya people who were escaping. He came to India with them. After crossing the border, he was arrested.

Satara Bibi was burnt while trying to save her belongings. Hospitals refuse to provide treatment to people who suffer burns. Saidul Golami, age 19, said that at the time of riots in 2012, bodies of murdered Rohingya were carried away by rivers. He also said that the permission of the army or border police was needed to bury the dead, as a result of which bodies kept piling up. Harun Rasid, 65, is one of two Rohingya who were in Myanmar in 1991–2. His house was set on fire. He left with his family and lived in Kutupalong camp in Bangladesh for two years. When the crisis was over, he returned to Myanmar. He built a house again, but ultimately he had to leave in 2008 with his family.

Jallal, Amina and Belua saw the violence of 1991–2 and 2012. Jallal, 53, escaped to Teknaf in Bangladesh in 1991. After a year and a half he returned to Myanmar, where his house had been taken over by Buddhists. He managed to build a hut, but in 2012 he decided to leave, in the face of increasing danger.

Women are victims of double discrimination – for being Rohingya and for being women. The rape of Rohingya women – even those who are pregnant – is common in Arakan, and Rohingya men are powerless to protest. Women are also abducted. Some are released, and some never return. Pregnant women can be murdered in hospitals, so they deliver at home. Those very near delivery are often attacked and eviscerated. At least ten respondents, both men and women, mentioned this. Some of them had witnessed such brutality. Minors are also tortured sexually. Parents of 'good-looking' women are required to pay exorbitant amounts to get marriage permits so that they cannot get married. These women are the main targets of the border police. Alima and Belua, both 60, who were in Myanmar in 1991–2, had seen soldiers cut the breasts of many women. Only three Rohingya men disclosed how women in their families were tortured.

Multiple causes, including forced labour, confinement to home, the fear of rape and the fear of being killed, have led to migration. Although 2012 and some other years are marked for extreme human rights violation and mass exodus, violence against Rohingya has continued over the years leading to continuous migration. Of the respondents in this study, seventy-eight had migrated in 2012 or after that.

In transit

Rohingya migration has been a serious concern for Bangladesh since 1978. The majority of the 250,000 Rohingya who fled in 1991–92 were initially sheltered in government-administered refugee camps in Cox's Bazar district. The Rohingya were recognized as prima facie refugees by executive order because they were Muslim. Not long after, Bangladesh and Myanmar signed a bilateral agreement to return those Rohingya who could establish bona fide residence. A controversial repatriation programme followed, in which almost all of the 250,000 were repatriated to Myanmar by 2000. Rohingya who had reached Bangladesh by mid-1992 were registered. The estimated 200,000 who arrived after that were not recognized as refugees and not permitted in the camps. At the same time, the porous border with Myanmar means there is a constant flow of persons who enter Bangladesh illegally. Consistent with the government's policy, UNHCR has not registered those outside the camps, nor does it actively engage with this self-settled population. Documentation is not provided to those outside the camps.

At present, the UNHCR provides support to around 32,000 registered Rohingya refugees in partnership with some non-governmental organizations (NGO). The refugees are not legally allowed to work or go outside the camps. But the number of undocumented Myanmar Rohingya in Bangladesh is 200,000–500,000. They live in unofficial settlements or in Bangladeshi villages with no legal protection from arrest or abuse and little or no humanitarian assistance. They are scattered over Chittagong, Bandarban, Rangamati, Khagrachari and Cox's Bazar city and survive mainly on daily wage labour. Some run small businesses. Traffickers are also found among this population. In one unofficial settlement, malnutrition rates were twice the emergency threshold. The lack of assistance for both unregistered refugees and host communities has increased tensions over scarce resources such as water and firewood, leading to physical and sexual violence against refugees, particularly women and girls. There is little security for undocumented refugees as they have no access to the UNHCR and other human rights organizations.[7]

Although 98 per cent of Rohingya refugees head into Bangladesh first, the latter is not their choice of destination. Of the 100 interviewed, sixteen wanted to be in Bangladesh while sixty-five preferred India. One Rohingya man, now 42, was born in Bangladesh and had never been to Myanmar. His parents, wife and children are in Cox's Bazar. He has come to India to earn more money. Seven Rohingya – BodiulAlam, Nur Kabir, Noor Alam, Ayesha Bibi, Ushnara Bibi, Hamida Begum and Nur Begam – migrated to Bangladesh in their childhood. BodiulAlam and Nur Kabir entered Bangladesh in 2008 when they were 11 and 12, respectively. After spending five years there, Bodiul came to India. Nur escaped from Myanmar with some neighbours, leaving his family behind. After living in Cox's Bazar for seven years he came in India to live in Jammu with his uncle. He does not know what happened to his parents, sisters and brothers. He has been in the Balurghat District Correctional Home since May 2015. Noor Alam spent twelve years in Bangladesh where he went with his parents in 1997 at the age of 5. In 2009, he left Bangladesh with almost all family members to settle in Delhi.

Ayesha Bibi, 21, and Ushnara Bibi, 22, had been in the Kutupalong camp since childhood. Both of them got married there. Ushnara Bibi has a Bangladeshi refugee card. Hamida Begum, 18, lived in a village in Bangladesh for ten years. Her parents have refugee cards in Bangladesh but she was not able to get one. Noor Begum, 20, has been in Cox's Bazar since she was a child. Her parents still live there. She knows many Rohingya people who are in Jammu and Delhi. None of these women can tell the exact year they left Myanmar. It appears that they migrated to Bangladesh between 2003 and 2005.

Among the reasons why Rohingya leave Bangladesh for India are the search for a livelihood and a better life; the presence of relatives, some of whom have refugee cards; harassment, including frequent arrests, in Bangladesh; and the fear of being sent back to Myanmar. Migration out of Bangladesh is evidently also caused by the fact that in a number of cases some members of a family get refugee status while others don't, forcing all of them to leave if they want to stay together.

After crossing the border, Faruk was in Bangladesh for a month. Then he was pushed back to Myanmar. After wandering for some days in the mountains, he entered Bangladesh again with sixteen other Rohingya who had also been forced back to Myanmar. Later, he came to India. Nur Sahatu, age 70, lived in Bangladesh for twenty years, fleeing there in 1991 with five children after her husband was murdered. She was in the Nayapara camp and had a refugee card in Bangladesh, but none of her children was registered. Because one of her daughters lived in Delhi, the whole family decided to relocate. They were arrested from English Bazar, Malda. Only two women of all the 100 people interviewed had Bangladeshi refugee cards: Nur Sahatu and Ushnara Bibi.

Negotiating borders

The first Rohingya reached India some twenty years ago, some of whom were asylum-seekers, now settled in Jammu; later arrivals have settled in different locations. Jammu city and its surrounding areas host the largest population of Rohingya in India with nearly 4,000 persons, followed by Hyderabad with about 1,300 persons. Smaller numbers from 250 to 700 persons, have settled in Delhi, Jaipur and Mewat. Even smaller groups live in Uttar Pradesh, including Muzaffarnagar, Saharanpur and Aligarh. The majority live in camp-like situations, while only a minority can afford rented rooms and are scattered among the local population. A few migrant clusters are located in slum areas where the Rohingya share space with local people. Rohingya who have arrived in India recently continue to move to Jammu because of the already established community networks in the area. Thirty-six respondents chose Jammu as their preferred settlement destination and the same number chose Delhi. Like other refugee groups, such as the Chin from Myanmar and Somalis, Rohingya feel safer living in a community. The UNHCR in India was approached by over 2,700 new Rohingya asylum-seekers during 2012 and 5,522 in 2013. As of 1 January 2014, 5,990 Rohingya refugees and asylum-seekers have been registered with UNHCR in India. Many more await registration.[8]

In West Bengal, there is no fixed settlement area for Rohingya. The largest identifiable number is concentrated in correctional homes. ABP Ananda, an electronic news channel headquartered in Kolkata, reported on 6 July 2015 that the number of Rohingya in the state is over 100,000 and that the union government is worried about the continuing migration.

Of those interviewed, ninety-eight had crossed two international borders to come in India, transiting through Bangladesh before entering West Bengal. South Dinajpur, Cooch Behar and North 24 Parganas are the three districts used by Rohingya as a gateway to West Bengal and India. The greatest volume of infiltration occurs through Hilli into South Dinajpur, which is surrounded by Bangladesh in the north, east and south. The Hilli railway station is in Bangladesh and is separated from India only by the tracks. Dinajpur-Dhaka and Dinajpur-Rajshahi trains have to cross Hili station. Many passengers get down from the overcrowded trains before reaching the station, after which it is easy to cross into Bengal without valid documents.[9]

Petrapole and Basirhat are in the North 24 Parganas district. Petrapole is the Indian side of the Petrapole-Benapoleborder checkpoint between India and Bangladesh. Two Rohingya men said they entered Basirhat from Satkhira, Bangladesh; seven who have come through Basirhat said they had taken shelter in Taki, a town in the same district, for some days. Changrabandha is another border crossing and a defunct rail transit point on the India-Bangladesh border in Cooch Behar district. The corresponding point on the Bangladesh side is Burimari in Lalmonirhat district. Only two men chose this border to enter in the state. Whereas Changrabandha and Hilli are in North Bengal, Petrapole and Basirhat are in South Bengal.

Rohingya follow different routes after crossing the border to reach their desired destinations. Among the sixty-four who crossed the border at Hilli, ten managed to reach Delhi, with six of them finally going to Jammu. The rest, who were arrested in Bengal, had planned to follow the same route. Crossing Hilli, they usually went to Balurghat. However, some informants said people sometimes travelled to Bardhaman, in south Bengal, to get a train to Delhi and evade arrest. Most of the twenty-two respondents who crossed the border at Petrapole also wanted to go to Delhi or Jammu. Rohingya who entered through Basirhat mostly wished to go to Hyderabad. Only one Rohingya man in this study tried to go to Mumbai after reaching the railway station in Howrah from Basirhat.

Jahid Hossain was among the six who found their way to Jammu. His Bangladeshi wife and five children were arrested at Hilli, however. Jallal Ahammad and Satara reached Jammu with their five children, leaving behind one child and others who were arrested in Balurghat. Md. Alam and BodiulAlam reached their destination with their families. Of the six, four have refugee cards, while Md. Alim, 25, who has lived in Jammu for three years, and BodiulAlam have not.

Md. Karim and his family reached Delhi safely. But Noor Islam, 26, lost his brother, who had mental problems at the time of the 2012 riots. Their eldest brother was murdered by the border police. A cousin went to Myanmar to bring them to India. They came through the Hilli border. After reaching Delhi, Noor applied for a refugee card and lived for six years in a Zakat Foundation camp with his parents, grandparents and others.[10] He then set off to scour Aligarh, Jammu, Meerut and Kanpur in search of his brother. He returned to Bengal thinking that his brother might be in the border area from where they entered. He was arrested at Hilli More.

Jahid and Abu Sidhi were in one of the Balapur camps in Hyderabad for some days. Jahid had been in different places: Delhi, Jammu, Rajasthan and Hyderabad. He was arrested in Balurghat, from where he had started his journey. Spending four months in Balapur, Abu, 18, wished to return to Bangladesh to his maternal uncle. He could not adjust in India. His parents and other family members were in Myanmar. He was arrested at the Petrapole border.

A 70-year-old woman was hiding with her family members in a village near Hilli border. They intended to go to Delhi to apply for a refugee card. But after fifteen days they were arrested on the way to Malda station in West Bengal. Md. Islam, Md. Amin and Jallal took shelter in Buniadpur, South Dinajpur. They were with their families and were engaged in jute cultivation as daily labourers. After four or five months, they were spotted by the police while going to Malda station with some other people to catch a train for Delhi. All of them were arrested. Harun Rasid was also engaged in jute cultivation in Buniadpur. Police arrested him from there. He has been awaiting trial for twenty-one months. His wife and children live in Jammu. All of them came to India in 2008 and they have refugee cards.

Nur Alam, 48, and Md. Faruk, 18 or 19, who are related, entered West Bengal through the Changrabandha border of Cooch Behar. They left Myanmar in 2011 in search of work and a better living. Nur Alam sold his land in Rakhine and paid the money to a tout who was supposed to help both of them to go to India and arrange for work. They entered Bangladesh and stayed there for about a fortnight before entering West Bengal. Instead of organizing work for them, the tout took them to Phuntsholingin Bhutan. There they worked for three months for practically no wages and were given food once a day. They left the job intending to return to Myanmar and went back to the same border crossing and approached Border Security Force (BSF) personnel to allow them to go to Bangladesh. At that point they were handed over to the police. They were then held in the Jalpaiguri Central Correctional Home. They wanted to be shifted to some other correctional home where they could live with fellow Rohingya. The other eighty-two Rohingya were spotted by BSF personnel or policemen as soon as they crossed into India, being noticeable because of their language. They were arrested near the borders within a couple of days of entering Bengal.

Thirty-eight Rohingya were arrested from or near the border areas, ten in Bongaon, five in Chandpara, one in Basirhat, six at the Kharagpur railway station and five at the Malda railway station. None of them faced any problems at the Howrah or Sealdah railway stations in Kolkata. Some Rohingya said BSF personnel let them go at the Benapole-Petrapole border even though they had no legal documents, but ultimately they were caught.

The 100 Rohingya in correctional homes in West Bengal in July 2015 were distributed across the Balurghat District Correctional Home, where there were forty-eight Rohingya; Berhampore Central Correctional Home, where there were eighteen; Jalpaiguri Central Correctional Home, where there were two; Midnapore Central Correctional Home, where there were six; and Dumdum Central Correctional Home, where there were twenty-six. Officials in these correctional homes said they had been brought in over the past three or four years, usually in family groups.

Rohingya in correctional homes belong to three categories: those under trial (eighty-two), those convicted (four) and those who have served their sentences but are still in prison because they cannot be released due to procedural reasons and who have to live on charity because the government doesn't provide rations (fourteen). Rohingya who are under trial are found in all the correctional homes except Jalpaiguri's. Convicted Rohingya are found only in Behrampore. Those who have served their sentences can be found in Jalpaiguri, Behrampore and Midnapore. Fifty-four of the Rohingya interviewed had been in correctional homes for under a year, all of them under trial; twenty-six had been incarcerated for thirteen to twenty-four months, of whom twenty-three were under trial and three had been convicted; thirteen had been incarcerated for twenty-five to thirty-six months, of whom five were under trial, one had been convicted and seven had served their sentences; and seven had been incarcerated for three to five years, all of whom had served their sentences.

Seven Rohingya remained imprisoned even though they have refugee cards, which they had shown to the police. They had been told that the cards are valid only in Delhi. Five of them were arrested near the Behrampore home, where they had gone to meet family members. Jallal Ahammad and his wife Satara, who managed to get to Jammu leaving one of their six children in Bengal, have been mentioned earlier. They got refugee cards there. After a couple of years they came to the Behrampore home to meet their lost child, having been told that the cards permitted free movement in India, but while returning to Jammu, the police arrested them and seized their cards. Now they are in the Behrampore home and their five children are in Jammu. They don't know what is happening to them. When asked why people with cards were being arrested, a police officer replied that the cards did not permit free movement and were for staying in a particular place. 'Why are people who have been given cards in Delhi coming to West Bengal again?' he asked.

Some Rohingya are allowed to keep their cards – two of them showed their cards during the interview. Correctional home officials admit that some of the people in custody have refugee cards, but the police flatly deny that. They say nobody is allowed to keep anything with them after being arrested. The police seem to be completely unaware of the fact that people with refugee cards sometimes come to meet relatives in correctional homes. Prejudice bred by linguistic differences makes the police even more intolerant.

The two Rohingya men who have refugee cards are in the Balurghat home. One of them is Harun Rasid, who repeatedly says he had been picked up at the Hilli border while waiting for someone. Other Rohingya in the correctional home said it was well known that he used to help people reach Jammu and Delhi after crossing the border. Noor Alam also has a card. In May 2015 he came to Patiram in South Dinajpur from Delhi, where he had been living for six years, to receive an uncle and other relatives who were coming to India from Myanmar via Bangladesh. The whole family was trying to shift to India.

Md. Ali had been living in Jammu for three years with his family and had applied for a UNHCR refugee card. He was arrested near the Hilli police station with his wife and child who were coming from Myanmar through Bangladesh. Ali had gone to Hilli to receive them. This is the story of thousands of Rohingya who are trying to shift to India. Because not all can afford to pay touts big sums of money, all members of a family do not come together, but make the crossing in groups following one another. So families get divided among Myanmar, Bangladesh and India. Abdul Hamid, 22, used to travel between Burma and Bangladesh clandestinely since he was 12. In 2007, he settled in Bangladesh. After staying there for a couple of years there he came to India to earn more money. One of his brothers, who is a labourer, still lives in Cox's Bazar with his parents, while four sisters and two brothers are in Rakhine. Bodiul lived in Jammu with his family for two years. In April 2015, he came to the Hilli border to meet friends who were in Bangladesh. Mention has been made of Noor Islam's cousin, who went to Myanmar to bring him to India, and the tout who took Noor Alam and Md. Faruk to Bhutan via Bangladesh and India.

In some cases, families get separated after coming to India, because while crossing the border some escape arrest and others do not. I met some Rohingya people who had spouses somewhere else in India. On the other hand, sometimes couples or families are arrested together and end up in Bengal's correctional homes. Those who suffer the most are the ones who are separated from their children. Children above age 7 are not allowed to stay with their mothers and are sent to children's homes.

A problem of invisibility is also noticeable. Md. Sarek and Md. Kharesh are two Rohingya men who have been in the Dumdum home for sixteen months, under trial. They were arrested from Bongaon station with their wives and children. Soon after, their wives were sent to Alipore Women's Correctional Home following a court order, although the Dumdum home had a female ward where these two women had been lodged. Their children were also separated, some staying in the Dumdum home and some going with their mothers. Now Sarek and Kharesh don't know how they can contact their wives. Members of a family can meet once in a week if they are in the same correctional home, but there is no such arrangement for inmates of separate correctional homes. Their complaint is that nobody asks them who they are and what they need. But the bigger problem is that the two Rohingya women have become invisible in the eyes of the government. When I wanted to work in correctional homes, I was granted permission to go to the Dumdum home and the Midnapore home, because these two places were known to house Rohingya. Alipore Women's Correctional Home was not mentioned because the authorities did not know about these women.

Still, some Rohingya feel life behind bars in Bengal is more secure than life in Arakan. The language problem is not insurmountable because the correctional homes have some Bangladeshis from Cox's Bazar who understand the language of the Rohingya, but a communication gap remains. New dresses are usually arranged by the authorities concerned as and when needed, but one man lamented that he had been wearing the same clothes for eight months. He had not been able to communicate his need to the relevant officials.

Of the 100 Rohingya interviewed, seven are refugees and the rest asylum-seekers. There are also twelve people in correctional homes who are stated to be Myanmar nationals in court documents, but they are not counted as Rohingya because they are actually Bangladeshis, by their own account. What could account for this mismatch is that some Bangladeshis say they are Rohingya when caught while crossing the border, but later admit to being Bangladeshis. The courts go by the original statement and treat them as Myanmar nationals. These people say they are Rohingya either in the mistaken belief that this will help get them refugee status or because that is the advice they get from touts. Whatever the reason, it makes it difficult to get back to Bangladesh, although eight of them have served their term, while two each are under trial and convicted.

Marriage between Bangladeshi women and Rohingya men is another facet of this problem. After crossing the border, women arrested with their Rohingya husbands and in-laws are labelled Rohingya. Margina Begum, 35, is from the Cox's Bazar. She has been married to Jahid Hossain, a Rohingya, for twenty-two years. Her husband has no Bangladeshi refugee card. At some point, Jahid got the idea that poor people could live a peaceful life in India and they made their way to India in the middle of 2012. While crossing the border, Margina was arrested at the Hilli border with five children. She has been in the Behrampore home for two years. Among her five children, two sons are in Behrampore, two daughters are in a correctional home in Malda and the youngest one is with her. After serving her term, she may have to remain incarcerated like Nur Sahatu, another woman from Cox's Bazar, who has been behind bars for four years although her detention period was for two years. Her husband, too, is a Rohingya. They got married in the Nayapara camp in Bangladesh. She was arrested from English Bazaar, Malda.

Refugees and asylum-seekers who are in detention have not committed any crime. Under international conventions they have the right to seek asylum in any place they can reach, even without valid documents if circumstances force them to. Refugees and asylum-seekers have legally distinct claims on hospitality. But such legal conventions are usually of no help.

Escaping confinement?

The tragic irony of the Rohingya in Bengal is that they end up incarcerated in a place they believed would free them from the confinement of the 'open prison' of Myanmar and the camps of Bangladesh. The United States, however, believes the 'real solution' to the Rohingya refugee issue lies in their going back to Myanmar when the situation changes in Rakhine State. Assistant Secretary of State of the Department of Population, Refugees and Migration Anne Richard has said, 'International pressure could play a part in changing that situation. The real solution for most Rohingya is that we should strive for this that they go home.'[11]

Myanmar has halted a national pilot project to verify the citizenship status of Muslim minorities in western Rakhine State. 'The Rakhine situation is too complicated. The verification process is difficult since applicants are applying [for] an identity which does not exist in the country,' said Rakhine Chief Minister Maung Maung in February 2015. This was a reiteration of the government's position that the Rohingya were illegal migrants from Bangladesh. Officials have said the verification process was being conducted under a 1982 law that bars citizenship registration using the term Rohingya instead of Bengali.

Shwe Maung, a Muslim MP from the western part of Rakhine, says there may be a way around the problem. 'I want to point out we should look at the generation of those who hold temporary citizenship cards,' he said. 'The problem will be solved in the short term if those who hold [temporary] citizenship cards and whose parents hold [temporary] citizenship cards are allowed to apply for citizenship [using] normal procedures, instead of a specific project.'[12]

Aiming to deal with the Rohingya crisis, the Commonwealth Human Rights Initiative in collaboration with the UNHCR organized a one-day training programme for officers of correctional homes in West Bengal on 'Human Rights and Refugee Protection' on 5 December 2014. The training was aimed at facilitating discussions and initiating a dialogue between them, the inmates of the homes and the UNHCR. Such discussion was aimed at enhancing coordination between prison administration and the UNHCR to enable seamless flow and exchange of information, thereby expediting the release of asylum-seekers in detention. The training focused on sensitization to the persecution of Rohingya in Myanmar; imparting appropriate knowledge about displaced people, asylum law and international principles; timely identification of asylum-seekers in detention through various identification tests relating to language, religion, education, occupation and so forth; creating a formal channel to direct the flow of asylum-seekers to the UNHCR; and India's position on asylum-seekers and refugees and the UNHCR's operational procedures in India.

Communication is a huge problem and language is only one part of it. The Rohingya cannot tell people about their history, which undermines their case for asylum. They either don't understand how the process works or are advised to share as little as possible. Involvement of NGOs can improve the situation somewhat. Although RCFI has provided some help to the Rohingya in Delhi, it is completely unaware about their problems in correctional homes in Bengal. Officials say that members of the Gour Bangla Human Rights Awareness Centre visit the correctional homes occasionally to discuss the Rohingya issue, but no NGO intervenes on a regular basis. The involvement of some opportunistic middlemen makes matters worse. Regular involvement of NGOs or the state human rights commission along with government support may produce positive results. The issues on which focus is necessary are providing refugee cards after quick verification; sensitizing police about the problems of Rohingya, especially the arrest and incarceration of people who have refugee cards and visit correctional homes to meet relatives; helping separated families, particularly when children are not with parents; and understanding that Rohingya are not satisfied with getting refugee cards for themselves – they want to bring family members, friends or other members of the community after securing some position in India, which is why Rohingya with refugee cards get sucked into correctional homes.

'We will never go home. They will kill us.' This is the standard reaction of Rohingya when asked whether they wish to return to Myanmar, because they are sure that their homeland will never be safe enough for them. Moreover, once outside Myanmar, Rohingya are systematically denied the right to return to their country. Twice every year, Rohingya in Myanmar are photographed by local authorities and those absent at the time are presumed gone and their names deleted from 'family books'. If such people are found by officials or the police, they are killed on the spot, the respondents say. Even people who have family members in Rakhine don't want to go back. They don't think their relatives are alive anymore. Most respondents were categorical that they wanted to be in India, most wanting to go to Jammu or Delhi where they have relatives or just people of their own community. The main reason for wanting to stay is that they are sure their lives are not in danger here.

The experiences of Rohingya are traumatic, uprooted as they are from one social setting and thrown into another, in the process undergoing untold sufferings. They spend years in refugee camps, where births, marriages and deaths take place within the confines of unfamiliar settings. Family lives are destroyed, with many Rohingya not even knowing whether their homes still exist and whether relatives are alive or dead. Generally, postcards are supplied to inmates of correctional homes so that they can write home. Many Bangladeshis send letters, but no Rohingya does. Acute depression is common in people who experience such a void in their lives. Depression causes suicidal tendencies, for which treatment, counselling and medication is provided.

When I think of the Rohingya I have met in the correctional homes, the first thing that comes to mind is the sadness and hopelessness that seems to mark them out.

Notes

1 B. Baseerat, 'Riot-hit Rohingya Muslims take refuge in Hyderabad', *Times of India*, Hyderabad, 15 April 2015, http://timesofindia.indiatimes.com/city/hyder abad/Riot-hit-Rohingya-Muslims-take-refuge-in-Hyderabad/articleshow/19551921.cms, accessed on 6 May 2015.
2 N. Kumar, 'Burmese Muslim refugees in Delhi, search for haven in J&K', *Sunday Guardian*, New Delhi, 2 November 2013, www.sunday-guardian.com/news/burmese-muslim-refugees-in-delhi-search-for-haven-in-jak, accessed on 5 August 2015.
3 Suvojit Bagchi, 'Rohingya influx – a brewing crisis', *The Hindu*, 17 march 2014 in www.thehindu.com/news/national/other-states/rohingya-influx-a-brew ing crisis/article5797314.ece, accessed on 20 February 2017.
4 From 1992, in accordance with the West Bengal Correctional Services Act, the jails/prisons in the state are known as correctional homes.
5 The RCFI has signed a memorandum of understanding with the Global Rohingya Centre (GRC) to support and rehabilitate Rohingya in India. The RCFI will be the only partner of GRC in India.
6 N. Kipgen, 'Addressing Rohingya problem', *Journal of Asian and African Studies*,49(2), 2014: 234–47.
7 Information about the number of Rohingya in Bangladesh, their living areas and their problems was provided by an officer of Ain O Salish Kendra, a leading human rights organization in Bangladesh.
8 See the report 'Rohingya Refugees and Asylum-Seekers in India: A situational analysis', February 2014. This report was jointly researched and written by four

national NGOs: Development and Justice Initiative (DAJI), BOSCO, Socio-Legal Information Centre and Confederation of Voluntary Associations, with UNHCR support.

9 The information about Hilli border was collected during fieldwork in 2015.

10 See Zakat Foundation of India, registered with the Government of India under the Indian Trusts Act, www.zakatindia.org/RohingiyaMuslims.html, accessed on 10 February 2015.

11 Senior correspondent, 'US pitches for Myanmar citizenship for Rohingya Refugees', *BDNews24*, Bangladesh, 24 January 2015, www.rohingyablogger.com/2015/01/us-pitches-for-myanmar-citizenship-for.html#sthash.WfWW9cQt.dpuf, accessed on 1 February 2015.

12 A. Y. Maung, 'Myanmar halts citizenship verification project for Muslim minorities', *Voice of America*, 5 February 2015, www.voanews.com/a/myanmar-halts-citizenship-verification-project-for-muslim-minorities/2630806.html, accessed on 6 February 2015.

5

ROHINGYA IN BANGLADESH AND INDIA AND THE MEDIA PLANET

Madhura Chakraborty

Stateless people, numbering about ten million according to United Nations High Commissioner for Refugees (UNHCR) estimates,[1] represent a rupture in the very fabric of our imagined geography of a world neatly divided into bordered nation states. Stateless populations, although non-citizens, are in most cases 'subjected non-subjects':[2] without rights, but not without the state's disciplinary interventions and discrimination. This chapter examines how nation states treat stateless non-citizens fleeing persecution, with particular reference to the Rohingya in Bangladesh and India.

Native to the Arakan area or Rakhine State of today's Myanmar, the Rohingya minority Muslim community has been the subject of controversy. The Burman-and Buddhist-dominated leadership of the country has long treated the Rohingya as illegal Bangladeshi infiltrators. Since the late 1970s, Rohingya have been present in large numbers in Bangladesh, particularly in the Teknaf area of Chittagong district across the Naf River separating the Rakhine State from Bangladesh, in refugee camps and elsewhere. Increasing hostility towards the Rohingya from the Awami League government in Bangladesh and continuing discrimination and violence against them in Myanmar has meant that large numbers of Rohingya are now seeking shelter in India.

This chapter is based on interviews as well as ethnographies, news chapter reports and theoretical writings. I have conducted group interviews with seven Rohingya girls at a shelter for minors in Kolkata, India, and an interview with a member of the Kozhikode-based Relief and Charitable

Foundation of India, which is a Muslim charitable organization working with Rohingya. In Bangladesh, I spoke with officials from various international organizations and local experts as well as some Rohingya. In the following sections I argue that the history of this region, coupled with the post-9/11 regime of securitization and the increasing currency of the discourse of terrorism and the concurrent rise of Islamophobia, have combined to make the plight of the Rohingya precarious in ways that are difficult to redress.

Myanmar, Bangladesh and India have a shared colonial past that has shaped their present borders and histories to a great extent. Looking at the colonial and post-colonial history of this region, starting with the Treaty of Peace between the British and the King of Ava in 1826 through the partition of 1947 and post-partition boundary-making through acts such as the North East Reorganisation Act of 1971 (India), Ranabir Samaddar writes:

> [W]hat is remarkable in this nearly two hundred years' history is that, with repeated boundary fixing in this huge region both as internal boundaries between different units of the country and as borders with outside regions/countries, and creation of different administrative-political units, we have in this region the incipient nations and nationalisms, territorialities and ethnicities, peoples and people-hood(s), which cannot live without the links of the past ages, yet cannot digest these links in light of their own emerging claims. They are in many ways therefore the 'divided peoples' – divided across international and the various internal political-administrative borders that cut what they consider now to be their nation. Inasmuch as they must now find out who they are in order to claim national status, they must to an equal degree demarcate who they are not in order to reinforce the claim.[3]

In the following sections I will examine how the Rohingya claims upon citizenship and humanitarian assistance are repeatedly repudiated through the discourses of (il)legitimacy and security that reinforce the tenuous and often arbitrary borders between these three nation states.

Rohingya in Bangladesh: insecure and a threat to national security

My co-researcher and I had the opportunity to meet some of the displaced Rohingya just outside one of the registered refugee camps in Teknaf, Bangladesh. About thirteen Rohingya women, all camp-dwellers, mostly from unregistered settlements around the official camp, sat around us in their black burqas. The translator was a young Rohingya man, one of the few attending college from his community. There was palpable discomfort, certain unease, even mistrust. We asked routine questions: Did you come from Myanmar? How long ago was that? Are there any family members left there? What kind of problems do you face? I had a camera, and to relieve the tension I started taking photographs of a toddler in a woman's lap and then showed it to the mother and child. There was curiosity; everyone smiled and the tension eased. Soon two of the most vocal women, one in her forties and the other in her twenties, took charge of the conversation. They clearly believed that narrating their tales of woes would get them some redress. As a result, they were eager to tell us about the lack of daily necessities that form part of the everyday camp life. We could get only a bare minimum about their travails in Myanmar.

Sensing that we were more interested in tales of trafficking, our young translator exhorted the youngest woman, a shy girl still in her teens, to tell us her tale of being smuggled to Malaysia. He himself, afterwards, talked about how he managed to escape from the clutches of the smugglers after being kept imprisoned in a small boat. From these tales of escape, it became clear that for the younger Rohingya, born and brought up in Bangladesh, the urgency to escape camp life was of paramount importance. For the boy, Rasool, it formed the leitmotif of his life – as a teenager he had escaped repeatedly to Dhaka to reach India but was unsuccessful. For Sahanara, the girl, the escape was coupled with romance. Her friend introduced her to a Rohingya man settled in Malaysia over the phone through the friend's fiancé. She was captured after landing in Malaysia and finally managed to get out of custody thanks to her fiancé; they both flew back to Bangladesh. In a twist of fate, it was there that Sahanara's husband got arrested under the Foreigners Act, and he faces now an uncertain future.

Both these youngsters have a lot of aspirations; they had been educated and worked with non-governmental organizations (NGO) within the camps. Clearly for the young Rohingya, escape, at any cost, is a means of survival, even if it might seem dangerous and even naive to board buses to reach India or trust a stranger and set out on the sea to Malaysia. Whereas the older women saw themselves as settled in Bangladesh, although complaining about lack of amenities, the young people could only envision life outside the constricting camps. Young Rohingya are increasingly frustrated with the restrictions of camp life and are constantly on the lookout for better prospects. We encountered parents in the community whose teenage sons had gone missing, and it was only later they found out that they had tried to take boats to Malaysia. Similarly we heard stories of nuclear family units who had left for India – mostly Jammu and Hyderabad. At least in one case there were reports of a smuggler/trafficker holding a family as bonded labourers till they worked off a sum 'owed' to him.

About 28,000 Rohingya live in the two UNHCR camps at Kutupalong and Nayapara in Cox's Bazar. An estimated 300,000 live outside the camps in villages or makeshift camps and are registered neither by the Government of Bangladesh nor UNHCR. They have stopped registering Rohingya since 1992. The insecurity and vulnerability of the unregistered Rohingya has increased following the voter registration verification process in 2007–8, when many unregistered Rohingya had their names struck off the voters' list. From interviews with a number of stakeholders and aid organizations, it turned out that villagers would often adopt a Rohingya family and provide an identity in exchange for free or cheap labour. Till now, marriage and citizenship through it is a possibility. However, a draft law banning marriage between Bangladeshis and Rohingya has been in the pipeline for some time now.

Older residents from the registered camps informed us that it was not so difficult to get help from locals. The most common favour was help in enrolling children in regular schools and colleges using the status of a Bangladeshi. Some government primary school teachers said that there were significant numbers of Rohingya children enrolled in school and that as teachers they could tell Rohingya children apart from Bangladeshi ones, often from linguistic clues. In the camps we heard stories of Rohingya children who did well enough to get scholarships but had their scholarships withdrawn after classmates revealed their true identity. For Rasool, this threat of betrayal came with his first job, where he quickly rose through the ranks and attracted the ire of some co-workers who threatened to get him arrested for leaving the camp.

In an interview with Barnaby Phillips of *Al Jazeera* on 27 July 2012, Bangladeshi Prime Minister Sheikh Hasina repeatedly asserted that it was not her country's problem to deal with the Rohingya and she could not intervene because it was unwise to meddle in the internal affairs of another country. She also said that the international community should insist on Myanmar taking back the Rohingya and not point an accusing finger at Bangladesh. Responding to accusations that fleeing Rohingya were forced back by Bangladeshi border guards, she said the guards had responded in a humanitarian way and offered money, medicine and food to the Rohingya and then 'persuaded' them to go back. As journalist Subir Bhaumik points out:

Today, Bangladesh's Awami League government sees them as Islamist extremists closer to their arch-rivals, the Jamaat-e-Islami. The United Nations High Commissioner for Refugees has been asked to shut down Rohingya refugee camps in southern Bangladesh.[4]

Bangladesh is becoming increasingly inhospitable to the Rohingya living there. In July 2014, law minister Syed Anisul Haque announced a draft law through which Rohingya marriages could no longer be solemnized in the country. This applied to marriages within the community as well as marriage between a Rohingya and a Bangladeshi national – the latter allegedly being 'used' by Rohingya to escape camp life and gain legitimacy as citizens.

In November 2014, Nigel O'Connor of *Al Jazeera* reported about the plans of the Bangladeshi government to intern and repatriate 270,000 undocumented Rohingya.[5] *Al Jazeera* also revealed a five-page foreign ministry document dated 31 March 2014, which said

> It has been suggested that a survey/listing of undocumented Myanmar nationals in Bangladesh would be carried out in order to identify them and determine their actual number and location . . . The listed individuals would be housed in temporary shelters in different suitable locations pending their repatriation to Myanmar through regular diplomatic/consular channels.

As the report pointed out, there was no indication in the document about what rights the interned Rohingya would have. In interviews with the legal officer at UNHCR, Dhaka, we were informed that there was no official communication between the Bangladeshi government and UNHCR about this and that the UNHCR too had found out from media reports.

At the same time, Rohingya provide cheap labour. According to a comprehensive report by the Danish Immigration Services (DIS),[6] Rohingya both in the camps and outside them (as well as the unregistered Rohingya outside the camps) are not allowed to work, but they do participate in the informal labour market. In 2009–10, a number of Rohingya were arrested and ultimately released through the intervention of their employers. In fact, as *Al Jazeera* reported, this has further alienated the Rohingya from the local population because the former sell their labour cheap.[7]

The DIS document showed that Bangladeshi government officials constantly harped on push and pull factors that brought Rohingya to Bangladesh. The district commissioner of Cox's Bazar was quoted as having said that the opportunity to travel to other countries from Bangladesh was a major factor in drawing the Rohingya to Bangladesh. Inherent in this statement is the denial that the Rohingya are political asylum-seekers and do not migrate only due to impoverishment. In fact, their political disempowerment in Myanmar is directly linked to their economic impoverishment. The DIS report further quotes various officials of international NGOs who posit that the Bangladeshi government suspended the policy of resettling the Rohingya in countries abroad through the UNHCR because it regarded this as a major reason for 'attracting' Rohingya to the country. An *Al Jazeera* report also pointed out that by neglecting the Rohingya in Bangladesh in order to discourage greater refugee influx from Myanmar, the government had created a population without access to healthcare, education, employment and basic means of survival.[8] Many articles by Bangladeshi scholars on the Rohingya 'problem' look at the situation from an internal security perspective. Utpala Rahman mentions the proximity of the Rohingya to various Islamist organizations and argues that the Rohingya camps in Cox's Bazar district are fertile ground for recruitment by Islamic militants and that the Rohingya are involved in smuggling drugs and arms smuggling from Myanmar.[9]

The Rohingya are also characterized as threatening the moral and economic fibre of Bangladeshi society:

> [A]ntisocial activities are increasing among the unregistered Rohingya refugee community. The social vices in the Rohingya community: commercial sexual exploitation, fake marriages, fake proposal of work, and the prevalence of sexually transmitted infections (STI) threaten the local social life and damage the stability of the Bangladesh-Myanmar border region . . . Undocumented Rohingya refugees use Bangladesh passport [*sic*]to travel abroad . . . Because Bangladesh depends on overseas remittance for its foreign currency reserve, the decline of the labor market could damage the country's economic stability.

Thus, Rohingya become characterized as a 'problem', a figurative disease carrier that literally infects Bangladesh (with sexually transmitted diseases, for instance) and metaphorically infects the country by strengthening the cause of Islamist fundamentalism. Meghna Guhathakurta writes:

> A new security era has emerged in the world after 9/11 and one in which the southern states[such as Bangladesh] have been caught up as pawns in the war against terrorism. Much of the dominant security

concerns of these states centre around following policies of counter-terrorism, which entail adopting strong vigilante technologies and techniques that bolster and reinvent dominant cartographic anxieties of the state. Needless to mention these technologies, sometimes derived directly for western economies fail to combat actual acts of terrorism and only manage to strengthen a xenophobia that ushers in a new security regime. Thus in a period of fluid population movements, states are compelled to engage with reinvented phobias of the cold-war instead of taking up creative policies of engagement.[10]

Bangladeshi scholars like Rahman,[11] Azad and Jasmin,[12] and Parnini[13] focus on how the Rohingya are a threat to security and national interests of Bangladesh and also how the influx of Rohingya is damaging strategic bilateral relations with Myanmar. In fact, Rahman recommends ensuring better educational and socio-economic opportunities for the Rohingya – not because they are political asylum-seekers facing a humanitarian crisis, but precisely because their impoverishment is seen as the destabilizing factor in the border region:

> If the situation of Rohingya Muslims is not addressed quickly, with an emphasis on justice and rights, the refugee camps can easily become a thriving breeding ground for terrorism and bring trouble for Bangladesh and the region.[14]

The Bangladeshi government does not seem to have the will to improve the lot of the Rohingya in any way. As a *Guardian* report from 2012 points out, the NGO Affairs Bureau in Dhaka has a policy of not approving plans for educational and health facilities in the Cox's Bazar district, even when it benefits local, non-refugee populations.[15] In fact, in 2011 the government rejected a USD 33 million joint initiative with the UN to develop the region with special focus on health and education.

Ethnographic researches conducted on the Rohingya open up a new way of looking at their problems beyond the paradigms of 'security' and 'protracted refugee problem', which have seemingly become buzzwords while referring to the Rohingya in Bangladesh. An article by Kazi Fehmida Farzana describes and analyses the 'cultural artefacts' (songs and paintings) of the Rohingya residing in Teknaf. Farzana argues that they help create a sense of community, maintain a collective memory of 'home' and are also a way of resisting dominant codes rewriting the Rohingya as disempowered, impoverished, nowhere people. Following James Scott's *Weapons of the*

Weak: Everyday Forms of Peasant Resistance,[16] Farzana argues that these songs and paintings are a way of registering protest against the mistreatment and oppression they have faced in both Myanmar and Bangladesh and in a context where other means of resisting is impossible.

In media reports, from local Chittagong dailies to national Dhaka-based news chapters, the Rohingya are most frequently mentioned in connection with the *yaba*[17] smuggling from Myanmar.[18] Even in connection with the boat people and trafficking networks, it is the plight of Bangladeshi migrants that is highlighted. From print to audiovisual media, Bangladeshi boat people were almost exclusively those interviewed in the aftermath of the crisis in the Bay of Bengal and Strait of Malacca in the early months of 2015. A senior journalist from the *Daily Star* who was present in Thailand as the crisis unfolded told us that the smuggling networks have only recently started abducting Bangladeshis because the Rohingya were too poor to pay a lucrative ransom. Further, Bangladeshis were either lured or kidnapped by smugglers and, therefore, were not really willing participants in these boat journeys in the way that Rohingya were. This was a version of events echoed by many other journalists. One of them recounted a story of a Bangladeshi man who broke down in tears after having confessed to initially introducing himself as a Rohingya in Malaysia in order to be able to stay on as an asylum-seeker. While it is true that many Bangladeshi people smuggled/ trafficked might have been lured with false promises, it is also true that Bangladesh is one of the highest migrant labour-exporting countries in the world. To say that the Rohingya had opened up this route and helped create a trap for unsuspecting Bangladeshis is both disingenuous and naive.

One of the main reasons for the increase in the number of boat people is Bangladesh's strict stance against taking in any more refugees from Myanmar. The failure of the Malaysia-Bangladesh agreement to send willing labourers to Malaysia through a legal route has also meant that many choose the illegal way to find a better life in Malaysia. In an article published in the *Dhaka Tribune* on 5 July 2015 titled 'Why Risk Your Life on the Open Seas?', Abid Azad and Adil Sakhawat cited the exact statistics: according to the Bureau of Manpower, Export, and Training (BMET), roughly 200,000 migrants have gone abroad legally till July 2015. The number was 425,000 in 2014.[19]

> After five years of closed doors, the Bangladesh government signed a deal with the Malaysian government on 22 October 2012 to send migrants to that country. The registration database shows that over 1.4 million had registered their names as applicants. Since then, 3,853

went to Malaysia in 2013, 5,134 in 2014 and 1,047 have gone in 2016 under this agreement. The database maintained by BMET also shows so far 1.45 million aspirants have already registered to go to another preferred destination, Saudi Arabia, which has opened its doors after seven years. But in the past five months [that is, between February and July 2015], only 9,726 aspirants have been able to go there through government initiative.[20]

An interesting distinction is made between Rohingya as victims and Bangladeshis as victims. A *Daily Star* report from 5 May 2015 titled 'Rohingyas Are the Easy Prey of Human Trafficking' provided this account from a Rohingya:[21]

> Zafar said that soon after they reached Malaysia sometime in 1992, he and some other Rohingyas were arrested and put in jail. Released after four months, he was handed over to the 'agents' in Thai bordering areas of Kelantan, northeastern state of Malaysia, only to be extorted twice.
>
> Eventually, he reached Kuala Lumpur and got registered with the UNHCR after months of efforts, but that was of no use as Malaysia neither has refugee camps nor provides aid to the refugees.
>
> With no passport or legal job document, life in Malaysia has always been difficult and humiliating for him. He was arrested a dozen times there.
>
> 'I sometimes work in construction, but the pay is very low. I have a wife and three children to look after, but I can't do much for them,' said Zafar.
>
> 'I have no state, no security of life. I feel very sad, frustrated. Often I cry and have sleepless nights,' he went on.

His tale sums up the plight thousands of stateless Rohingyas go through.

On 29 May 2015 the same newspaper published a report titled 'Traffickers Kidnap Bangladeshis and Send to Malaysia as Slave Labour', in which words like *kidnapped, tricked* and *trapped* featured repeatedly. It seemed that the two groups of migrants were distinguished by levels of voluntariness. While Rohingya are 'easy prey', Bangladeshis have to be tricked into migrating.

However, looking at facts and figures provided by the International Organization for Migration (IOM), just under half of the boat people rescued earlier in 2015 were Bangladeshis while the rest were Rohingya.[22] In fact, it was repeatedly asserted by various journalists we interviewed in

Dhaka that Bangladeshi migrants consisted exclusively of young and able-bodied men whereas the women and children were all Rohingya. And as the reasons for migration listed in the *Dhaka Tribune* infographic show, political and religious persecution is not the cause why the Bangladeshis are choosing perilous sea and land journeys to South and Southeast Asia. The need to constantly separate these two groups seems paramount in Bangladesh, while the impossibility of this attempt becomes clear in the face of this mixed and massive population outflow from the region.

This mixed and massive flow has given rise to unique problems for the Rohingya. Whereas the Southeast Asian and Bangladeshi governments are eager to separate the Rohingya from the Bangladeshis, the boat people often get clubbed together in the international arena, much to the chagrin of the Bangladeshi government. For Bangladeshi migrants, adopting a Rohingya identity is often more beneficial for getting legal asylum as the account of the Bangladeshi journalist mentioned above shows. Rahman's article expresses anxiety over the fate of remittances by Bangladeshi migrants when Rohingyas take advantage of these migrant networks. She writes:

> Undocumented Rohingya refugees use Bangladesh passport[s] to travel abroad. Because Bangladesh has no law, regulation, or formal policy regulating the confinement of refugees and asylum seekers,[23] influential people patronize Rohingyas and help them get passports in exchange for bribes. Bangladesh has already started to suffer from the practice. Around 700 Rohingyas traveling on Bangladeshi passports were arrested in Saudi Arabia after becoming involved in various crimes. Saudi authorities have been holding them in a deportation center in Jeddah . . . Saudi Arabia, the largest labor market for Bangladeshi migrant workers, also hinted that they would not address Bangladeshi workers' problems if the arrested Rohingyas were not taken back. Because Bangladesh depends on overseas remittance for its foreign currency reserve, the decline of the labor market could damage the country's economic stability.[24]

Rahman's article, thus, shows that Rohingya in Bangladesh are seen in mainstream opinion as people who steal jobs and give the country a bad name through their illicit activities. However, through our personal interviews, particularly with the Rohingya in Bangladesh, we came to know that not only are Rohingya used as cheap labour, there are also gangs that extort money from them for gathering articles of daily necessity. Further, Bangladeshis have been using the sea route to illegally migrate to Malaysia, which was initially opened because of the desperation of Rohingya trying to find asylum in Southeast Asia. Lisa Brooten,[25] analysing a series of reports by Reuters on Rohingya in Myanmar, identifies the 'savage-victim-saviour trope' drawing on Mutua's[26] analysis of how the Western liberal human rights discourse frames developing world crises. Drawing from that analysis, I would argue that the creation of the Bangladeshi victim necessitates the erasure of Rohingya as victims. Rohingya become footnotes in the Bangladeshi boatpeople story. However, in domestic reportage, often tangentially connected to the boat people crisis, they are certainly the savage perpetrators. A June 2015 report published in *ProthomAlo*, a leading Bengali daily published from Dhaka, charged the Teknaf-based parliamentarian Abdur Rahman Badi of being involved with a crime syndicate operating from Teknaf. He was charged with involvement in human trafficking and smuggling, the illegal yaba trade from Myanmar, and accused of getting Rohingya included in the Bangladeshi voters' list.[27] All three of these crimes were related to and perpetrated by Rohingya to a greater or lesser degree. The article also indirectly alleged that Badi was involved in helping Rohingya cross over to Bangladesh, letting them stay there and arranging for illegal identity and travel documents. In fact, while talking to the locals in Teknaf and Cox's Bazar, we also came to know that it is rumoured that Badi himself is a Rohingya.

Rohingya in India: victims or terrorists?

[C]an there be a policy for hospitality, a policy to be kind? . . . The pertinence and the impossibility of the question suggest for us, of course, the need for a dialogic approach to the issue of care and hospitality. New rules can be built only on such dialogic awareness that will tell us of the need for continuous conversation within the country and internationally; among shelter-seekers, shelter-givers, and the institutions of care and justice, including public and community bodies.[28]

According to the UNHCR, New Delhi, roughly 8,000 Rohingya in India are undergoing the process of determination of refugee status. An accurate estimate is hard to come by. Rohingya are a mobile group of refugees spread out in settlements across Hyderabad, Delhi, Mewat, Jaipur and Jammu as well as some rural areas in North India – and of course, in jails in West Bengal.

Since the violence in Myanmar in 2012, Bangladesh has not been admitting any more Rohingya refugees (see Sheikh Hasina's interview cited earlier). Thus, most of the desperate refugees take to boats trying to find refuge in Southeast Asia. But a smaller group (and again there are no actual numbers) choose to come to India through Bangladesh. Hamida Hossain, vice chairperson of Research Initiatives Bangladesh,[29] recalled that Rohingya would cross into Pakistan through Jammu and Kashmir till the 1990s. Anwar's work on the Bangladeshi and Rohingya fishing settlements in Karachi corroborates this claim.[30] However, with the increasing securitization of the northwestern border with Pakistan, for many Rohingya India has become the final destination. Subir Bhaumik points out that the plight of the Rohingya came into sharp focus in India when the coast guard rescued a boatload of 109 Rohingya in Northern Andaman in March 2013.[31]

The mixed flow of Rohingya and Bangladeshis through the porous eastern border has thrown up a number of challenges for the state. Samaddar talks about the state's dichotomous tendency to provide care while exerting power:

> [A] game of protection, hospitality, security, morals, nation-making, citizenship-conferring; a game of states, human rights, rights of citizens, and of statecraft – in short, a game of care and power . . . Which is to say, the game of care produces power.[32]

The 'calculated hospitality' of the Indian state towards displaced populations,[33] despite not being a signatory to the 1951 Refugee Convention, is well documented. In fact, in the 'calculated hospitality' that Samaddar mentioned is something that is not accounted for in the Global North–centric approach to humanitarian aid to refugees/forced population: not being bound by laws defining issues connected to refugees (the 1951 Convention, for instance, does not recognize gender as a category on which discrimination can be premised whereas the 1966 Bangkok Protocols, to which India is a signatory, do).

The ethics of international law and the imperatives of hospitality directly clash with the post-9/11 securitization regime producing a schizophrenic oscillation between asserting sovereign power and providing hospitality. The media mirrors this.

Looking at reports across the country since 2012, two distinct strands of reportage about Rohingya are noticeable. In the coverage of the crisis in Myanmar, the Indian media is unflinchingly critical of the Government of Myanmar. An editorial on 9 November 2012in the *Anandabazar Patrika*, a leading Bengali daily published from Kolkata, for instance, pointed out that Thein Sein's government was faltering in its first steps towards democracy, because violence perpetrated by the majority over the minority Rohingya continued unabated. It went on to criticize the refusal to grant citizenship to Rohingya by both Myanmar and Bangladesh, as a result of which 800,000 people were virtually rendered stateless.[34] The editorial was interesting because of three things. First, it linked violence against Rohingya in Myanmar with revenge attacks on minority Buddhist Chakmas in the Chittagong Hill Tracts by the Muslim majority.[35] Second, while critiquing Aung San Suu Kyi and the United States' role in the region, it remained silent on India's role. Lastly, it pointed out that desperate Rohingya refugees were taking to the seas in small boats and blamed Bangladesh border guards for deaths during maritime transit. Another editorial on 3 June 2013 talked about democracy in Myanmar and the condition of minorities, particularly Rohingya, in the country. Interestingly, it compared the bottom-up democratization brought about by the Arab Spring with the top-down democracy in Myanmar and expressed scepticism about the latter. It also pointed out that the opening up of Myanmar meant that human rights issues would be ignored in the rush for a share of the pie by multinational corporations.[36]

Between these two editorials, the *Hindu* reported in December 2012 the setting up of a consulate in Sittwe, which made India the first country with three consulates in Myanmar. As the report went onto state:

> Sittwe port, about 550 km from Kolkata, is slated to see considerable Indian activity soon after it becomes the mouth of a maritime-cum-road route to India's North-East as an alternate to India's sole link to the region via the congested Siliguri corridor . . . The External Affairs Minister discussed four other major economic issues – a trilateral highway linking Myanmar and India to Thailand by 2016, the Rhi-Tiddim road connecting both countries, gas exports to India and the possibility of supplying power from the India-assisted Tamanthi and Shwezaye projects on the Chindwin river basin.[37]

The Rohingya came into the media spotlight again in July 2013 in the context of the serial blasts in Bodh Gaya. Supposedly perpetrated by the Indian Mujahideen group, it was seen as a reaction to Buddhist persecution of Rohingya in Myanmar. A *Times of India* report after the Bodh Gaya blasts of 7 July, titled 'Rohingyas in Hyderabad Live in Fear', talks about fear of police harassment.[38] In the report, a Rohingya refugee named Abdullah is quoted as having said, 'We were unaware of the attack as most of us cannot read, write or even speak local languages. We are first concerned about earning money to buy food and get refugee status.' The report goes on to say that

> a substantial number [of Rohingya] chose Hyderabad as their new home. They believed the city, on account of its substantial Muslim population, would welcome them with arms wide open. Little did they think about police questionings and needless interrogation each time a Hindu shrine or a Buddhist structure comes under attack.[39]

The report also quotes the executive director of Hyderabad-based Confederation of Voluntary Organisations, Mazher Hussain, as having said:

> To think that these illiterate and hapless people could be behind any terror attack is unbelievable. Whoever has engineered the blasts has damaged the cause of Rohingya. This act could lead to another wave of violence against Rohingya population not only in Myanmar, but also in India.[40]

Another *Times of India* report on 15 April 2013 titled 'Riot-Hit Rohingya Muslims Take Refuge in Hyderabad'[41] talked about the Rohingya and the support they got from local NGOs. Interestingly, it referred to the Rohingya as 'asylum-seekers', directly putting the burden of their protection on the state, although the state is an absent actor in the narrative. The report ended with a reference to police harassment, but while discussing cross-border flows from Bangladesh into West Bengal, issues of illegality and/or security (except for the insecurity of the Rohingya and their hardships) did not feature.

Soon after the blasts, Firdaus Ahmed wrote in the *Kashmir Times*:

> [I]n the Bodh Gaya case, the readiness to lap up the theory that this is [a] Muslim backlash for the Buddhist suppression of Rohingya[s] and Sri Lankan Muslims owes to the success of the narrative of Muslim extremism [*sic*]. This completes the circle in which there is then no compulsion to look for evidence.[42]

An *Anandabazar Patrika* report on 8 July 2013 about the Bodh Gaya blasts not only linked the Rohingya issue to the attacks but also to the infamous terrorist outfit Lashkar-e-Toiba and Pakistan. The second line of the report said that the Rohingya were 'allegedly' being tortured by the Buddhist majority.

On 14 July 2013, the same daily ran a short piece with a photo from Meiktila, Myanmar, which showed a cycle being ridden among the ruins of settlements destroyed in riots in 2012. It reported that the courts were giving harsher punishments to Muslims. While Rohingya were not directly mentioned, it demonstrated how security issues in national contexts overrode any humanitarian impulses. The absence of the national security issue, when the focus was on other countries, made it possible to sympathetically portray the Muslim 'others' who once within the borders represented a threat to sovereign integrity. I would argue that this dichotomy in reportage is a manifestation of the 'calculated hospitality' that Samaddar talked about. The prerogative of the state to care is invisibilized in the media, but by reflecting public discourse the duality between care and power is constantly in balance in these reports.

The next reports about the Rohingya surfaced in two leading dailies, the *Anandabazar Patrika* and the *Hindu*, seven days apart in March 2013. The *Hindu* reported on 17 March 2014 that:

> A steady influx of Rohingya Muslims into West Bengal via Bangladesh is causing concern to the security establishment . . . A senior intelligence official told The Hindu that 'more than one thousand' Rohingya refugees had been detained and sent to prisons in the State in the last six months . . . The refugees detained under the Foreigners Act, 1946 are now supposed be sent to the Tihar jail in New Delhi as the UNHCR has jurisdiction only in Tihar. Once they get refugee status, they will be sent to India's only refugee camp, which is in Jammu. 'But we do not know when that will happen, as it is not easy to send so many people,' said an official at Alipore jail here.[43]

The *Anandabazar Patrika* report on 10 March 2014 presented a more realistic figure of over eighty incarcerated Rohingya in West Bengal.[44] The report raised the question of Rohingya who had escaped the 'strict border policing by BSF' and mingled with the general populace and the possibility of such people being used in terrorist attacks, such as the one in Bodh Gaya. These pronouncements prove almost prophetic, with a Rohingya suspect being arrested from Hyderabad in connection with the Khagragarh blast in West Bengal in November 2014.[45]

Discussions on Rohingya in India, following the Khagragarh blast, were predictably focused on 'Muslim infiltrators' destroying a Hindu nation in the wake of the earlier theme of Bangladeshi infiltrators destroying national integrity. At the same time, many articles in both the Indian and international media on Rohingya living in settlements in Delhi, Jammu and Hyderabad have sympathetically portrayed these beleaguered people. In Hyderabad, Islamic charitable organizations and philanthropists, including a local Member of Legislative Assembly (MLA), have come forward to help the Rohingya. A report from India together states that in 2012 during Ramzan a lot of donations had poured in. A hefty sum also came from the Iranian government. In Delhi, as in Hyderabad, land on which Rohingya have been allowed to settle belongs to Muslim charitable organizations – for example, the Zakat Foundation near Madanpur Khadar[46] – or Muslim individuals.[47] This can further fuel the paranoia about Muslim 'others' out to destroy the Hindu nationhood.

Following the Khagragarh blast, Rohingya camps in Hyderabad have experienced increased surveillance from the police and harassment as reported in *DNA*[48] and the *Times of India*.[49] Passi points out that 'the state-centred naturalization of space is produced and reproduced, and how the exclusions and inclusions between "We" and "Them" that it implies are historically constructed and shaped in relation to power, various events, episodes and struggles.'[50] The partition of 1947 and the logic of minorities being proxy citizens of neighbouring countries have constructed economic migrants as well as political asylum-seekers crossing the eastern borders as suspect and threats to security. A Reuters report dated 15 September 2014 states:

> New Delhi has twice blocked draft laws on refugee recognition. Because of its porous borders, often hostile neighbours and external militancy, it wants a free hand to regulate the entry of foreigners without being tied down by any legal obligation, analysts said.[51]

The reiteration of the need for strictly policing the border with Bangladesh also reveals that the subjects of state scrutiny are Muslim aliens. The *Hindu* reported that on 17 December 2014 the Supreme Court of India expressed concern over the insecure borders with Bangladesh. It said in a judgement:

> We are at a loss to understand why 67 years after independence the eastern border is left porous. We have been reliably informed that the entire western border with Pakistan, 3300 km long, is not only properly fenced, but properly manned as well, and is not porous at any point.[52]

The *Deccan Herald* was the only newspaper among those reviewed that consistently portrayed India's lacklustre treatment of refugees in an unfavourable light.On17 June 2012, on the eve of World Refugee Day, in a report titled 'Refugees Subjected to Discrimination in India: Activists', the news chapter highlighted the plight of the Rohingya living in Delhi and the discrimination they face and compared their fate with other refugees in India, saying:

> When young Ziaur Rehman entered India to escape persecution in Myanmar he thought he could finally live his dream of a better future, little knowing his struggles were far from over as he would be scorned as a pariah, a thief and a terrorist in his host country.[53]

Activists and experts claim 30-year-old Rehman is just one among thousands of the 200,000-plus refugees in India who are subjected to discrimination and arbitrary detention as a result of the lack of a comprehensive legal framework to govern asylum-seekers in the country.

This theme was further elaborated in a report dated 20 October 2012 titled 'Refugees Denied Basic Facilities'.[54] It showed how difficult it was for refugees in India to access basic facilities like education and how often the most vulnerable sections – women and children – end up being trafficked and having to take to sex work to survive.

On 2 August 2012, a report criticizing Bangladesh's handling of the Rohingya issue was published. Titled 'Bangladesh Bans Foreign Charities Helping Rohingya', it said:

> France's Doctors without Borders (MSF) and Action Against Hunger (ACF) as well as Britain's Muslim Aid UK have been told to suspend their services in the Cox's Bazaar district bordering Myanmar, local administrator Joynul Bari said. 'The charities have been providing aid to tens of thousands of undocumented Rohingya refugees illegally. We asked them to stop all their projects in Cox's Bazaar following directive from the NGO Affairs Bureau,' he told AFP. Bari added that the charities 'were encouraging an influx of Rohingya refugees' from Myanmarin the wake of recent sectarian violence that left at least eighty people killed.[55]

The *Deccan Herald* was also the only newspaper which carried an alternative perspective of the Bodh Gaya blasts, in a report dated 7 July 2013:

> So far, no terrorist organisation has claimed responsibility for the serial explosions, but the police suspect the involvement of Indian

Mujahideen (IM) modules. Police sources said it could also be fallout of the tussle between Buddhists and Muslims in Myanmar.

Another theory doing the rounds is that it was terror tactics adopted by IM modules to spread panic rather than cause actual harm. Yet another unconfirmed report said that it was the 'internecine war among monks' which led to the explosions.[56]

On 5 October 2013, the chapter reported that the Supreme Court had issued a notice to the central government on the condition of Rohingya living in camps in Delhi and Mewat:

> The Supreme Court has issued notice to the Centre on a PIL seeking direction to ensure proper health facilities for women and children of Rohingya tribes of Myanmar, residing in refugee camps in Delhi and Haryana . . . A bench of Justices H L Dattu and Gyan Sudha Misra also sought response from Delhi and Haryana governments on the petition filed by Jaffar Ullah.
>
> According to the petitioner, almost 150 Rohingya refugee families, staying in the camps at Delhi and Haryana's Mewat district did not have access to basic medical care, clean water, nutritious food and secure shelters.
>
> The petitioner sought humanitarian assistance to ensure the survival and wellbeing of the refugees as guaranteed under the Constitution.[57]

Prime Minister Narendra Modi was quoted on 7 May 2014 by the *Hindu* as having said: 'There are two types of people who have come in – infiltrators and refugees. Those who are refugees are our family. It is the responsibility of all of India, whether Gujarat or Rajasthan to rehabilitate them with all respect.'[58]

Going back to Brooten's classification of savage-victim-saviour,[59] it is increasingly clear that the Rohingya cannot simply be the victims but must embrace the duality of being victims as well as being in some way the savage. They are never the victims who can be recipients of state's munificence and are only characterized as victims when they are external to the state or the state is an indirect actor.

Similarly, Bangladesh's focus on maintaining strategic relations with Myanmar[60] has meant that its government will not force Myanmar's hand in stopping the persecution against Rohingya as they continue to remain a people that have fallen between two stools – neither citizens nor asylum-seekers, they are internally displaced or stateless people. They are, in fact, asylum-seekers who have been invisibilized.

Sanlaap, an NGO working with trafficked women and children, reported that Rohingya children started coming into their shelter homes in large numbers since 2012. At one point they were providing shelter to over forty children, mostly girls, who came to them through the state Child Welfare Committee. Usually large groups of Rohingya being smuggled across the borders are captured and sent to correctional homes under the Foreigners Act. Men, women and children are separated and the children end up in shelter homes. Sanlaap conducted a study in Rohingya settlements in Jammu and Delhi as more and more relatives came to the shelter from settlements in these two states, claiming the children as their wards. Their reports from the settlements talked about the insecurity of the Rohingya, particularly the children going back from the shelter to be reunited with their families in the unsanitary condition of the camps, with little access to basic health care, clean water and other facilities, and exposed to trafficking and other dangers.[61]

In an interview with seven minor girls residing in the Sanlaap Shelter Home in Kolkata, the ideas of security and insecurity were thrown into sharp contrast. On the one hand, in their imagination their native villages in Arakan were idylls where they had freedom to roam, swam in lakes, took buffaloes to the pastures and where the food was wholesome unlike what they got in the shelter. On the other hand, the idea of Jammu, a mythical place where everything would become all right, had also captured their imagination. In her 1943 essay 'We Refugees', Hannah Arendt wrote about the ubiquitous Mr Cohn, the prototype of a stateless German Jew in Europe, who tried to adapt to every new country by becoming the model, patriotic citizen but was suspect everywhere and denied citizenship because of his Jewishness, which he tried so much to hide.[62] The Rohingya girls, with their slightly accented Bangla and refusal, at least initially, to talk in their mother tongue and constantly trying to fit in with what they imagined to be my narrative as an Indian reminded me strongly of Mr Cohn. They refused to criticise the Indian children in the shelter, instead choosing to focus on the Bangladeshi girls who made their lives miserable and treated them as outcasts. When I asked about their choice of destination when they fled their homes and whether their families ever considered going to Pakistan, one of the girls responded uncertainly: 'But isn't Pakistan an enemy of Hindustan?' In the course of the three-hour-long interview, the girls began to open up, teaching me words in the Rohingya language and then singing songs for me. I was recording their conversation, and eager to listen to themselves they started by first displaying their knowledge of English and Bangla nursery rhymes and eventually a Rohingya love song, followed by a song which called for Rohingya brothers to come together across nations. As they exhausted their repertoire, they recited Quranic verses learnt at madrassas they attended in Arakan. After reciting a verse from the Quran – whose meaning they could not recall – one of the girls asked me whether I was Muslim. She looked crestfallen when I said I was not. Perhaps having the relative freedom of being able to express themselves freely without being ridiculed about their strange language and customs, they had tried to find in me a kindred soul and the closest approximation to what they could imagine would be a sympathetic Muslim. In a world where they have only faced rejection as Rohingya, as girls brought up in conservative social environments where boys but not girls are allowed to venture out and watch Bollywood films, as illegal trespassers in a country, as aliens in their shelter homes, it must have been difficult for them to imagine kindness outside the family. Forced to live in a shelter, separated from their families, they only dreamt of Jammu where they would be reunited with their families. The better health, education, clothing and shelter they got at the shelter did not at the moment hold any attraction for them. They named their favourite television serials and their favourite actors, soon after saying it was *gunah* for girls to wear make-up or watch Bollywood films back in Arakan. I asked them if they would miss these when they went to Jammu. They all replied that they would not and they knew it was gunah, but it was OK to watch television at the shelter because they were suffering. They would never miss these when they were with their families in Jammu. While some of this was performed for my benefit, to show loyalty to their families, it is also true that these girls viewed their families as their only refuge and shelter. Being together as a family, in a world which only displayed hatred and indifference, was beyond everything.

Conclusion

In 'We Refugees', Arendt writes:

> We lost our home, which means the familiarity of daily life. We lost our occupation, which means the confidence that we are of some use in this world. We lost our language, which means the naturalness of reactions, the simplicity of gestures, the unaffected expression of feelings. We left our relatives in Polish ghettos and our best friends have been killed in concentration camps, and that means the rupture of our private lives.[63]

The words still ring true, applicable to persecuted, stateless people across the world. Efforts to curb statelessness after World War II through international covenants have failed as the number of stateless people continues to grow. Arendt writes that ultimately the life of a stateless non-citizen is reduced to the 'abstract nakedness of being human',[64] or what Agamben calls 'bare life', or reduction to just biological life without a political voice. Interpreting Arendt's work in context of asylum-seekers in Holland, Borren[65] writes that citizenship is the basis on which we are granted human rights, and it is almost impossible for a sovereign nation state to grant human rights to a non-citizen. Civil and political rights in today's world of nation states are premised on citizenship, nationality and nativity.[66]

Interpreting Arendt's work, particularly in Eichmann in Jerusalem,[67] Butler says that our precarity as humans leads to interdependency, and the only way to avoid genocide is not to choose with whom we cohabit in this world:

> We might think that interdependency is a happy or promising notion, but it is often the condition for territorial wars and forms of state violence . . . [U]nwilled proximity and unchosen cohabitation are preconditions of our political existence, the basis of [Arendt's] critique of nationalism . . . [F]rom unchosen cohabitation, Arendt derives notions of universality and equality that commit us to institutions that seek to sustain human lives without regarding some part of the population as socially dead, as redundant, or as intrinsically unworthy of life and therefore ungrievable.[68]

To translate such a philosophy into a viable policy to reverse genocidal violence in Arakan, and the rest of the world, is a challenge facing us all.

Notes

1 UNHCR, *Stateless People Figures*, www.unhcr.org/pages/49c3646c26.html, accessed on 5 October 2015.
2 C. Ryan, 'The subjected non-subject: Security, subjectification and resistance in the occupied Palestinian territories', *Critical Studies on Security*, 1(3), 2013: 295–310.
3 P. Banerjee and R. Samaddar, *Migrations and Circles of Insecurity*, New Delhi: WISCOMP: An initiative of the Foundation for Universal Responsibility, 2012.
4 S. Bhaumik, 'No country for Rohingyas', *India Today*, 22 March 2013, http://indiatoday.intoday.in/story/rohingya-muslims-rakhine-myanmar-bordering-bangladesh/1/259014.html, accessed on 5 October 2015.

5 N. O'Connor, 'Bangladesh proposes interning, repatriating up to 270K Rohingyas', *Al Jazeera*,2014, http://america.aljazeera.com/articles/2014/11/26/bangladesh-proposesinterningrepatriatingupto270krohingyatomyanma.html, accessed on 5 October 2015.

6 Danish Immigration Services, *Rohingya refugees in Bangladesh and Thailand: Fact finding mission to Bangladesh and Thailand*, 2011, www.nyidanmark.dk/NR/rdonlyres/B08D8B44-5322-4C2F-9604-44F6C340167A/0/Factfindingrapport Rohingya180411.pdf, accessed on 5 October 2015.

7 *Ibid*.

8 O'Connor, 'Bangladesh proposes interning, repatriating up to 270K Rohingyas'.

9 U. Rahman, 'The Rohingya refugee: A security dilemma for Bangladesh', *Journal of Immigrant & Refugee Studies*, 8(2), 2010: 233–9.

10 M. Guhathakurta, 'Cartographic anxieties, identity politics and the imperatives of Bangladesh foreign policy peace prints', *South Asian Journal of Peacebuilding*, 2(3), Winter 2010.

11 Rahman, 'The Rohingya refugee'.

12 A. Azad and F. Jasmin, 'Durable solutions to the protracted refugee situation: The case of Rohingyas in Bangladesh', *Journal of Indian Research*, 1(4), 2013: 25–35.

13 S. N. Parnini, 'The crisis of the Rohingya as a Muslim minority in Myanmar and bilateral relations with Bangladesh', *Journal of Muslim Minority Affairs*, 33(2), 2013: 281–97.

14 U. Rahman, 'The Rohingya refugee: A security dilemma for Bangladesh', *Journal of Immigrant & Refugee Studies*, 8(2), 2010: pp. 233–9.

15 S. Z. Al Mahmood, 'Burma's Rohingya refugees find little respite in Bangladesh', *Guardian*, Teknaf, 2012, www.theguardian.com/global-development/2012/jun/29/burma-rohingya-refugees-bangladesh, accessed on 5 October 2015.

16 J. C. Scott, *Weapons of the Weak: Everyday Forms of Peasant Resistance*, New Haven, CT: Yale University Press, 1985.

17 *Yaba* is an illegal drug containing methamphetamine and caffeine in pill form. It is smuggled from Myanmar to neighbouring countries like Bangladesh and Thailand.

18 See for instance: *Prothom Alo*, 'Yaba Shebon 6 Bochhore 77 Goon Berechhe', 9 December 2014, www.prothomalo.com/bangladesh/article/392629/%E0%A6%87%E0%A6%AF%E0%A6%BC%E0%A6%BE%E0%A6%AC%E0%A6%BE-%E0%A6%B8%E0%A7%87%E0%A6%AC%E0%A6%A8-%E0%A7%AC-%E0%A6%AC%E0%A6%9B%E0%A6%B0%E0%A7%87-%E0%A7%AD%E0%A7%AD-%E0%A6%97%E0%A7%81%E0%A6%A3-%E0%A6%AC%E0%A7%87%E0%A6%A1%E0%A6%BC%E0%A7%87%E0%A6%9B%E0%A7%87, accessed on 5 October 2015.

19 A. Azad and A. Sakhawat, 'Why risk your life on the open seas?', *Dhaka Tribune*, 30 July 2015, www.dhakatribune.com/bangladesh/2015/07/05/why-risk-your-life-on-the-open-seas/, accessed on 5 October 2015.

20 *Ibid*.

21 Porimol Palma with Walid Bin Habib, 'Rohingyas are the easy prey of human trafficking', *The Daily Star*, Dhaka, 5 may 2016 in https://www.thedailystar.net/frontpage/rohingyas-the-easy-prey-80514, accessed on 30 April 2018.

22 International Organization for Migration, 'IOM sees progress in SE Asia Migrant crisis, but warns more must be done', 22 May 2015, www.iom.int/

news/iom-sees-progress-se-asia-migrant-crisis-warns-more-must-be-done, accessed on 5 October 2015.

23 This is not true. The nearly 30,000 registered Rohingya under the UNHCR mandate are legally speaking supposed to be confined to the camps, although in practice they do move around more freely but not entirely without risk of capture and confinement. In fact, one of the main points of advocacy for the UNHCR Bangladesh with the country's government is to release Rohingya prisoners currently confined under the Foreigners Act in Cox's Bazar prison who have already served their term of punishment.

24 Rahman, 'The Rohingya refugee'.

25 L. Brooten, 'Blind spots in human rights coverage: Framing violence against the Rohingya in Myanmar/Burma', *Popular Communication*, 13(2), 2015: 132–44.

26 M. Mutua, *Human Rights: A Political and Cultural Critique*, Philadelphia: University of Pennsylvania Press, 2002.

27 S. Hasan, 'Teen Talikatei Shangshod Body', *Prothom Alo*, 18 June 2015, www. prothomalo.com/bangladesh/article/556429/%E0%A6%A4%E0%A6%BF% E0%A6%A8-%E0%A6%A4%E0%A6%BE%E0%A6%B2%E0%A6%BF%E0%A 6%95%E0%A6%BE%E0%A6%A4%E0%A7%87%E0%A6%87-%E0%A6%B8% E0%A6%BE%E0%A6%82%E0%A6%B8%E0%A6%A6-%E0%A6%AC%E0% A6%A6%E0%A6%BF, accessed on 5 October 2015.

28 R. Samaddar (ed.), *Refugees and the State: Practices of Asylum and Care in India, 1947–2000*, New Delhi: Sage, 2003, p. 60.

29 Personal Interview, Dhaka: 5 July 2015.

30 N. H. Anwar, 'Negotiating new conjunctures of citizenship: Experiences of 'illegality' in Burmese-Rohingya and Bangladeshi migrant enclaves in Karachi', *Citizenship Studies*, 17(3–4), 2013: 414–28.

31 Bhaumik, 'No country for Rohingyas'.

32 Samaddar, *Refugees and the State*.

33 R. Samaddar, 'Refugees and dynamics of hospitality: The Indian story', in U. A. Segal, D. Elliott and N. S. Mayadas (eds.), *Immigration Worldwide Policies, Practices, and Trends*, New York: Oxford University Press, 2009.

34 'Gorishthyer Adhipatyo', *Anandabazar Patrika*, 9 November 2012, http:// archives.anandabazar.com/archive/1121109/9edit2.html, accessed on 5 October 2015.

35 This claim that the Rohingya are responsible for the attacks on the Buddhist minority in Bangladesh is debatable and all the experts that I spoke to in Bangladesh – from professors in Dhaka University to UNHCR officials – pointed this out repeatedly, especially with reference to incidents of violence against Buddhist minorities in Ramu, Bangladesh.

36 'Ganatantra o Myanmar', *Anandabazar Patrika*, 3 June 2013, http://archives.anandabazar.com/archive/1130603/3edit1.html, accessed on 5 October 2015.

37 'India to open third mission in Myanmar', *Hindu*, 16 December 2012, www. thehindu.com/news/international/india-to-open-third-mission-in-myanmar/ article4204046.ece?ref=relatedNews, accessed on 5 October 2015.

38 S. Mohammed, 'Rohingyas in Hyderabad live in fear', *Times of India*, 9 July 2013, http://timesofindia.indiatimes.com/city/hyderabad/Rohingyas-in-Hyderabad-live-in-fear/articleshow/20980972.cms, accessed on 5 October 2015.

39 *Ibid.*

40 *Ibid.*

41 B. Baseerat, 'Riot hit Rohingyas take refuge in Hyderabad', *Times of India*, Hyderabad, 15 April 2013, http://timesofindia.indiatimes.com/city/hyderabad/ Riot-hit-Rohingya-Muslims-take-refuge-in-Hyderabad/articleshow/19551921. cms, accessed on 5 October 2015.

42 F. Ahmed, 'Distancing from cloak and dagger', *Kashmir Times*, 19 July 2013, www.kashmirtimes.in/newsdet.aspx?q=8775, accessed on 5 October 2015.

43 S. Bagchi, 'Rohingya influx: A brewing crisis', *Hindu*, 17 March 2014, www. thehindu.com/news/national/other-states/rohingya-influx-a-brewing-crisis/ article5797314.ece, accessed on 5 October 2015.

44 'Jele Rohingya Koyedir Bohor Dekhe Mathay Haat Shorasthro Montroker', *Anandabazar Patrika*, 10 March 2014, www.anandabazar.com/state/%E0%A6%B0- %E0%A6%9C-%E0%A6%AF-%E0%A6%B0-%E0%A6%B9-% E0%A6%99-%E0%A6%97-%E0%A6%95%E0%A7%9F-%E0%A6%A6- %E0%A6%B0-%E0%A6%AC%E0%A6%B9%E0%A6%B0-%E0%A6%A6-% E0%A6%96-%E0%A6%9A-%E0%A6%A8-%E0%A6%A4-%E0%A7%9F- %E0%A6%95-%E0%A6%A8-%E0%A6%A6-%E0%A6%B0-%E0%A7%9F- %E0%A6%B8-%E0%A6%AC%E0%A6%B0-%E0%A6%B7-% E0%A6%9F-%E0%A6%B0-%E0%A6%AE%E0%A6%A8-%E0%A6%A4- %E0%A6%B0%E0%A6%95-1.9264#, accessed on 31 August 2015.

45 J. Gupta, 'Khalid's arrest sparks off debate on Rohingyas in India', *Times of India*, 20 November 2014, http://timesofindia.indiatimes.com/india/Khalids-arrest-sparks-off-debate-on-Rohingyas-in-India/articleshow/45220794.cms, accessed on 5 October 2015.

46 Personal interviews with staff of Sanlaap, February 2015.

47 M.A.R. Fareed, 'Rohingya exiles struggle to survive in India', *Al Jazeera*, 6 January 2014, www.aljazeera.com/indepth/features/2014/01/rohingya-exiles-struggle-survive-india-201416143243337187.html, accessed on 5 October 2015.

48 'Rohingya Muslim refugees in Hyderabad are under surveillance, say police', *DNA*, 27 December 2014, www.dnaindia.com/india/report-rohingya-muslim-refugees-in-hyderabad-are-under-surveillance-say-police-2047456, accessed on 5 October 2015.

49 Gupta, 'Khalid's arrest sparks off debate on Rohingyas in India'.

50 Paasi, 'Boundaries as social processes'.

51 N. Bhalla, 'Myanmar's Rohingya stuck in refugee limbo in India', *Reuters*, 15 September 2014, www.reuters.com/article/2014/09/15/us-foundation-stateless-india-rohingya-idUSKBN0HA07F20140915, accessed on 5 October 2015.

52 K. Rajagopal, 'SC: Why is eastern border still porous?', *Hindu*, 18 December 2014, www.thehindu.com/todays-paper/tp-national/sc-why-is-eastern-border-still-porous/article6702655.ece, accessed on 5 October 2015.

53 'Refugees subjected to discrimination in India: Activists', *Deccan Herald*, 17 June 2012, www.deccanherald.com/content/257575/archives.php, accessed on 5 October 2015.

54 'Refugees denied basic facilities', *Deccan Herald*, 20 October 2012, www.deccanherald.com/content/286895/refugees-denied-basic-facilities.html, accessed on 5 October 2015.

55 'Bangladesh bans foreign charities helping Rohingya', *Deccan Herald*, 2 August 2012, www.deccanherald.com/content/268792/bangladesh-bans-foreign-charities-helping.html, accessed on 5 October 2015.

56 A. Kumar, 'Nine explosions rock Bodh Gaya', *Deccan Herald*, 7 July 2013, www.deccanherald.com/content/343424/nine-explosions-rock-bodh-gaya.html, accessed on 5 October 2015.

57 'SC notice to centre on Myanmar refugees', *Deccan Herald*, 5 October 2013, www.deccanherald.com/content/361432/sc-notice-centre-myanmar-refugees. html, accessed on 5 October 2015.

58 'Bangladeshi "infiltrators" would have to go back: Modi', *Hindu*, 7 May 2014, www.thehindu.com/elections/loksabha2014/bangladeshi-infiltrators-would-have-to-go-back-modi/article5986165.ece, accessed on 5 October 2015.

59 Brooten, 'Blind spots in human rights coverage'.

60 See, for instance, Parnini, 'The crisis of the Rohingya as a Muslim minority'.

61 Personal interviews with staff of Sanlaap, February 2015.

62 H. Arendt, 'We refugees', in M. Robinson (ed.), *Altogether Elsewhere: Writers on Exile*, London: Faber & Faber, 1994.

63 *Ibid.*, p. 111.

64 *Ibid.*

65 M. Borren, 'Towards an Arendtian politics of in/visibility', *Ethical Perspectives*, 15(2), 2008: 213.

66 *Ibid.*

67 H. Arendt, *Eichmann in Jerusalem*, Penguin, 1963.

68 J. Butler, 'Precarious life, vulnerability, and the ethics of cohabitation', *Journal of Speculative Philosophy*, 26(2), 2012: 134–51.

6

LEGAL BRIEF ON STATELESSNESS

Law in the Indian context

Charlotte-Anne Malischewski

Statelessness poses one of the most complex problems both in terms of humanitarian intervention and for the creation and implementation of legal protection. By its very nature, statelessness challenges the citizen–state relationship of the contemporary state model in which provisions for formal membership either through nationality or citizenship laws are the state's prerogative, and international norms and commitments are largely effectuated through the enactment and implementation of laws, policies, and practices at the state level. Indeed, 'the very notion of statelessness exposes the essential weakness of a political system that relies on the state to act as the principal guarantor of human rights.'[1] Without a legal bond with any state, stateless people are left vulnerable to a variety of forms of exploitation and abuse, poverty and marginalization.

Addressing statelessness

In the United Nations High Commissioner for Refugees' (UNHCR) much belated attempt to respond to the plight of an estimated fifteen million stateless people around the world,[2] the organization has suggested a four-pronged approach to statelessness involving identification, prevention, reduction and protection.[3]

Identification: The number of stateless people worldwide remains unclear, and the complexity of their experiences in different regions remains underdocumented. A number of factors complicate assessments of the global reality of statelessness, including the facts that the term 'statelessness' remains ambiguous, that governments are reluctant to study and share findings about stateless populations, that some stateless people may opt not to register for fear of persecution from state actors, that some people prefer to remain stateless than to have to take a particular citizenship, and that little is known about statelessness in detention facilities.[4] Therefore, the identification of stateless people and those at risk of statelessness is important. Mapping the complexity of the problem is the first step to developing appropriate responses.

Prevention: According to the UNHCR's António Guterres and UN High Commissioner for Human Rights Louise Arbour, prevention is 'the easiest and most effective way to deal with statelessness is to prevent it from occurring in the first place.'[5] Indeed, responding to statelessness means looking at ways to avoid there being new cases of statelessness.

Reduction: This element of addressing stateless is focused on existing cases of statelessness. Essentially, reduction of statelessness refers to group and individual acquisition of nationality or citizenship.

Protection: Being stateless should not mean being without rights. Protection of stateless people means working to respect, protect and fulfil their rights, including but not limited to education, healthcare, judicial and travel rights.

Defining citizenship

There is a distinction between the legal meaning of the terms 'nationality' and 'citizenship' and the conceptual debates around their meanings in political theory, international relations and sociology. Shared ideologies, customs, institutions, feelings of belonging or associations with particular territory, which may constitute a nation,[6] do not necessarily align with a particular state. In many contexts, the term 'nationality' is tied to the idea of a nation and is thus distinguished from a legally recognized bond with a particular state. However, because some countries use the term 'nationality' and others 'citizenship' to refer to persons who have a legal bond with a state by operation of law, and because this chapter is primarily concerned with the law, the terms 'nationality' and 'citizenship' will be used interchangeably in reference to persons with such bonds. Bonds of nationality and citizenship are both the result of applications of enacted legal instruments at the state level.

Citizenship in India

Unfortunately, mounting international pressures to respect a universal right to nationality have not coincided with an increased respect for the principle in India. Instead, India's changing citizenship laws demonstrate an increasingly strict approach to the granting of citizenship. In the wake of independence, India's 1955 citizenship laws were relatively inclusive. Except for those people whose fathers were diplomats or 'enemy aliens', citizenship was accorded at birth to everyone 'born in India on or after the 26th January, 1950, regardless of their descent, ethnicity, or national identity.'[7] By the mid-1980s, this had begun to change.

Following the large-scale illegal migration of Bangladeshis into India and the resulting disaffection of the internally displaced and increasingly economically excluded local Assamese population, the Indian legislature adopted the Citizenship (Amendment) Act, 1987, which restricted the *jus soli*[8] mode of citizenship acquisition established in 1955.

The Government of India took 'a serious view of the entry of persons clandestinely into India', citing 'fear about adverse effects upon the political, social, cultural and economic life of the State' and expressing concern over what it considered to be 'a large number of persons of Indian origin [who had] entered the territory of India from Bangladesh, Sri Lanka, and some African countries'.[9]

The amendments made it easier for those who were outside India and whose parents were citizens to gain citizenship than for those who reside in India and whose parents were not Indian citizens to do so. This change marks an important shift with regard to migrant stateless populations because, in general, it is more difficult to incorporate provisions for granting citizenship to migrants and their children in countries whose citizenship laws are built on *jus sanguinis*. Indeed, the new centrality of Indian nationality to the granting of citizenship overwhelmingly limits citizenship to those who descend from existing nationals, leaving stateless people and their children significantly more likely to be caught in a cycle of statelessness.

Furthermore, since 2004 a new amendment to the citizenship laws has further restricted stateless populations' access to Indian citizenship. In addition to increasing the residency requirements and limiting the meaning of the expression 'ordinarily resident in India', these new laws forbid those who are 'illegal migrants' from accessing citizenship registration and naturalization procedures, which are the only two ways of acquiring Indian citizenship for those who cannot do so by birth or descent, or by being a national of a territory incorporated into India. While not all stateless people have migrated, unless they became stateless after their migration, stateless migrants are very likely to have entered into India without the required documents and so they are deemed 'illegal migrants'.

'Illegal migrant' in India

Under Indian law, an 'illegal migrant' is

> a foreigner who has entered into India without a valid passport or
> other travel documents and such other document or authority as may
> be prescribed by or under any law in that behalf; or with a valid pass-
> port or other travel documents and such other document or authority
> as may be prescribed by or under any law in that behalf but remains
> therein beyond the permitted period of time.[10]

The language of this provision suggests two requisite elements. First, in
all circumstances, the term 'entered' suggests a cross-border movement from
another jurisdiction into India. Second, people must find themselves without the required legal documents to validate their presence under India law,
either from the moment they entered India or from the point at which the
documents with which they entered India become no longer valid. While
being deemed an 'illegal migrant' does not necessary entail statelessness, as
those migrants judged 'illegal' may retain an effective or ineffective bond
with another state, people who are stateless are very likely to also be illegal migrants. Unless the person was either born in India or found herself
or himself in India during independence such that s/he would not fulfil
the cross-border movement requirement, or they hold residency documents
(such as an Overseas Citizen of India [OCI] card) that do not amount to citizenship, de jure stateless people will also be categorized as 'illegal migrants'.
Illegal migrants may also not be de jure stateless but may be de facto by
virtue of their inability to access effective citizenship from the state with
which they hold a formal legal bond.

Being categorized as 'illegal migrants' places stateless people in a precarious position. While India does not have any legislation in place to protect
stateless people from being deported to regularize their status or grant them
citizenship, it does have legislation in place that allows the state to deport
illegal migrants. Since the Supreme Court of India deemed the legislation
ultra vires,[11] the Constitution of India, striking it down in 2005,[12] the Illegal
Migrants (Determination by Tribunal) Act, 1983 (hereinafter IMDT Act
1983), which gave migrants a right to appeal and placed the burden of proof
on the government rather than on the migrants themselves, is no longer
valid. Illegal migrants now find themselves again more vulnerable to deportation under the more liberal powers granted to the government in the

Foreigners Act, 1946. This legislation grants the government wide powers, including the ability to deport illegal migrants, which some argue have even been used in border regions against Muslim Indian citizens who were too poor to contest their deportation.

Children of those categorized as illegal migrants are also severely limited in their ability to acquire citizenship, as was alluded to earlier on the granting of citizenship in India. Furthermore, on a discursive level, the categorization of certain people as 'illegal' conflates the actions undertaken by people with their character. By using this term to describe them, India justifies their exclusion from the practice of the rule of law. The fewer rights they are granted in relation to citizens, the less their legal personality can be considered effective.[13]

Despite these many concerns, it can be argued that the term 'illegal migrants' has been rendered practically redundant, because the very legislation that associated the term with a legal category ceased to exist when with the abolition of the IMDT Act 1983. Now, if people find themselves unable to prove that they are a citizen of India, they will be deemed a foreigner by the authorities vested with the power for such determinations. However, because the Supreme Court ruling that struck down the IMDT Act 1983 was enacted in 2005, two years after the latest amendment to Indian citizenship laws, the term 'illegal migrant' remains a legal category in Section 2(e) of the Citizenship (Amendment) Act, 2003, as defined above. It is now unclear if the limitations imposed by the 2003 amendment in relation to 'illegal migrants' now only apply to those who were determined as such before the 2005 ruling or whether any of those considered 'foreigners' under the Foreigners Act, 1946, and their children are also affected by the 2003 amendments.

Indian overseas citizen

Under Indian law, an 'Indian overseas citizen' is

> a person who is of Indian origin, being a citizen of a specified country, or was a citizen of India immediately before becoming a citizen of a specified country, and is registered as an overseas citizen of India by the Central Government.[14]

Overseas Citizen of India (OCI) cards must not be mistaken for Indian citizenship. First, unlike Indian citizenship, OCIs may be held in conjunction with citizenship or nationality. An OCI is granted certain privileges not usually available to non-residents of India, such as the right to work, study and own property not used for agriculture or plantations; however the holder is ineligible for an Indian passport, has no voting rights in India and cannot work in government.[15]

Defining statelessness

International law

Article 1 of the Convention Relating to the Status of Stateless Persons, 1954 (1954 Statelessness Convention) defines a stateless person as one 'who is not considered as a national by any State under the operation of its law'.[16] This definition is now widely understood to be customary international law. This means that it should be applied by all states even if, like India, they are not party to the convention. Indeed, domestic processes of recognizing people as 'stateless' should use this definition as their basis.[17] It would, however, be misleading to suggest that there is global consensus on the definition of statelessness or acceptance of a set manner in which it should be applied. Due to varied attempts to respond to the complexity of lived realities and to the often tense geopolitics of nationality, procedures and requirements that govern the recognition of people as stateless differ around the world.

As matter of law, the 1954 Statelessness Convention definition is clear and allows for a relatively straightforward application, given that bonds of nationality are themselves legal connections. Yet it is very restrictive. The binary opposition of the national or citizen versus the stateless person on which it rests oversimplifies the reality of nationality as it is experienced by people the world over.

De jure vs. de facto statelessness

Those who satisfy the 1954 Statelessness Convention definition are considered *de jure* stateless. This type of statelessness covers those who do not have a legal bond with any state. As such, it generally covers those who are not automatically granted nationality at birth by the application of state legal instruments, those without nationality who are unable to obtain it through established legal provisions for its acquisition, and those whose nationality is revoked or terminated for any reason and who do not have a second nationality.

De facto statelessness, on the other hand, remains an area of open debate. Broadly speaking, it refers to those who are unable to disprove the assumption that they have nationality and those whose legal bonds of nationality are ineffective.[18] However, there is no legal meaning for the term '*de facto* statelessness'. In fact, by virtue of its distinction from de jure statelessness, the term necessarily refers to people who are not stateless under the 1954 Statelessness Convention definition of statelessness in international customary law. However, given the strong similarities in their plight to those who are *de jure* stateless, there are a number of practitioners and scholars who advocate for their inclusion in international legal protection frameworks for statelessness.

Former UNHCR Legal Adviser on Statelessness and Related Nationality Issues Carole Batchelor argues that the history of the 1954 Statelessness Convention serves to explain that its definition is so narrow and that the 'technical distinctions between *de jure* and *de facto* stateless persons should not be significant if the principles and intent of international law are fully recognized.'[19] She argues that the drafters of the 1954 Statelessness Convention assumed that those for whom nationality bonds had become ineffective would be considered refugees when they adopted this restrictive definition of statelessness. Yet, the Convention Relating to the Status of Refugees, 1951 (1951 Refugee Convention) limits the definition of refugee to those whose experiences of persecution are based on one of five convention grounds. A refugee is one who, owing to well-founded fear of being persecuted for reasons of race, religion, nationality, membership of a particular social group or political opinion, is outside the country of his nationality and is unable or, owing to such fear, is unwilling to avail himself of the protection of that country.[20]

In 1961, Paul Weis further warned the international community that the 'borderline between what is commonly called de jure statelessness and de facto statelessness is sometimes difficult to draw'.[21] More recently, Batchelor married this practical angle with a concern for the ethics of protection. On the basis that the central concern in addressing statelessness must be one of protection, she argues that protection on the grounds of the simple existence or non-existence of legal bonds creates an arbitrary exclusion of de facto refugees whose ineffective nationality puts them in a comparable situation to *de jure* ones.[22] In the end, however, the 1954 Statelessness Convention is unambiguous in its definition. Legally, it only covers *de jure* stateless people. That said, concerns about the lack of protection available to *de facto* refugees give good reason to question the appropriateness of this narrow definition and to consider ways to address the existing protection gap.

Stateless refugees

It is important to note that while some people may be both stateless and refugees, the two words are not coterminous. A stateless refugee is someone who is not considered to be a citizen or national under the operation of the laws of any state and satisfies the definition of a refugee under Article 1 of the 1951 Refugee Convention. Stateless refugees fall under the UNHCR's refugee mandate and are legally entitled to the protections of the 1951 Refugee Convention. When stateless refugees ceases to be refugees, they remain stateless if the resolution of their refugee status does not include acquisition of nationality or citizenship.

Prevention and reduction of statelessness

Attribution of nationality

Because de jure statelessness is by definition a lack of nationality, acquiring nationality is its clear legal solution. However, closing nationality gaps requires action by the state, which in some cases is the very agent which has rendered the persons stateless in the first place through its policies of deprivation of nationalities considered legal by domestic laws.

Nationality legislation generally follows family links such as links to the state through one's parents or spouse, or territorial links such as links to the state through one's place of birth or residence. In some cases of statelessness, these modes of acquisition are unavailable either by the language of the law or because there exist insufficient procedural guarantees. In other cases, stateless people have acquired nationality in these traditional ways, but because the laws in place allow for the deprivation or renunciation of nationality even in situations in which such actions render the person without a nationality, they do not in fact acquire it.

While there has been a move away from the strict view that it is 'for each State to determine under its own law who are its nationals'[23] such that the 'manner in which states regulate matters bearing on nationality cannot today be deemed within their sole jurisdiction',[24] the Government of India retains the power to grant citizenship. The right to nationality is framed by citizenship laws. This is why, for example, the UN Commission on Human Rights' 2007 call 'to adopt and implement nationality legislation with a view to preventing and reducing statelessness'[25] was directed towards states.

The right to nationality in international law

The very notion of statelessness is at odds with the right to nationality, which is guaranteed under international law. The idea that everyone has a right to nationality as a basic human right *was* developed in early twentieth-century conventions and treaties and is now found under Article 15 of the Universal Declaration of Human Rights (UDHR), which states that 'no one shall be arbitrarily deprived of his [*sic*] nationality nor denied the right to change his [*sic*] nationality.'[26]

Since then, the 1954 Statelessness Convention and the Convention on the Reduction of Statelessness, 1961 (1961 Statelessness Convention) have further developed this right. While India has not ratified either of these conventions, it did accede to the International Covenant on Civil and Political Rights, 1966 (ICCPR) in 1979, which also affirms that 'every child has the right to acquire a nationality.'[27] Other conventions have also reinforced the universality of the right to nationality. For example, Article 5(d)(iii) of the Convention on the Elimination of Racial Discrimination, 1965 (CERD), which India ratified in 1968, explicitly prohibits racial discrimination in applications of the right to nationality and the Committee on the Elimination of Racial Discrimination has further held that deprivation of citizenship on the basis of race, colour, descent, or national or ethnic origin is a breach of state parties' obligations to ensure non-discriminatory enjoyment of the right to nationality.[28]

Factors of statelessness

Blitz's typology: primary and secondary statelessness

In his policy chapter 'Statelessness, Protection, and Equality', founder of the International Observatory on Statelessness Dr Brad Blitz suggests a conceptual division be made between primary and secondary sources of statelessness. In his typology, primary sources of statelessness are those which are the direct result of discrimination, while secondary sources of statelessness are those which 'relate to the context in which national policies are designed, interpreted, and implemented'.[29] Because all causes of statelessness are in some way the result of forms of discrimination and inequality, it is often hard to distinguish between them. Blitz suggests that primary sources of statelessness are those which are the result of direct discrimination while secondary sources are the result structural discrimination. In his analysis, denial, deprivation and loss of citizenship are primary sources, and political restructuring, environmental displacement and barriers that impede accessing rights are secondary sources.

For Blitz, the denial and deprivation of citizenship caused by state discrimination either through explicit laws and onerous provisions is a primary source of statelessness. For example, citizenship laws based on ethnicity, religion, gender, lineage or other identity factors may prevent certain people from obtaining citizenship. Moreover, provisions that impose particular requirements, such as proof of birth or marriage on those seeking citizenship, can prevent people who do not have those documents from accessing their right to citizenship.[30] He also refers to the 'revocation of laws and forced removals following xenophobic campaigns' as a 'withdrawal and loss of citizenship', which he describes as a primary source of statelessness.[31]

Again, state succession that may result in violent nationality contests that forcibly displace people into other states or may not cause displacement, but may mean that people remaining in the same geographic area find themselves living in new jurisdictions, is considered to be a secondary source of statelessness. In these cases, statelessness may result from 'ill-defined nationality laws following conflict, de-federation, secession, state succession, and state restoration in multinational situations'.[32]

Further forms of structural discrimination, such as onerous requirements in the procedures for acquiring necessary identity documents, high feeds, witness certification requirements and lack of registration opportunities, constitute another secondary source of statelessness for Blitz.[33] He also warns that it is possible that, with the physical disintegration of certain states, populations will become stateless.[34] The possibility of displacement was certainly emphasized at the UN Conference on Climate held in 2009. While the possibility of an entire state ceasing to exist such that its population would become de jure stateless may not appear imminent, but it is certainly a prospect with which the international community may someday need to reckon. Meanwhile, it is foreseeable that climate change could result in more than just displacement. Situations where the state would no longer be able to provide effective citizenship to its citizens as a result of climate change are foreseeable. With the Intergovernmental Panel on Climate Change (IPCC) warning of rising sea levels in the Netherlands, Guyana, Bangladesh, and the islands of Oceania,[35] Blitz's warning of the possibility of de facto statelessness as a result of climate change must not be dismissed.

Factors of statelessness in India

Primary factors in India: denial, deprivation and loss of citizenship

In India, a number of explicit provisions provide the legal means by which a person in possession of Indian citizenship may lose that legal bond. Specifically, the Citizenship Act of India, 1955, states that Indian nationality may be lost through renunciation, termination or deprivation.

Renunciation

Under the Citizenship Act of India, 1955

If any citizen of India, who is also a national of another country, renounces his Indian citizenship through a declaration in the prescribed manner, he ceases to be an Indian citizen on registration of such a declaration. If the person making the declaration is a male then when the person loses his Indian citizenship, every minor child of his also ceases to be a citizen of India. However, such a child may within one year after attaining full age, become an Indian citizen by making a declaration of his intention to resume Indian citizenship.[36]

This presents two serious problems for statelessness. First, it deprives children of their Indian citizenship on the basis of their father's actions in such a way that may leave them stateless until they reach the mandated age to resume their Indian citizenship by declaration. Second, both in the case of the children who lose their Indian citizenship and the adults who renounce them, there is no provision to safeguard against statelessness. A person is in all circumstances entitled to renounce his or her citizenship, even if by doing so they would become *de jure* stateless.

Termination

Under the Citizenship Act of India, 1955

Any person who acquired Indian citizenship through naturalization, registration or otherwise, if he has voluntarily acquired the citizenship of another country at any time between 26 January 1950, the date of commencement of this Act, will cease to be a citizen of India from the date of such acquisition.[37]

The Supreme Court of India's Constitution Bench held in 1962 that if a 'person has acquired foreign citizenship either by naturalization or registration, there can be no doubt that he ceases to be a citizen of India in consequence of such naturalisation or registration'.[38] While this does not pose a problem for *de jure* statelessness, as the language of the provisions is such that termination comes only when citizenship of another state has been acquired, there is certainly the possibility that this termination provision could result in *de facto* statelessness because there is no guarantee that the non-Indian citizenship that has been voluntary acquired is, in fact, an effective one. Furthermore, it is important to note that a person may well satisfy the legal requirement of voluntary acquisition implied by the provision while still feeling varying degrees of social, political, or other pressures. Here gender, generation, class and other markers of identity are likely to have an effect on the experience of citizenship acquisition that cannot be recognized by the voluntary/involuntary binary of the legal provision.

Deprivation

Under the Citizenship Act of India, 1955, the Government of India may deprive a citizen of citizenship if it is 'satisfied that it is not conducive to the public good that the person should continue to be a citizen of India'[39] and

> the registration or certificate of naturalization was obtained by means of fraud, false representation or concealment of any material facts; or that the citizen has shown himself by act or speech to be disloyal or disaffected towards the Constitution of India as by law established; or that citizen has, during any war in which India may be engaged unlawfully traded or communicated with an enemy or been engaged in, or associated with, any business that was to his knowledge carried on in such manner as to assist an enemy in that war; or that citizen has, within five years after registration or naturalisation, been sentenced in any country to imprisonment for a term of not less than two years; or that citizen has been ordinarily resident out of India for a continuous period of seven years, and during that period, has neither been at any time a student of any educational institution in a country outside India or in the service of a Government in India or of an international organisation of which India is a member, nor registered annually in the prescribed manner at an Indian consulate his intention to retain his citizenship of India.[40]

In no uncertain terms, this provision creates statelessness. It is prescribed as punishment for certain actions. In other circumstances, where the person is deemed to have established themselves outside of India according to certain temporal and geographic criteria and is guilty of inaction of sorts by failing to register, no consideration is given to the ease with which the person will be able to acquire another citizenship. This provision is irreconcilable with India's human rights obligations and is a grave impediment in the prevention of statelessness.

Secondary factors: state succession and lack of access [41]

Secondary factors of statelessness are often particularly difficult to pinpoint, because unlike primary factors, no single specific laws, policies or regulations can be identified as these secondary factors. In India, as in many other states, state succession and lack of access to rights are interwoven with factors of statelessness and informed by the complexities of decolonization in the region.

In India, state succession is of particular importance in the creation of statelessness. The 1947 partition of India into the sovereign states of India and Pakistan and the 1971 secession of Bangladesh are two key periods in this regard. For example, most of those displaced by the partition in 1947 have since been granted citizenship in either India or Pakistan, but there are exceptions. Estimates suggest that approximately 20,000 Hindu refugees and over 100,000 Punjabi refugees from Pakistan remain stateless in India.[42] In many cases, their descendants are unable to acquire citizenship.[43]

In other situations, without political change at the level of state succession and without positive state action against discriminatory laws, people may find themselves in de jure and de facto situations of statelessness, because a lack of infrastructure to implement action has led to deprivation of citizenship,[44] or because the political, social or geographic context in which they find themselves makes it impossible for them to access citizenship acquisition mechanisms. A prime example of the latter is the case of those who live in the Bangladeshi Chitmahals in India, which are enclaves within enclaves along the India-Bangladesh border. Although India introduced passport and visa controls in 1952, the government did not provide for those living in these enclaves.

Other factors of statelessness in India: displacement, migration and trafficking

The situation of statelessness is complicated by various forms of movement, be it forced or voluntary. Forced migration during periods of political development may 'generate new minority groups and give rise to subsequent stateless populations' and can 'raise nationality problems'.[45] Some argue that the human trafficking results in incomplete citizenship that is de facto statelessness.[46] Identity factors such as gender, generation, class, ethnicity and religion often lead to additional forms of discrimination, which further complicates experiences of movement for stateless people.

Legal remedies

Formal legal remedies

Under international law, the resolution to stateless *is* implied by the very way de jure statelessness is defined. Because statelessness is a lack of formal legal bonds, and the acquisition of such bonds is its remedy. Indeed, in legal terms, the formal legal remedy to stateless is the granting of citizenship or nationality. Processes for the acquisition of citizenship in India are defined by the Citizenship Act of 1955 and its 1986 and 2003 Amendment Acts.

Informal legal remedies

Extra-judicial processes

The focus on state and international implementation agencies in the articulation of an international and regional statelessness framework may give the impression that stateless people cannot themselves resolve their precarious legal situation. It would be erroneous to assume that they are passive actors in this regard. Instead, stateless people often demonstrate a great deal of agency. In India, by putting the right amount of money in the hands of the right person, many stateless people work outside the legal framework to find informal solutions to the difficulties of being stateless. From paying off a bank employee for the ability to open an account to bribing an election bureau official for an election identification card, there are numerous illegal means by which people acquire the elements that make up legal citizenship. In some cases, elected officials deliberately turn a blind eye to these processes because they know that the populations fraudulently gaining the ability to vote are the very voters ensuring their re-election. Thus, the democratic nature of Indian elections becomes fuel for a 'selective blindness' of sorts.

Unofficial citizenship

Situations in which people come to enjoy many of the rights associated with citizenship, such that they are effectively treated as though they were citizens, has led some to use the term 'de facto citizenship'. Yet, as Batchelor warns, this term does not carry any legal meaning, and as such its use can be misleading.[47] Indeed, being described as having de facto citizenship can act as a discursive mask that hides the reality that people remains de jure stateless. Because their status is not officially recognized, these people are especially vulnerable to changing political and social contexts in which their unofficial citizenship may cease to be recognized by those around them. In addition, because the means by which they acquired this unofficial citizenship are likely to have included illegal actions, these people may be more likely to find themselves in the criminal justice system, which may increase their chances of deportation and may lead to prolonged incarceration, abuse or exploitation.

Protection of stateless persons

Statelessness status and status determination procedures

As a matter both of law and of policy, status determination procedures are generally conceived of as being the key to ensuring that those who are stateless are able to enjoy the rights to which they are entitled under international law. Indeed, in a system in which legal protection is afforded on the basis of legal status, such procedures are a necessary precursor to accessing rights. Therefore, those who are de jure stateless by application of the international customary law definition may be denied the relevant protection if they do not have access to procedures by which they can be recognized as such by those who would offer them protection. It is, therefore, a matter of primary concern for the protection of stateless people that there currently exist no statelessness status determination procedures in India.

The most basic distinction between those who are stateless and those who are not is that, at least by law if not in practice, those who are citizens of a state should have access to a number of rights guaranteed by that state. While not all states grant the same legal protection of rights to their citizens and many states are unable or unwilling to enforce rights that are legally guaranteed, the legal bond between a citizen and a state remains the basic means by which people are able to enjoy rights.

Recently, however, a move away from citizen rights towards human rights developed through a series of international legal instruments in the twentieth century such that there has been an uncoupling of nationality from rights, meaning that there are international legal mechanisms that, if applied, ensure the enjoyment of certain rights for all people, including those who are stateless. The UDHR specifies in Article 15 that nationality must be a guarantee of equal access to human rights.

Civil and political rights

The civil and political rights guaranteed by specific statelessness instruments are considerably more limited than those found in broader human rights mechanisms. In terms of civil and political rights, the 1954 Statelessness Convention provides for the right to freedom of religion,[48] the right to legal personhood,[49] the right to property,[50] the right to access courts[51] and the right to freedom of movement.[52] It is, therefore, of great relevance that stateless people's rights are not only based on the Statelessness Conventions, but also on other human rights instruments that have since been created in so far as they are applicable to stateless people. The ICCPR is of great importance in this regard, especially because India has ratified it. According to the UN Human Rights Committee, the civil and political rights outlined in the ICCPR are 'available to all individuals, regardless of nationality or statelessness [. . .] who may find themselves in the territory or subject to the jurisdiction of the State Party'.[53] So, unless otherwise specified, the rights outlined in the ICCPR should apply to stateless people.

The civil and political rights to which stateless people are entitled to include 'freedom of religion', which was considered of great importance in the post–Second World War context of the 1954 Statelessness Convention;[54] 'freedom of movement', which is most broadly espoused in the UDHR, which states that '[e]veryone has the right to freedom of movement and residence within the borders of each state;'[55] 'legal personhood', addresses issues of jurisdiction in matters of personal status, but it does not do so in the explicit way human rights law instruments do; and the 'right to access courts', which is an important right for stateless people because courts can be the means by which they seek redress for other human rights violations they have faced and because courts can provide the very means by which they resolve their status and have their right to nationality or citizenship legally recognized in a particular state.[56]

Civil and political rights absent from the Statelessness Convention

It is important to note that there are a number of rights to which the drafters of the 1954 Statelessness Convention do not make explicit reference. The right to life and protections against torture and slavery were omitted from the 1951 Refugee Convention because they were considered sufficiently established,[57] and so the same is likely true of the 1954 Statelessness Convention. They are, therefore, rights to which the stateless are entitled.

Other rights are omitted and cannot as easily be read into any of the provisions. As Van Waas aptly points out, both protections against arbitrary detention and minority rights are absent from the 1954 Stateless Convention, but are rights protected under human rights mechanisms that are of particular relevance to stateless populations.[58] The ICCPR explicitly provides that '[n]o one shall be subjected to arbitrary arrest or detention.'[59] Upon ratification, India made a twofold declaration regarding this provision, which limits its generous language in its application to India. First, India declared that the provision would be 'applied as to be in consonance with the provisions of clauses (3) to (7) of article 22 of the Constitution of India', which authorize preventative detention of enemy aliens and of those envisioned by preventative detention legislation for up to three months with the possibility of longer detention if an advisory board that includes a High Court judge finds sufficient cause for such an extension. Despite this clarification of the forms of detention that India will not consider arbitrary, the Constitution provides a protection to all those detained such that they are to promptly communicate the grounds on which the person is being detained unless it would go against public interest to do so. Second, India limited the remedies for unlawful arrest or detention, holding that neither is to result in compensation from the state.[60]

With regard to minority rights, the ICCPR states that they

> shall not be denied the rights, in community with the other members of their group, to enjoy their own culture, to profess and practice their own religion, or to use their own language.[61]

Assessment of civil and political rights of the stateless

As demonstrated in this brief overview of the civil and political rights of stateless people under the 1954 Statelessness Convention as compared to other human rights mechanisms, the Statelessness Convention provides no more protection than other human rights mechanisms. Therefore, in this regard, the fact that India has not signed the 1954 Statelessness Convention should not prove influential at the level of civil and political rights to which stateless populations in India should have access. In fact, the UDHR, which India participated in drafting, and the ICCPR, notwithstanding the limiting declarations India made when acceding, both provide more substantial rights protection for the stateless which India is bound to protect.

It must, however, be remembered that rights of stateless people do not amount to those of citizens with political rights under any of these instruments. Free speech protections and the right to participate in organized governmental politics are not granted to the stateless.

Economic, social and cultural rights

Much like civil and political rights, the economic, social and cultural rights guaranteed by the 1954 Statelessness Convention are considerably more limited than those found in broader human rights mechanisms. The International Covenant on Economic, Social, and Cultural Rights, 1966 (ICESCR), to which India acceded on 10 April 1979,[62] is an especially important part of human rights law in this regard, because its interpreting committee, the Committee on Economic, Social and Cultural Rights, has forcefully asserted that no group should be denied the 'minimum core content' of the ICESCR rights.[63]

The following is an overview of the economic, social and cultural rights to which stateless people are entitled.[64]

Right to work

Under the 1954 Stateless Convention,

> the Contracting States shall accord to stateless persons lawfully staying in their territory treatment as favourable as possible and, in any event, not less favourable than that accorded to aliens generally in the same circumstances[65] with regards to remuneration, hours of work, overtime arrangements, holidays with pay, restrictions on home work, minimum age of employment, apprenticeship and training, women's work and the work of young persons, and the enjoyment of the benefits of collective bargaining.[66]

Much like the aforementioned limitation of the protection of freedom of movement, this provision is limited to those who are lawfully on the territory, which inherently excludes a great number of stateless people who by virtue of their lack of citizenship or other circumstances find themselves unlawfully in a given territory.

The labour rights mechanisms that have evolved as part of human rights law offer an incomparable number of rights provisions, many of which apply to stateless people. The right to work and to just and favourable work conditions set out in the UDHR[67] are reflected in the ICESCR and have been elaborated in nearly 100 work-related conventions by the International

Labour Organization (ILO),[68] which are meant to apply irrespective of citizenship, meaning they apply to those who are stateless.[69]

Article 6 of the ICESCR, for example, grants everyone

> the right to work, which includes the right of everyone to the opportunity to gain his living by work which he freely chooses or accepts, and will take appropriate steps to safeguard this right.[70]

Right to an adequate standard of living

The idea of an 'adequate standard of living' is considerably more fleshed out in human rights instruments than it is in the 1954 Statelessness Convention, which includes only 'adequate food, clothing and housing, and [. . .] continuous improvement of living conditions'.[71]

While the meaning of the right to clothing has not been authoritatively expounded, the meaning of 'adequate' in relation to food and housing has been expounded in human rights conventions and by their associated committees. The right to food is not only a right to be 'free from hunger',[72] but also a guarantee of a 'quantity and quality sufficient to satisfy [. . .] dietary needs'[73] and the right to housing is 'the right to live somewhere in security, peace and dignity'.[74]

Right to social security

Social security benefits were not traditionally understood as universal, but rather were seen as part of the state-citizen relationship, extended only to those citizens of other countries if there was a reciprocal arrangement between the state from which they were coming and the state in which they then found themselves.[75] Stateless people were, therefore, precluded from the traditional model in which social security provisions are provided to those not citizens of the given state.

Therefore, at first glance, the 1954 Statelessness Convention appears generous in this regard. Article 23 grants a right to 'public relief and assistance' and Article 24 a right to

> legal provisions in respect of employment injury, occupational diseases, maternity, sickness, disability, old age, death, unemployment, family responsibilities and any other contingency which according to national laws or regulations, is covered by a social security scheme.[76]

In contrast, the ICESCR recognizes 'the right of everyone to social security, including social insurance',[77] which has been understood to include virtually the same entitlements as the 1954 Statelessness Convention, but which applies to everyone without regard to the lawfulness of the person's presence in a given state. Therefore, under the ICESCR, stateless people are guaranteed 'medical care, cash, sickness benefits, maternity benefits, old-age benefits, invalidity benefits, survivors' benefits, employment injury benefits, unemployment benefits [and] family benefits'.[78] This is, however, only a progressive obligation rather than an immediate one, and there is a widespread implied understanding that social security benefits are only achieved by participating in contributory mechanisms.[79] As for non-contributory social security schemes, the UN Committee on Economic, Social and Cultural Rights holds that 'refugees, stateless persons and asylum-seekers, and other disadvantaged and marginalized individuals and groups should enjoy equal treatment' and specifically supports 'reasonable access to health care and family support, consistent with international standards'.[80]

Right to education

The 1954 Statelessness Convention distinguishes between the right to education as it regards elementary education and as it regards more advanced education. Article 22 grants 'the same treatment as is accorded to nationals with respect to elementary education',[81] while 'access to studies, the recognition of foreign school certificates, diplomas and degrees, the remission of fees and charges and the award of scholarships'[82] for non-elementary education is only granted on par with similarly situated non-citizens.

In human rights law, however, non-citizens were first granted equal access to education as the citizens of the given state with the adoption of the UNESCO Convention Against Discrimination in Education.[83] While India has not ratified this convention, it has ratified the ICESCR which also addresses the right to education. Article 13 of the ICESCR extensively expands the components of the right to education so that it is 'directed to the full development of the human personality',[84] so that it include compulsory primary education as well as progressively implemented free secondary and higher education,[85] so that it protects of the liberty of legal guardians to choose schools,[86] and so that it affords people the right to 'establish and direct educational institutions'.[87] As Hathaway explains,

> while poorer states may rely on the Economic Covenant's general duty of progressive implementation to justify an overall insufficiency

of secondary education opportunities or the failure to progressively make such education free of charge, there must be no discrimination against non-citizens in granting access to [. . .] education.[88]

Assessment of economic, social and cultural rights of the stateless

As demonstrated in this brief overview of the economic, social and cultural rights of stateless people under the 1954 Statelessness Convention as compared to other human rights mechanisms, namely the ICESCR, the Statelessness Convention provides no more protection than human rights mechanisms. Therefore, much as was the case with civil and political rights, the fact that India has not signed the 1954 Statelessness Convention does not lower the bar for the level of civil and political rights to which stateless populations in India should have access. In fact, on the contrary, the UDHR, which India participated in drafting and the ICESCR to which India acceded in 1979 both provide more substantial rights protection for the stateless.

Access to documents

There is no general right to documentation in human rights law, but the 1954 Stateless Convention ensures that those individuals who qualify for protection by satisfying the definition articulated in Article 1 are provided with documentation confirming their status as stateless persons.[89] The right to identity chapters is found in Article 27 of the 1954 Statelessness Convention. Some identity documents are necessary to prove that a person is stateless and that s/he has a right to reside in the state, while other identity documents are useful in preventing statelessness by demonstrating a person's connection with a given state such that the state may not deny him or her citizenship.

First, registration certificates (RC) are a form of documentation available in India for those who are not citizens to legalize their residency in the state. While there exists specific documentation for people from particular regions or with particular relationships to India, which are afforded on criteria other than the person's citizenship status, RCs are not inherently limited to any one group. These are cards which designate the holder as a foreigner within India. Valid for either six months or a year, there is no guarantee of their renewal. In practice, RCs are a form of informal status that enables the holder to reside in designated regions of India. RCs can also allow for limited domestic travel and, in certain situations, travel abroad.

They are regulated by the Registration of Foreigners Act, 1939, and the Foreigners Act, 1946. The implementation of changing policies with regard to RCs is inconsistent across India. Those stateless people who are successful in obtaining an RC would not be considered 'illegal' during the period in which their cards are valid.

Second, documentation of births and marriages are another form of identity documents, on which people may rely to prevent and resolve statelessness. Birth certificates can have an important role in legitimizing a person's claim to citizenship if the person was born in the state and the state follows *jus soli* methods of granting citizenship. Indeed, the UNHCR standing committee explains that:

> while nationality is normally acquired independently and birth registration in and of itself does not normally confer nationality upon the child concerned, birth registration does constitute a key form of proof of the link between an individual and a State and thereby serves to prevent statelessness.[90]

Marriage, on the other hand, may have an effect on the likelihood a person will be granted citizenship, especially if the person they have married is a citizen of the state. With regard to the registration of marriages in the Indian context, the Convention on the Elimination of All Forms of Discrimination Against Women (CEDAW) committee has expressed its concern 'that India has not yet established a comprehensive and compulsory system of registration of births and marriages'.

Conclusion

The legal situation of stateless people in India cannot be understood simply by the fact that India has not acceded to either of the Statelessness Conventions. While this certainly demonstrates the state's reluctance to commit to addressing the issue of statelessness, it must not be understood as meaning that India has no statelessness law. Instead, if we are to accept that statelessness law includes both the law which produces situations of statelessness and the law which seeks to address it, then it is clear that India has a wealth of statelessness law. First, India has numerous legal provisions with actively produce statelessness in the form of citizenship laws that allow for the denial, deprivation and loss of Indian citizenship. Second, India is a party to numerous human rights conventions which offer protection to stateless people.

While acceding to the two Statelessness Conventions would no doubt be a decision welcomed by the international community of agencies and organizations concerned with statelessness, there is much for India to do to address the plight of those who are stateless besides considering accession to either convention. First, India must stop legally sanctioning the production of statelessness. It must revise its citizenship laws such that citizenship cannot be revoked from those who would be rendered stateless by such an act. Second, India must act on its human rights commitments. By acceding to the ICCPR and the ICESCR conventions, India has already promised to protect a wide range of civil, political, social, cultural and economic rights of the stateless. It must turn those international commitments into domestic law and policy.

In the end, however, addressing statelessness in India, like elsewhere in the world, is not merely a legal question. While the de jure statelessness definition is defined by the existence or non-existence of a legal bond, the experience of statelessness is about much more than citizenship in name. It is about citizenship in practice. Indeed, the existence of effective rights and entitlements goes much beyond the courtroom, to the political arena and socio-cultural milieu. Statelessness is more than its de jure definition. It is a multi-faceted issue that requires a multi-faceted response.

Notes

1 B. Blitz, 'Statelessness, protection, and equality', *Forced Migration Policy Briefing* 3. Oxford: Refugee Studies Center, 2009, www.refworld.org/pdfid/4e5f3d572. pdf, last accessed on2 December 2014.

2 UNHCR, 'The world's stateless people', *Refugees Magazine*, 147(3), 2007. It is, however, worth noting that ascertaining a clear number is difficult and UNHCR estimates have varied greatly. Practical difficulties in calculating numbers as well as continued disagreements about the definition of statelessness amongst political and academic actors serve to muddy the picture.

3 UNHCR, *UNHCR Executive Committee, 'Conclusion No. 78 on Prevention and Reduction of Statelessness and the Protection of Stateless Persons'*, www.unhcr. org/41b4607c4.pdf, last accessed on27 August 2014.

4 M. Lynch, *Lives on Hold: The Human Cost of Statelessness*, Washington: Refugees International, 2005, p. 7.

5 A. Guterres and L. Arbour, *The Hidden World of the Stateless*, Geneva: UNHCR, 2007.

6 W. Connor, 'A nation is a nation is a state is an ethnic group is a . . .', in J. Hutchinson and A. D. Smith (eds.), *Ethnic and Racial Studies*, Oxford and New York: Oxford University Press, 1994.

7 The Citizenship Act of India, 1955 (India), 1955, s 3.

8 *Jus soli* is Latin for 'right of the soil'. It refers to practices in citizenship law in which the right to citizenship is afforded by virtue of the person being born on the given state's territory.

9 Statement of Objects and Reasons of the Amendment from the Citizenship (Amendment) Act, 1987 (India), 1987.

10 The Citizenship (Amendment) Act 2003 (India), 2003, s 2(b).

11 Latin legal term meaning 'beyond the powers of'.

12 A. Roy, *Mapping Citizenship in India*, Oxford: Oxford University Press, 2010, p. 193.

13 For a more on universal look at the way foreigners are not considered complete legal subjects, see F. Crépeau and R. Samaddar, 'Recognizing the dignity of migrants', *Refugee Watch*, 37, 2011, www.mcrg.ac.in/rw%20files/RW37/5.Fran çois.pdf, last accessed on 5 May 2014.

14 Supra note 10, s 2(e).

15 India Country Specific Information, Online: US Department of State, www. travel.state.gov/travel/cis_pa_tw/cis/cis_1139.html#special_circumstances, accessed on 12 November 2013.

16 1954 Convention relating to the Status of Stateless Persons, 360 UNTS 117, art 1.

17 See UNHCR, *Regional Expert Roundtable on Good Practices for the Identification, Prevention and Reduction of Statelessness and the Protection of Stateless Persons in South East Asia*, Bangkok: National Human Rights Commission of Thailand and United Nations High Commissioner for Refugees, 2011.

18 *Charlotte-Anne Malischewski,* 'How Indian Law Produces Statelessness', in http:// blogs.mcgill.ca/humanrightsinterns/2013/07/17/how-indian-law-produces- statelessness/, accessed on 30 April 2018.

19 Supra note 18 at 172–5.

20 1951 Convention relating to the Status of Refugees, 189 UNTS 137, art 1.

21 P. Weis, 'Elimination or reduction of future of statelessness', Speech delivered at the Speech to the United Nations Conference on 25 August 1961 [unpublished].

22 C. Batchelor, 'Stateless persons: Some gaps in international protection', *International Journal of Refugee Law*, 7, 1995: 252.

23 1930 Convention on Certain Questions relating to the Conflict of Nationality Laws 179 LoNTS 89, art 1.

24 UNHCR, 'Statelessness and citizenship', in *The State of the World's Refugees: A Humanitarian Agenda*, Oxford: Oxford University Press, 1997, p. 251.

25 Resolution 2005/45 on Human Rights and Arbitrary Deprivation of Nationality, UN Commission on Human Rights, 57th Meeting, UN Doc E/CN.4/ RES/2005/45 (2005).

26 Universal Declaration of Human Rights, GA Res 217 (111), UNGAOR, 3d Sess, Supp No 13, UN Doc A/810 (1948), art 15.

27 *International Covenant on Civil and Political Rights,* 19 December 1966, 999 U.N.T.S. 171, Can. T.S. 1976 No. 47 (entered into force 23 March 1976), art. 24.

28 UN Committee on the Elimination of Racial Discrimination, *General Recommendation 30: Discrimination against Non-Citizens,* 1 October 2004, para. 14.

29 Supra note 1 at 1.

30 Supra note 1 at 10.

31 *Ibid.*at 16.

32 *Ibid.*

33 *Ibid.*

34 *Ibid.* at 14.

35 IPCC, *Climate Change 2007: Impacts, Adaptation and Vulnerability*, Geneva: IPCC, 2008.

36 Supra note 7, s 8, https://indiancitizenshiponline.nic.in/Ic_GeneralInstruction. pdf accessed on 30 April 2018.

37 Supra note 7, s 9, Foreigners Division, Ministry of Home Affairs, Government of India, https://indiancitizenshiponline.nic.in/citizenshipact1.htm, accessed on 30 April 2018.

38 Izhar Ahmad Khan v Union of India, 1962 AIR 1052 at 248.

39 Supra note 7, s 10(3).

40 *Ibid.*, 10(2).

41 As the assessment of extra-legal factors in statelessness is beyond the scope of this brief, please refer to the Mahanirban Calcutta Research Group research programme on statelessness for more case-based analysis of these factors.

42 The International Observatory on Statelessness, 'India', 22 May2013, www. nationalityforall.org/india, last accessed on 24 March 2014.

43 For further explanations of the effects of state succession in India, please refer to the three Mahanirban Calcutta Research Group reports on statelessness available at www.mcrg.ac.in.

44 Supra note 1 at 10.

45 Supra note 1 at 13.

46 See P. McLean, *Incomplete Citizenship, Statelessness and Human Trafficking: A Preliminary Analysis of the Current Situation in West Bengal*, Kolkata: Calcutta Research Group, 2005.

47 Supra note 18 at 171.

48 Convention Relating to the Status of Stateless Persons, 1954, Article 4. For details see www.unhcr.org/3bbb25729.pdf, last accessed on28 March 2014.

49 *Ibid.*, art 12.

50 *Ibid.*, art 13.

51 *Ibid.*, art 13(1).

52 *Ibid.*, art 26, 31.

53 Human Rights Committee, General Comment 31: Nature of the General Legal Obligation Imposed on States Parties to the Covenant, Geneva: 26 May 2004, para.10. It must, however, be acknowledged that several of the ICCPR provisions are explicitly more limited, e.g. 'juvenile offenders' or 'pregnant women' (Art. 6).

54 For a more in-depth analysis of each of these rights, please refer to supra note 19 at 235.

55 UN General Assembly, Universal Declaration of Human Rights, 1948, Article 15. See www.ohchr.org/EN/UDHR/Documents/UDHR_Translations/ eng.pdf, last accessed on 23 June 2014.

56 Supra note 19 at 266.

57 J. Hathaway, *The Rights of Refugees Under International Law*, Cambridge: Cambridge University Press, 2005, p. 94.

58 Supra note 19 at 285.

59 International Covenant on Civil and Political Rights, 1966, Article 9. For details see www.ohchr.org/en/professionalinterest/pages/ccpr.aspx, last accessed on 2 August 2014.

60 *Ibid.*

61 *Ibid.*, art 27.

62 It should be noted that unlike the ICCPR, the ICESCR allows for progressive achievement. See International Covenant on Economic, Social, and Cultural Rights,1966, Article 2(1). For details see www.ohchr.org/Documents/ ProfessionalInterest/cescr.pdf, last accessed on 21 March 2014.

63 *Ibid.*
64 For a more in-depth analysis of each of these rights, please refer to supra note 19 at 301.
65 Convention Relating to the Status of Stateless Persons, 1954, Article 17.
66 Article 24, paragraph 1(a) of the 1954 Convention Relating to the Status of Stateless Persons.
67 See Articles 23 and 24 of the Universal Declaration of Human Rights, 1948.
68 Supra note 19 at 312.
69 Hathaway, *The Rights of Refugees Under International Law*, p. 485.
70 Article 6, paragraph 1 of the ICESCR.
71 ESC Committee, General Comment 4: The right to adequate housing, 13 December 1991, para. 6.
72 Article 11, paragraph 2 of the International Covenant on Economic, Social and Cultural Rights.
73 ESC Committee, General Comment 12: The right to adequate food, 12 May 1999, para. 8.
74 ESC Committee, General Comment 4: The right to adequate housing, 13 December 1991, para. 6.
75 Hathaway, *The Rights of Refugees Under International Law*, p. 773.
76 Article 24, paragraph 1(b) of the 1954 Convention Relating to the Status of Stateless Persons.
77 Article 9 of the ICESCR.
78 ESC Committee, Revised general guidelines regarding the form and contents of reports to be submitted by state parties under Articles 16 and 17 of the International Covenant on Economic, Social and Cultural Rights, E/C.12/1991/1, 17 June 1991.
79 Supra note 19 at 238.
80 ESC Committee, General Comment No. 19 – The Right to Social Security, Advanced unedited version, 4 February 2008, para. 38. in Van Waas, p. 331.
81 Article 22(1) of the 1954 Convention relating to the Status of Stateless Persons.
82 Article 22(2) of the 1954 Convention relating to the Status of Stateless Persons.
83 Article 3, paragraph e of the UNESCO Convention Against Discrimination in Education, 14 December 1960.
84 Article 13(1) of the ICESCR.
85 Article 13(2) of the ICESCR.
86 Article 13(3) of the ICESCR.
87 Article 13(4) of the ICESCR.
88 Hathaway, *The Rights of Refugees Under International Law*, pp. 611–12.
89 Supra note 19 at 375.
90 UNHCR, 'Birth registration: A topic proposed for an executive committee conclusion on international protection', *EC/61/SC/CRP.5*, www.refworld.org/docid/4b97a3242.html, last accessed on 25 January 2015.

7

REDUCING STATELESSNESS

A new call for India

Shuvro Prosun Sarker

> Moder kono basha nai, Moder kono desh nai . . .
> Moder kono disha nai, Moder kono dyash nai.[1]
> —Bengali folk song by Abbasuddin

The principal objective behind any research on statelessness in India should be to find out the communities/groups within India that are lacking nationality, rather protection of nationality, and to find out the means and methods to cover them under state protection or international protection. However, there is the possibility that this kind of research may trace communities/groups from both ways that 'do not have the nationality of any state legally' or 'do not count on their state for protection'. It is noteworthy for a country like India that the second category has emerged from the neighbouring states in relation to episodes of irregular migration because of sustained or systemic violation of basic human rights towards some communities/groups by their own state/majority community. The situation actually leaves the victims virtually unprotected by the agencies of the state. This category of persons indicates that effective statelessness may no longer reflect in the relationship between the state and the person concerned. On one side there is hope that the host state will play a compassionate role, and on the other side there are strict laws of the land which define the nature of nationality. All these factors raise the question of protection for this vulnerable class which may be called on by advocating for a new international protocol or evocative acts or advocacy for a regional pact or direct national legislation.

Although there are two UN conventions on statelessness, these cannot make India liable to go by their terms, as India has not acceded/ratified/adopted/signed the conventions. The limitation of these conventions to reduce statelessness for a country like India is a writ of bit large as there is a growing number of people who are stateless de facto.[2] Their human rights are more vulnerable as they have left the state to which they have a formal connection and also do not get protection by the host state as doubtful citizens. The relationship between protection of these stateless persons and human rights is one of the primary issues in India. It is necessary to consider alternative protection for these stateless persons under the two human rights covenants as the hierarchy of non-citizens in a state highlights the gap between protection and human rights. There is expansion of non-derogable rights and the concept of social, economic and cultural rights started in the twentieth century, along with international affirmation of universality, indivisibility, interdependence and interrelatedness of human rights. All these should come together to consider the identification of specific groups/communities whose human rights require special protection.

With regard to customary practices of international law, non-refoulement is the principle with regard to refugees and stateless-refugees which is non-derogable in nature. Apart from that there is a significant body of international law that has elaborated the principle of non-discrimination as a non-derogable norm that prohibits discrimination on the basis of race, ethnicity and related criteria. India's acceding to ICCPR,[3] ICESCR,[4] CRC[5] and ratification of ICERD[6] and CEDAW[7] have excelled the quantum of protection from the idea of compassion to rights. This development of a body of international law which triggered the prohibition of nationality-based discrimination has been further encouraged by the advocacy efforts of international organizations, non-governmental actors, and particular states. Also the recent increase in public information and advocacy has served to remind international bodies and non-governmental organizations (NGO) that the persistence of statelessness is a complex matter that underlines the centrality of effective protection. There is a growing pressure from international NGOs, refugee organizations, and human rights monitoring bodies to provide protection to those who do not fall under either the refugee convention or the conventions on statelessness. There is a specific case decided by the Supreme Court of India in the matter of Chakmas from Chittagong Hill Tracts (CHT), East Pakistan (presently Bangladesh) where the Court decided the case in favour of the Chakmas with specific direction to process their citizenship application through the process established by law.[8] It is mentionable here that a new public interest litigation, *Swajan & Anr. v. Union of India & Anr.*,[9] is pending before the Supreme Court asking for specific direction to confer citizenship/refugee status to the Bangladeshi minorities staying in the State of Assam and the Court has already issued notice to the respondents Union of India and State of Assam. So it is evident that the expansion of human rights regime of stateless persons of the second category has positive momentum in India along with the expansion of locus standi of foreigners staying in India.[10] Now it is time to see whether the Supreme Court comes out with a decision based on human rights consideration or on the grounds of internal security and economic constraint of India.

A countless number of deemed stateless or deemed nationals are looking forward to obtaining justice!

This chapter will focus on defining statelessness and its implication to the Indian scenario. Thereafter, India's obligation to protect the stateless persons from discrimination and inequality will be followed. Various cases decided by the Indian judiciary and debates in the parliament will be analysed to determine emergence of protection of the stateless persons.

The Indian scenario and statelessness

Citizenship has become a political weapon and treatment to non-citizens is worsening precisely as states are increasingly bestowing, denying, or retracting citizenship through various acts.[11] It is difficult to determine the number of stateless persons in the world as there is a lack of a systematic method of collecting data, and most importantly the lack of consensus on inclusion-exclusion policy.[12] Here the dilemma begins.

Historically, a state has the right to determine or define who is a citizen of that state.[13] A person who is under the confusion of the citizenship laws about his status as a non-national is called de jure stateless,[14] and 'it is a purely legal description; the characteristics and value of a particular person's nationality as it is realized in his particular home state is irrelevant to the definition'.[15] The 1954 Convention in Article 1 defines stateless as a person 'who is not considered as a national by any State under the operation of its law'.[16] This *de jure* situation is also recognized by the 1961 Convention on the Reduction of Statelessness.[17] It is believed by many legal scholars that the concept of statelessness should encompass more than *de jure* statelessness. The conventional definition is too narrow and limited, as this does not cover those persons who have a nationality technically but not fruitfully or cannot prove their nationality on the basis of evidence.[18] The prior statement should be well understood with the following statement:

The definition of statelessness outlined in the 1954 Convention precludes full realization of an effective nationality because it is a technical, legal definition which can address only technical, legal problems. Quality and attributes of citizenship are not included, even implicitly, in the definition. Human rights principles relating to citizenship are not delineated, despite the inspiration of the Conventions themselves by article 15 of the Universal Declaration of Human Rights. The definition is not one of quality, simply one of fact.[19]

The same author further clarifies her opinion as follows:

The definition of a *de jure* stateless person was chosen in order to exclude the question of whether the person has faced persecution, as there are conflicts of legal issues which might result in statelessness without any willful act of neglect, discrimination, or violation on the part of the State. *de facto* statelessness, on the other hand, was presumed to be the result of an act on the part of the individual, such as fleeing from the country of nationality because of persecution by the State. The drafters of the 1954 and 1961 Conventions felt that all those who faced persecution, and who did not have an effective nationality, would be considered refugees and would receive assistance from the international community under the terms of the 1951 [Geneva] Convention relating to the Status of Refugees. Quite intentionally, then, the drafters of the 1954 Convention relating to the Status of Stateless Persons adopted a strictly legal definition of stateless persons.[20]

From this point it may be argued that persons without effective nationality should be treated as stateless.[21] These persons may have a legal bond with a country but no longer be able to utilize it or enjoy the benefits for various socio-political reasons or cannot prove it with sufficient evidence.[22] In this regard, the definition of statelessness should be broadened to include de facto statelessness.[23] Categorically there are three groups who may be considered as de facto stateless:[24]

1 Persons who do not enjoy the rights attached to their nationality
2 Persons who are unable to establish their nationality, or who are of undetermined nationality
3 Persons who, in the context of state succession, are attributed the nationality of a state other than the state of their habitual residence.

In this context a definition of de facto stateless adopted by the Council of Europe's Group of Specialists on Nationality may be considered as timely with regard to the expansion of statelessness regime:[25]

> persons [who] do possess a certain nationality, but where either the state involved refuses to give the rights related to it, or the persons involved cannot be reasonably asked to make use of that nationality, yet it has to be underlined, that it is up to the states to determine what de facto statelessness is and thus which persons are to be covered.

The Inter-American Court on Human Rights in the *Case of the Yean and Bosico Children v. The Dominican Republic*[26] held that:

> States have the obligation not to adopt practices or laws concerning the granting of nationality, the application of which fosters an increase in the number of stateless persons. This condition arises from the lack of a nationality, when an individual does not qualify to receive this under the State's laws, owing to arbitrary deprivation or the granting of a nationality that, in actual fact, is not effective.

As the primary responsibility of states includes prevention and reduction of statelessness,[27] the case of India should be to attempt to identify effectively stateless persons and find ways to reduce it. In India, it is fact that we will find people without effective nationality due to the effects of partition, decolonization, internal politics and security issues in India, negative legislative intent and civil war in Sri Lanka and Bhutan, Indo-Chinese relationship and so forth, and finally the lack of measures in Indian citizenship law to deal with this grave situation. At the same time, India is not bound by the terms of any of the conventions relating to statelessness as India has not acceded/ratified/adopted/signed them. However, India is a party to various other international instruments, which on the other hand brings responsibility to protect the stateless population in India.

The general comment under the International Covenant on Civil and Political Rights (ICCPR) on the issues of position of aliens upholds that the rights guaranteed under this covenant should guarantee without distinction to aliens and citizens.[28] The general rule is that each one of the rights of the covenant must be guaranteed without discrimination between citizens and aliens. Aliens receive the benefit of the general requirement of non-discrimination in respect of the rights guaranteed in the covenant.[29] Exceptionally, some of the rights recognized in the covenant are expressly applicable only to aliens. However, the committee's experience in examining reports shows that in a number of countries other rights that aliens should enjoy are denied to them or are subject to limitations that cannot always be justified under the covenant.[30]

The drafters of the Convention on the Elimination of All Forms of Discrimination Against Women (CEDAW) were preoccupied with ensuring that women attain equality with men in regard to their own nationality and that of their children.[31] It is assumed that if women do not receive equal treatment with men, then that amounts to discrimination and again women may face discrimination for which they may not find adequate redress.[32]

The Convention on the Rights of the Child (CRC) provides, among others, that the child shall have the right to acquire a nationality, while state parties have to implement these rights according to their national law and obligations under relevant international instruments to prevent the child from becoming stateless.[33] This convention further provides that state parties undertake to respect the right of the child to preserve his or her nationality as recognized by law without 'unlawful interference', and declares that state parties shall provide assistance and protection to a child 'legally deprived' of, in this case, nationality, for its speedy restoration.[34]

Parliamentary discussions and judicial pronouncements

The issue of granting citizenship of India to the various effectively stateless persons has stormed both houses of the Indian Parliament. In various occasions Members of Parliament (MP) asked specific questions about Indian citizenship granting process to the Chakma and Hajongs, Pakistani, and Bangladeshi migrants in various Indian states and so forth. There has been a continuous discussion starting from 1993 to the present day where MPs actually showed interest in reducing statelessness in India. However, there has been no discussion on the definitional aspect, and by and large it is derived from the discussion that MPs are considering any group who are present in India without an effective nationality as stateless, as they are continuously insisting the government to grant citizenship, expedite the citizenship granting process, propose a new bill, delegate powers and so forth. The following paragraphs will be addressing these parliamentary proceedings in a nutshell.

Nyodek Yonggam MP asked the Minister of Home Affairs to provide details of granting citizenship to Chakma refugees settled in various parts of India.[35] The Minister of State for Home Affairs replied that the issues of granting citizenship to Chakma refugees who are resident of Arunachal Pradesh and arrived in India before 25 March 1971 has been under consideration of the Ministry. However, Chakma refugees living in other parts of India have not been considered for citizenship. Drupad Borgohain MP asked the Minister of Home Affairs about the latest decision of the Ministry to grant Indian citizenship to Chakmas and Hajongs who had migrated from Bangladesh to Arunachal Pradesh and if there would be any bill to come before the parliament on this issue.[36] The Minister of State for Home Affairs replied that the granting of citizenship was under consideration but there was no such proposal to introduce a bill in the parliament regarding this issue.

A. Vijayaraghavan MP asked the Minister of Home Affairs whether the Ministry had received any representation to grant Indian citizenship to Pakistani citizens settled in Malappuram district of Kerala during the time of independence and whether there was any attempt in denying ration cards by the district magistrate in 2003 to family members of these persons who are citizens of India by birth.[37] The Minister of State replied that the Ministry did not receive any such representation. If they apply for Indian citizenship, proper action will be taken by the central government as per the Indian Citizenship Act, 1955, and Citizenship Rules, 1956. However, no such information on denying ration cards was available at that time and the Minister of State assured that the information would be collected and laid down in the table of Rajya Sabha. Mr Vijayaraghavan MP again in 2005 asked the Minister of Home Affairs whether the Ministry extended time frame of the delegated powers of the district magistrates of Gujarat and Rajasthan to grant Indian citizenship to persons who came from Pakistan, and the statewise number of persons who were granted Indian citizenship in the last year.[38] The Minister of State replied that the Ministry extended the time frame of this delegated power by one year and the number of Indian citizenship granted in the last one year to migrants from Pakistan in Gujarat and Rajasthan are 1,469 and 11,298, respectively.

Motilal Vora MP asked the Minister of Home Affairs whether due to the laxity of Indian laws and carelessness of Indian security agencies Bangladeshi and Pakistani migrants are living in India, the government's reaction to this and the number of pending application from Pakistani citizens for granting Indian citizenship.[39] The Minister of State replied that the government was aware of the illegal immigrants mostly from Bangladesh and state governments were empowered under Section 3(2)c of the Foreigners Act, 1946, to detect and deport those foreign nationals staying illegally. However, the minister could not provide any data about the pendency figure.

Rajeev Chandrasekhar MP asked the Ministry of Home Affairs to provide a data on citizenship applications received by the Ministry up to 1
September 2007 from the citizens of Bangladesh, Pakistan and Myanmar.[40]
The Minister of State replied his question saying that there is no centralized
data maintained by the Ministry regarding this, and so it is not possible to
provide any estimate of how many applications may be cleared by the ministry by the end of 2007.

Man Mohan Samal MP in the Lok Sabha asked the Minister of Home
Affairs about the refugees from Bangladesh in the State of Odisha.[41] He
specifically wanted to know about their rehabilitation and citizenship granting process. The Minister of State replied that the Government of Orissa
informed the Ministry that illegal Bangladeshi migrants were a major concern for the law and order situation in the Nabarangpur district of Orissa.
During the 1960s and 1970s Bangladeshis were rehabilitated by the Government in Malkangiria, Koraput, Nabarangpur, Bhadrak, Jagatsinghpur,
Kendrapara, Khurda and Balasore districts and all Bangladeshi settlers who
were thus rehabilitated were given citizenship rights.

The Minister of State for Home Affairs in 2013, while discussing the resolution and answering the questions related to formulation of an action plan
to rehabilitate persons displaced from Pakistan finally requested the members
to withdraw the resolution. For the convenience of readers, the reply of the
Minister of State has been put below in his own words in the Lok Sabha:

The Minister of State in the Ministry of Home Affairs (Shrimullappally Ramachandran)

A very important issue has been raised by Shri Meghwal relating to
the rehabilitation of displaced Hindu families presently coming from
Pakistan. It is worthwhile to mention that in order to solve the massive problem of mass influx of displaced persons from the erstwhile
West Pakistan – as a result of partition in 1947 and to rehabilitate
them – the Government of India, during 1950's, had taken a series of
measures by enacting a series of Acts. As the major works of claims,
compensation and also rehabilitation, more or less, had been completed by 1970, the Central Government repealed all these Acts in
2005. At present, we do not have any Act in this connection because
this august House has repealed all these Acts.

[. . .]

I would like to state that the Central Government has been very
sensitive to the issues faced by the Pakistan nationals who migrated

to India at various point of time. For instance, it has been decided that the cases of the Pakistan nationals who entered India prior to 31.12.2004 would be processed on a case to case basis, and if an applicant files an Affidavit before the authority prescribed under Rule 38 of the Citizenship Rules, 2009, that is, the Collector, District Magistrate and Deputy-Commissioner, it may be accepted in lieu of the Renunciation Certificate. The State Governments and UTs concerned have been duly requested to deal with these matters as per instructions given by the Ministry of Home Affairs. In fact, the Ministry has also stipulated a Standard Operating Procedure for dealing with foreign nationals who claim to be refugees. Madam, another important issue has been raised, that is, delegation of power to the District Collectors in the States of Gujarat and Rajasthan for grant of Indian Citizenship to Pakistan nationals. This is a very important issue which has been raised by some Members. The powers to grant Indian Citizenship to nationals of Pakistan belonging to minority Hindu community were delegated to the Collectors of Kutch, Patan, Banaskantha, Ahmedabad of Gujarat and Barmer and Jaisalmer of Rajasthan in 2004 for one year to grant citizenship to Pak nationals of minority community staying in the border districts of Rajasthan and Gujarat as a special case. This delegation was extended up to2007 on year to year basis. Such powers were not delegated to any other State. Sufficient time was given to these two States to decide such pending cases.

[. . .]

The provisions of applying for Indian Citizenship continue to be available as per provisions of Citizenship Act of 1955. Normally, the Central Government takes about four months in processing cases and issuing acceptance letter in consultation with security agencies. In order to make the procedure simpler, faster and transparent, the Home Ministry has decided to introduce what is called online submission of application for grant of citizenship with effect from 1.12.2001.

[. . .]

I would like to reiterate that the Government of India is very sensitive to the issue related to the welfare of all foreign nationals in India including Hindu Pak nationals who deserve support and attention subject to the laws of the land and policies of the Indian Government.

[. . .]

It clear from the abovementioned questions by the Members of the Parliament and the answers of the Ministry of Home Affairs clearly indicates that the parliamentarians of India and also the Government of India are not concerned about the two conventions of statelessness and precisely they have clubbed these two identities while dealing with them. They have never tried to get reference of these two conventions anywhere during these proceedings which primarily denote that statelessness in India is in such a unique situation that the conventional definition could not serve the purpose of reducing statelessness in India.[42]

If these proceedings are analysed, it will be found that while the Government of India was not denying any responsibility to reduce statelessness or granting citizenship to these groups present in the country, it was not addressing these issues with in a specific normative framework or legislative action in a proper and timely manner.

India is not a party to the stateless conventions, however this does not reduce India's obligation to protect. The principle of non-refoulement has been accepted as a principle of customary international law. This goes on to add that the other principles regarding refugees enumerated in various international law instruments have to be taken into consideration. This leads to the international law and municipal law debate. Thus stands out a question: why would a nation respect international principles and policies unless they have been incorporated in the municipal laws of that nation? The Supreme Court of India deserves a laud in this regard. The way Supreme Court of India has interpreted the Constitution in its decisions to highlight the duty of the state to accord refugee protection is phenomenal.

In its two major decisions the Supreme Court referred to Article 14 of the Universal Declaration of Human Rights and Article 13 of the International Covenant on Civil and Political Rights to uphold the obligation of refugee protection.[43] The first instance was the case of *KhudiramChakma v. State of Arunachal Pradesh*,[44] where the Supreme Court of India referred to the Universal Declaration of Human Rights in the context of refugees in India in the following words:

> Article 14 of the Universal Declaration of Human Rights, which speaks of the right to enjoy asylum, has to be interpreted in the light of the instrument as a whole, and must be taken to mean something. It implies that although an asylum seeker has no right to be granted admission to a foreign State, equally a State which has granted him asylum must not later return him to the country whence he came. Moreover, the Article carries considerable moral authority and embodies legal prerequisite of regional declarations and instruments.[45]

The pro-refugee protection approach was further reflected in the case of *National Human Rights Commission v. State of Arunachal Pradesh.*[46] The Supreme Court of India held that Chakma refugees who had come from Bangladesh due to persecution cannot be forcibly sent back to Bangladesh as they may be killed or tortured or discriminated, and in result of this they would be deprived of their right to life under Article 21[47] of the Constitution of India. The Supreme Court in the same case made a number of observations relating to the protection of Chakma refugees in India:

> We are a country governed by Rule of Law. Our Constitution confers certain rights on every human being and certain other rights on citizens. Every person is entitled to equality before the law and equal protection of the laws. So also, no person can be deprived of his life or personal liberty except according to the procedure established by law. Thus the State is bound to protect the life and personal liberty of every human being, be he a citizen or otherwise, and it cannot permit anybody or group of persons . . . to threaten the Chakmas to leave the State, failing which they would be forced to do so . . . the State government must act impartially and carry out its legal obligations to safeguard the life, health and well being of Chakmas residing in the state without being inhibited by local politics. Besides, by refusing to forward their applications, the Chakmas are denied rights, constitutional and statutory, to be considered for being registered citizens of India.[48]

A subtle derivation from the above trend would stand to claim that the obligation to protect refugees or particularly the stateless persons is paramount. The importance of Article 21 of the Constitution can be well inferred from the decisions rendered by the Supreme Court. Article 21 is a non-derogable right. It would be therefore not incorrect to claim that the term 'reducing statelessness' with regard to the groups who are staying in India for a long period or for generations have been fully incorporated into Indian law via Article 21 of the Constitution of India.

However, with regard to illegal migration from Bangladesh, the Supreme Court has declared the Illegal Migrants (Determination by Tribunal) Act, 1983, unconstitutional in the decision given in *Sarbananda Sonawal v. Union of India.*[49] The Act was enacted by the Indian government, partly to prevent a witchhunt against illegal migrants, but also with the professed aim of making the detection and deportation of illegal migrants easier. This Act resulted in the establishment of tribunals to determine whether or not a person is an illegal migrant. This was specifically and exclusively applicable to foreigners in Assam, while foreigners in the rest of India covered under the provisions of the 1946 Foreigners Act.[50] While the Foreigners Act specifically provides that the onus of proving citizenship status rests on the person accused of being a non-citizen,[51] the 1983 Act contained no such provision, and in effect, its provisions accorded greater protection to anyone accused of being a foreigner in placing the burden of proof on the prosecution to establish that he or she is not a citizen of India. In this case, the petitioner, a former president of the All Assam Students Union, stated that the 1983 Act was unconstitutional as it discriminated against a class of citizens of India, making it impossible for citizens resident in Assam to secure the detection and deportation of foreigners from India. The petitioner claimed that the Act had actually ended up protecting illegal migrants. The Court declared the Act unconstitutional on the ground that it violated Article 355 of the Indian Constitution.[52] This judgement has a very long-standing effect in determining the issue of granting citizenship in India where on one side there is threat to security and in another side there is a possibility of social integration.

Conclusion

It is noteworthy that stateless persons have not been historically distinguished from refugees; however, refugees are identified through various categories; and stateless persons are mostly unidentified.[53] For a country like India, statelessness emerges mainly for the following reasons: rigidity of Indian citizenship laws, administrative obstacles by Indian authorities and neighbouring countries, laws that revoke citizenship in some of the neighbouring countries, arbitrary and discriminatory denial of citizenship in India in case of children, State withdrawal of citizenship in some of the neighbouring countries, laws affecting women rights of nationality and subsequent rights, transnational migration and so forth. This is the time for India to deal with this situation of effective statelessness, else in near future the number will grow in such huge numbers that the government machinery will not be able to deal with the demand for protection and grant of citizenship for each and every group. In this present world political scenario it may not be possible to adopt any of the conventions of statelessness by the Indian government as there is a growing concern over the third world approaches to international law, precisely public international law.[54]

So, it should be possible to deal with statelessness in India with a human rights approach. After all, humanism and compassion have been India's ageless heritage and are considered a fundamental duty under Article 51 of the Indian Constitution.[55] The recent judgements[56] of the Delhi High Court and Karnataka High Court dealing with citizenship rights of Tibetan children born in India from 1950 to 1987 and now exercising their right to vote, have increased the opportunity for other groups present in India to make their way towards Indian citizenship.

Notes

1 This Bengali folk song may be translated as 'we have no residence, we have no village; we have no direction, we have no country.' This song with its excellent lyrics and music portrayed the misery and sorrow of every person who became homeless, rather refugee, during the dawn of independence of India. Even today this song has relevance with regard to misery and sorrow of refugee and stateless persons staying in India. The song is available at www.youtube.com/watch?v=LrwYo5-DLpI.

2 On de facto statelessness, see for example Section II.A. of United Nations High Commissioner for Refugees, Expert Meeting on the Concept of Stateless Persons under International Law (Summary Conclusions), 2010 (hereinafter referred to as the 'Prato Conclusions'):

> 1. *De facto* statelessness has traditionally been linked to the notion of effective nationality and some participants were of the view that a person's nationality could be ineffective inside as well as outside of his or her country of nationality. Accordingly, a person could be de facto stateless even if inside his or her country of nationality. However, there was broad support from other participants for the approach set out in the discussion paper prepared for the meeting which defines a de facto stateless person on the basis of one the principal functions of nationality in international law, the provision of protection by a State to its nationals abroad. 2. The definition is as follows: de facto stateless persons are persons outside the country of their nationality who are unable or, for valid reasons, are unwilling to avail themselves of the protection of that country. Protection in this sense refers to the right of diplomatic protection exercised by a State of nationality in order to remedy an internationally wrongful act against one of its nationals, as well as diplomatic and consular protection and assistance generally, including in relation to return to the State of nationality.

Available at www.unhcr.org/refworld/pdfid/4ca1ae002.pdf accessed on 7 March 2015.

3 International Covenant on Civil and Political Rights, 1966. India acceded to the convention on 10 April 1979.

4 International Covenant on Economic, Social and Cultural Rights, 1966. India acceded to the convention on 10 April 1979.

5 Convention on the Rights of the Child, 1989. India acceded the convention on 11 December 1992.

6 International Convention on the Elimination of All Forms of Racial Discrimination, 1965. India ratifies the convention on 3 December 1968 with reservations.

7 Convention on the Elimination of All Forms of Discrimination Against Women, 1979. India signed the convention on 30 July 1980 and ratified it on 9 July 1993 with reservations.

8 National Human Rights Commission v. State of Arunachal Pradesh, 1996 AIR 1234.

9 W.P.(C)No.243/2012, pending before the Supreme Court of India.

10 Chairman, Railway Board & Ors. v. Chandrima Das & Ors., 2000 AIR 988.

11 J. A. Goldston, 'Holes in the rights framework: Racial discrimination, citizenship, and the rights of noncitizens', *Ethics & International Affairs*, 20, 2006: 321–2.

12 UNHCR estimates there to be at least twelve million people around the world. See www.unhcr.org/pages/49c3646c155.html.

13 The International Court of Justice held in the Nottebohm Case that 'it is for every sovereign state to settle by its own legislation the rules relating to the acquisition of its nationality.' Nottebohm (Liechtenstein v. Guatemala), Judgment, 1955 I.C.J. 4, at 20 (Apr. 6, 1955). See also Alice Edwards and Laura van Waas (eds.), *Nationality and Stateless under International Law*, Cambridge: Cambridge University Press, 2014; *Citizenship and the minority rights of non-citizens*, Working paper/submitted by Asbjorn Eide, 1999.

14 Article 1(1) of the 1954 Convention sets out the definition of a stateless person as: 'For the purpose of this Convention, the term "stateless person" means a person who is not considered as a national by any State under the operation of its law.'

15 D. Weissbrodt and C. Collins, 'The human rights of stateless persons', *Human Rights Quarterly* 28, 2006: pp. 245, 251. 'While there may be complex legal issues involved in determining whether or not an event has occurred by operation of law, national courts have means of resolving such questions.' See C. A. Batchelor, 'Stateless persons: Some gaps in international protection', *International Journal of Refugee Law* 7, 1995: p. 232.

16 Convention Relating to the Status of Stateless Persons, adopted 28 July 1951, G.A. Res. 429 (V), 360 U.N.T.S. 117 (entered into force 6 June 1960).

17 H. Massey, 'Legal and protection policy research series: UNHCR and de facto statelessness', *Legal and Protection Policy Research Series* (UNHCR, April 2010), www.refworld.org/pdfid/4bbf387d2.pdf. UNHCR Action to Address Statelessness: A Strategy Note, *UNHCR Division of International Protection*, 4 (UNHCR, March 2010), www.refworld.org/cgi-bin/texis/vtx/rwmain?docid=4b9e0c3d2, 'UNHCR's responsibilities for stateless persons began with refugees who are stateless under paragraph 6(A)(11) of its statute and Article 1(A) (2) of the 1951 Convention relating to the Status of Refugees, both of which refer to stateless persons who meet the criteria of the refugee definition. UNHCR's mandate responsibilities concerning statelessness were expanded following the adoption of the 1954 Convention relating to the Status of Stateless Persons, and the 1961 Convention on the Reduction of Statelessness. General Assembly resolutions 3274 (XXIV) and 31136 designated UNHCR as the body mandated to examine the cases of persons who claim the benefit of the 1961 Convention and to assist such persons in presenting their claims to the appropriate national authorities.'

18 David Weissbrodt and Clay Collins, 'The Human Rights of Stateless Persons', in *Human Rights. Quarterly*, Vol. 28, 2006, p. 270.

19 Carol A. Batchelor, 'Statelessness and the Problem of Resolving Citizenship Status', Paper Presented during UNHCR Conference entitled "People of Concern" during 21–23 November 1996, http://repository.forcedmigration.org/pdf/?pid=fmo:1527, accessed on 30 April 2018.

20 *Ibid*. Despite the reluctance of the drafters of the 1954 Convention to acknowledge de facto statelessness, the Final Act of the 1961 Convention recommends that 'persons who are stateless *de facto* should as far as possible be treated as stateless de jure to enable them to acquire an effective nationality.' United Nations Conference on the Elimination or Reduction of Future Statelessness, 30Aug. 1961, Final Act, 91 23, U.N. Doc. A/Conf./9/14 (1961).

21 David and Clay, 2006.

22 *Ibid.*, p. 270.

23 However, UNHCR's mandate on de facto stateless persons is: 'The extent to which de facto stateless persons who do not fall within its refugee mandate qualify for the Office's protection and assistance is largely determined by UNHCR's mandate to prevent statelessness. It was noted that unresolved situations of de facto statelessness, in particular over two or more generations, may lead to de jure statelessness.' Op cit. 2, at p. 8.

24 Massey, supra note 17, at iii.

25 As quoted by Massey, supra note 17, at 30.

26 Judgment of 8 September, 2005, www.refworld.org/docid/44e497d94.html, accessed on 7 March 2016.

27 UN General Assembly Resolution No 61/137, adopted on 19 December, 2006, www.un.org/en/ga/search/view_doc.asp?symbol=A/RES/61/137&Lang=E, accessed on 10 March 2016.

28 General Comment No. 15, The position of aliens under the Covenant, 4 November 1986, www.unhchr.ch/tbs/doc.nsf/MasterFrameView/bc561aa81bc5d86ec12563ed004aaa1b?Opendocument.

29 Article 2:

    1   Each State Party to the present Covenant undertakes to respect and to ensure to all individuals within its territory and subject to its jurisdiction the rights recognized in the present Covenant, without distinction of any kind, such as race, colour, sex, language, religion, political or other opinion, national or social origin, property, birth or other status.

    2   Where not already provided for by existing legislative or other measures, each State Party to the present Covenant undertakes to take the necessary steps, in accordance with its constitutional processes and with the provisions of the present Covenant, to adopt such laws or other measures as may be necessary to give effect to the rights recognized in the present Covenant.

    3   Each State Party to the present Covenant undertakes:

        (a)   To ensure that any person whose rights or freedoms as herein recognized are violated shall have an effective remedy, notwithstanding that the violation has been committed by persons acting in an official capacity;

        (b)   To ensure that any person claiming such a remedy shall have his right thereto determined by competent judicial, administrative or legislative authorities, or by any other competent authority provided for by the legal system of the State, and to develop the possibilities of judicial remedy;

(c) To ensure that the competent authorities shall enforce such remedies when granted.

30 General Comment, supra note 17, para. 2.

31 Article 9:

1 States Parties shall grant women equal rights with men to acquire, change or retain their nationality. They shall ensure in particular that neither marriage to an alien nor change of nationality by the husband during marriage shall automatically change the nationality of the wife, render her stateless or force upon her the nationality of the husband.

2 States Parties shall grant women equal rights with men with respect to the nationality of their children.

32 T. L. Lee, 'Refugees from Bhutan', *International Journal of Refugee Law*, 10, 1998: 118, 142.

33 Article 7:

1 The child shall be registered immediately after birth and shall have the right from birth to a name, the right to acquire a nationality and. as far as possible, the right to know and be cared for by his or her parents.

2 States Parties shall ensure the implementation of these rights in accordance with their national law and their obligations under the relevant international instruments in this field, in particular where the child would otherwise be stateless.

34 Article 8:

1 States Parties undertake to respect the right of the child to preserve his or her identity, including nationality, name and family relations as recognized by law without unlawful interference.

2 Where a child is illegally deprived of some or all of the elements of his or her identity, States Parties shall provide appropriate assistance and protection, with a view to re-establishing speedily his or her identity.

35 Question No. 169, Proceeding 2821, Rajya Sabha, 22 December 1993.

36 Question No. 197, Proceeding 2127, Rajya Sabha, 11 December 2002.

37 Question No. 198, Proceeding 617, Rajya Sabha, 26 February 2003.

38 Question No. 204, Proceeding 3634, Rajya Sabha, 27 April 2005.

39 Question No. 207, Proceeding 1699, Rajya Sabha, 8 March 2006.

40 Question No. 211, Proceeding 2369, Rajya Sabha, 5 September 2007.

41 Question No. 194, Proceeding 1714, Rajya Sabha, 5 December 2001.

42 Resolution of 17 August 2012, Discussion on 13 May 2013; however, the International Law Commission observed that Article 1(1), definition of stateless, of the 1954 Convention relating to the Status of Stateless Persons can 'no doubt be considered as having acquired a customary nature'. Op cit. 2, at p. 2.

43 Article 14(1) of the Universal Declaration of Human Rights states 'Everyone has the right to seek and to enjoy in other countries asylum from persecution.' Article 13 of the International Covenant of Civil and Political Rights states: 'An alien

lawfully in the territory of a State party to the present Covenant may be expelled therefrom only in pursuance of a decision reached in accordance with law and shall, except where compelling reasons of national security otherwise require, be allowed to submit the reasons against his expulsion and to have his case reviewed by, and be represented for the purpose before, the competent authority or a person or persons especially designated by the competent authority.' The Supreme Court used these international mechanisms to hold that it is the duty of the state to protect refugees.

44 (1994) Supp (1) SCC 615.
45 *Ibid.*
46 (1996) 1 SCC 742.
47 Article 21: 'No person shall be deprived of his life and personal liberty except according to the procedure established by law.'
48 National Human Rights Commission, supra note 8.
49 (2005) 5 SCC665.
50 The Foreigners Act confers wide-ranging powers to deal with all foreigners, prohibiting, regulating, or restricting their entry into India or continued presence in the country including through arrest, detention, and confinement. The Foreigners Act, No. 31 of 1946.
51 Section 9 reads as follows:

> Burden of proof – If in any case not falling under section 8 any question arises with reference to this Act or any order made or direction given thereunder, whether any person is or is not a foreigner or is or is not a foreigner of a particular class or description the onus of proving that such person is not a foreigner or is not a foreigner of such particular class or description, as the case may be, shall, notwithstanding anything contained in the Indian Evidence Act, 1872 (1 of 1872), lie upon such person.

52 Article 355: 'It shall be the duty of the Union to protect every State against external aggression and internal disturbance and to ensure that the Government of every State is carried on in accordance with the provisions of this Constitution.' On the broad meaning of aggression, the Court referred to the US Supreme Court decision in *Chae Chan Ping*: 'To preserve its independence, and give security against foreign aggression and encroachment, is the highest duty of every nation, and to attain these ends nearly all other considerations are to be subordinated. It matters not in what form such aggression and encroachment come, whether from the foreign nation acting in its national character or from vast hordes of its people crowding in upon us.' See Sonawal, (2005) 5 S.C.C. 665, para. 57 (citing Chae Chan Ping v. United States, 130 U.S. 581 (1930). The Court also quoted Lord Denning, former Justice of the U.K. Court of Appeals: In recent times England has been invaded not by enemies nor by friends, but by those who seek England as a haven. In their own countries there is poverty, disease and no homes. In England there is social security, a national health service and guaranteed housing all to be had for the asking without payment and without working for it. Once here, each seeks to bring his relatives to join him. So they multiply exceedingly. See Sonawal, (2005) 5 S.C.C. 665, para. 59.
53 Guy S. Goodwin-Gill, 'Rights of refugees and stateless persons: Problems of stateless persons and the need for international measures of protection', in K. P.

Saksena (ed.), *Human Rights Perspectives and Challenges*, New Delhi: Lancer Books, 1994.

54 B. S. Chimni's work in the area of third world approaches to international is well regarded.

55 Article 51: Promotion of international peace and security. The State shall endeavour to:

(a) promote international peace and security;

(b) maintain just and honourable relations between nations;

(c) foster respect for international law and treaty obligations in the dealings of organised peoples with one another; and encourage settlement of international disputes by arbitration.

56 See 'Children of Tibetan refugees can now vote', *Indian Express*, 11 February 2014, http://indianexpress.com/article/india/india-others/children-of-tibetan-refugees-can-now-vote/. See also Karnataka High Court Judgment in Tenzin L. C. Rinpoche vs. Union of India & Anr., WP No. 15437/2013 (GMPASS) and Delhi High Court Judgment Namgyal Dolkar vs. Govt. of India, WP (C) 12179/2009.

EPILOGUE

The regional dimensions

*Sabyasachi Basu Ray Chaudhury and
Ranabir Samaddar*

Regional initiatives

The chapters in this book make clear the regional dimension of statelessness, and in this case of the Rohingya refugees. Yet, the regional dimension is the most neglected part of the issue. Commentators have noted the fluctuating attitudes and policies of great powers like the United States and the United Kingdom, neighbouring power India and China, plus the United Nations towards the policies of suppression of the Rohingya and other ethnic minorities by the State of Myanmar, but the regional dimension of the problem has been ignored. By focusing on Rohingya in India, this book wanted to bring to light this neglected aspect. As Rohingyas fled in large numbers to neighbouring Bangladesh, India, Thailand, and Malaysia, and some even tried to reach Australia, the regional dimension of the issue of statelessness became clearer. Perhaps part of the solution lies in regional policies for the protection of the stateless population groups. In case of several stateless groups who were rehabilitated and resettled in India (or Sri Lanka in case of Tamil plantation workers or protection of Afghan escapees in India, Pakistan and Iran) a bilateral framework and a spirit of regional understanding worked. So why should this not be the case for the Rohingya, and why should not states of South and Southeast Asia along with other Asia Pacific countries deliberate on the issue of the rights of the Rohingya, and see how the issue of statelessness can be resolved? Of course involving Myanmar will be important and essential in this exercise. We may recall how the issue of Balkan refugees and ex-Yugoslav stateless groups were resolved in the framework of Europe.

Yet regional initiatives often fail. For instance, in the wake of the growing international focus on the Rohingya issue, the Royal Thai government called for a regional meeting to address the migrant crisis on 29 May 2016 involving 15 nations. These included Bangladesh, Myanmar, Indonesia, Malaysia and host Thailand as well as Australia and the United States. Several countries wanted the root causes of the flow of migrants to be discussed in the meeting. However, the Myanmar government said that it would boycott the meeting and accused others of being soft on human trafficking. This blame game did not help. As the current migrant crisis came under further regional and international scrutiny, Myanmar was asked to recognize that its transition to democracy would be judged by how it treated its minority communities. In this connection it is important to note that the Indian navy was involved in several relief and rescue operations in the Bay of Bengal in the past. The current humanitarian crisis in the Bay of Bengal requires from India a more proactive policy in the sea to rescue the boat people.

Before this initiative was taken, there was another regional initiative, taken in 2002, known as the Bali Process on People Smuggling, Trafficking in Persons and Related Transnational Crime. It attempted to raise regional awareness of the consequences of the smuggling of people, trafficking in persons and related transnational crimes. Accordingly, it developed and implemented strategies and practical cooperation in response. More than forty-five members, including the UNHCR, the International Organization for Migration (IOM) and the United Nations Office of Drugs and Crime (UNODC), as well as a number of observer countries and international agencies participate in this voluntary forum.[1] The core objectives of the Bali process were:

- The development of more effective information and intelligence sharing;
- Improved cooperation among regional law enforcement agencies to deter and combat people smuggling and trafficking networks;
- Enhanced cooperation on border and visa systems to detect and prevent illegal movements;
- Increased public awareness in order to discourage these activities and warn those susceptible;
- Enhanced effectiveness of return as a strategy to deter people smuggling and trafficking through conclusion of appropriate arrangements;
- Cooperation in verifying the identity and nationality of illegal migrants and trafficking victims;
- Enactment of national legislation to criminalise people smuggling and trafficking in persons;

- Provision of appropriate protection and assistance to the victims of trafficking, particularly women and children;
- Enhanced focus on tackling the root causes of illegal migration, including increasing opportunities for legal migration between states;
- Assisting countries to adopt best practices in asylum management, in accordance with the principles of the Refugees Convention;
- Advancing the implementation of an inclusive non-binding regional cooperation framework under which interested parties can cooperate more effectively to reduce irregular movement through the region.[2]

Later, an ad hoc group was set up to develop and pursue practical measures to inform future regional cooperation on people smuggling, trafficking in persons and the irregular movement of people.[3]

In 2009, some Southeast Asian countries agreed to use the Bali process to solve the Rohingya issue. Earlier, Thailand's Prime Minister Abhisit Vejjajiva said in February 2008 that the issue of Rohingya needed greater discussion in a regional forum. He told reporters in Jakarta during his visit to Indonesia then that the regional governments would take up the issue of the Rohingya at the Bali process.[4] In fact, all the countries of the region that are affected by the Rohingya issue are both members as well as ad hoc group members of the Bali Process.

However, during the 2014 ASEAN Summit in Naypyidaw, the first one to be held in the new capital of Myanmar, the plight of the Rohingya Muslims was left out of the agenda. The Government of Myanmar's decision in March 2014 to expel humanitarian groups and prevent them from providing health care and aid has increased the number of Rohingya moving to other countries.

When the rickety boats carrying Rohingya, with depleting food and drinking water, hit the newspaper headlines in May 2015, at least Malaysia and Indonesia bowed to international pressure, and said they would no longer turn away migrant boats, offering instead to take in a wave of asylumseekers, provided they could be resettled or repatriated within a year. But Australian Prime Minister Tony Abbott's comments were a massive blow to efforts to ensure an effective regional response to the worsening humanitarian crisis on the Bay of Bengal and the Andaman Sea.[5] Prime Minister Abbott categorically stated that they wanted other countries to help with resettlement, but Abbott said those seeking a better life in Australia needed only to come through the 'front door'. He said that while Australia stood ready to assist in other ways, there was no way any of those fleeing would be allowed to settle in Australia. 'Nope, nope, nope,' he said, shaking his head.[6] He went on to say, 'If we do the slightest thing to encourage people to get on boats, this problem will get worse, not better.' He said: 'Australia will do absolutely nothing that gives any encouragement to anyone to think that they can get on a boat, that they can work with people-smugglers to start a new life.' Without batting an eyelid, Abbott further said, 'Our role is to make it absolutely crystal clear that if you get on a leaky boat, you aren't going to get what you want', although Indonesia's foreign ministry spokesman, Arrmantha Nasir, said Australia was obliged to help as a signatory to the United Nations Refugee Convention. According to Abbott, 'This is quite properly a regional responsibility and the countries that will have to take the bulk of the responsibility are obviously the countries which are closest to the problem.' In his opinion, 'Australia can show leadership and compassion, just as it did after the Tiananmen Square massacre and the Vietnam War, by authorising special intake of refugees fleeing war and persecution.'

Therefore, it became absolutely clear that none of the more than 8,000 Rohingya refugees caught in a weeks-long standoff at sea would be resettled in Australia, even on humanitarian grounds, in spite of Greens Senator from Australia Sarah Hanson-Young saying: 'The asylum seekers, many suffering from starvation, are in desperate need of assistance, and Australia, as a regional leader, has an international responsibility to provide leadership and provide immediate assistance.'[7] The fact remains that Australia would prefer to resettle the Rohingya asylum-seekers and/or refugees in the poorer countries. Australia, indeed, is already running prisons on the Pacific island nation of Nauru and having a multimillion-dollar deal with Cambodia for this purpose.[8]

The Refugee Council of Australia (RCOA) has expressed its deep dismay at the Australian Prime Minister's stand. RCOA chief executive officer Paul Power said, 'No nation in the Asia-Pacific region is better placed than Australia to assist with this resettlement (of Rohingya refugees).' He rightly said, 'If the Australian Government wants to see more order and control in the movements of desperate people across borders, then surely it has a particular responsibility to help a multi-country effort such as this.' He also said, 'The way in which the Prime Minister dismissed the request leaves serious questions about the (Australia) Government's commitment to protecting persecuted people.'[9]

It is worth mentioning that the coalition government elected in September 2013 reiterated Australia's previously introduced restrictive policy changes. The introduction of (regional) offshore processing in Papua New Guinea and Nauru in 2012, with no prospect of durable settlement in Australia, was combined with Operation Sovereign Borders to implement the government's policy of intercepting and returning boats to Indonesia. Under the Australian government policy, all people who try to reach Australia by boat as refugees are held in offshore centres such as the one in Nauru.[10] In short, Australia does not allow the asylum-seekers or refugees onto its shores. Rather, Canberra would detain them at the facilities on the island nation of Nauru and Manus Island in Papua New Guinea.

The Abbott government, in fact, reduced the humanitarian programme from 20,000 resettlement places in the fiscal year 2012–13 to 13,750 places in 2014–15. Over and above, in September 2014 Australia and Cambodia signed a memorandum of understanding for the relocation of recognized refugees from Nauru to Cambodia.[11] Australia also set aside about AUD 55.5million(USD 40 million; GBP 15 million) for the deal, including a $40m aid package, which means almost AUD 14million per refugee so far, according to figures from the Australia Associated Press.[12]

On the other hand, Thailand for instance was quick to recognize the regional imperative in finding a solution to the Rohingya issue. In a meeting held as part of the Bali process (24–25 February 2009), Thailand noted the entry of Rohingya as illegal migrants. The Thai representative noted that over 5,000 boat arrivals were recorded in 2008, and the potential migrant stock would be several hundred thousand. With a burden of three million illegal migrants, Thailand could not be either a country of transit or country of destination. Hence it pressed for a regional approach. It was a 'a collective problem that the countries concerned in the region – countries of origin, transit and destination – have to collectively address, and in a comprehensive manner. We have proposed to the other affected countries (Bangladesh, India, Indonesia, Malaysia and Myanmar) to join hands with Thailand in constituting a contact group to coordinate and cooperate on this matter.' Thailand also advocated several overlapping approaches, and declared its readiness to facilitate the work of a small group of relevant stakeholders towards a solution. It also declared that it was seeking cooperation of the United Nations High Commissioner for Refugees (UNHCR) and the International Organization for Migration (IOM).[13]

In the same meeting at Brisbane, the UNHCR representative added,

> The situation of the Rohingya, with its refugee protection and economic dimensions, therefore presents, in critical form, a case study of the broader problem of onward movement affecting the region. The situation of the Rohingya needs both an immediate response and a broader solutions strategy. Any movement of people for protection related reasons requires access to territory and to an assessment of

protection needs based on international standards. The issue also needs a regional approach that addresses the entire range of push and pull factors and the full cycle of displacement, which includes countries of origin, transit and destination. In the absence of such cooperation and of efforts to address root causes and stabilize the population through measures to improve both rights and livelihoods at the points of origin, there is a likelihood that onward movements will continue.'[14]

The presence of Rohingya as undocumented labour migrants was also noted by the Regional Support Office of the Bali Process in a paper on 'Pathways to Employment: Expanding Legal and Legitimate Labour Market Opportunities for Refugees'.[15]

The Andaman Sea refugee crisis in 2015–16 finally left no one in doubt that the Rohingya crisis called for a regional approach. Sea and the oceans are always regional. Indeed they make regions. That the Andaman Sea crisis was therefore seen as a call to the region did not surprise those working for human rights and humanitarian protection. Yet, and this is what causes surprise and anguish, little advance has been made on the Rohingya, and the Indian and Bangladesh governments have done little to strengthen a regional framework.

We must recapitulate some of the aspects of the crisis mentioned in course of this book in order to emphasize the regional aspect of the issue. We have to recall that more than 25,000 had fled Myanmar and Bangladesh by boat, and around 8,000 were stranded at sea. Around 400 possibly died. Many paid great deal of money for their passage. On 1 May 2015, a mass grave containing the remains of more than thirty bodies was discovered in the Sadao district of Thailand, a few hundred metres from the Malaysia border. On 5 May, three Thai officials and a Myanmar national were arrested in Thailand for suspected involvement in human trafficking. Thereafter boats began to be intercepted. Thai, Malaysian and Indonesian authorities reportedly intercepted boats of asylum-seekers and pushed them back out to sea. Consequently boatloads of people were abandoned on the water. An estimated 6,000 Rohingya and Bengalis were stranded by 12 May – without food or water. Some were rescued by Indonesian and Malaysian local officials and fishermen, or they swam to shore. On 26 May, Malaysian policemen found the remains of approximately 140 bodies, perhaps of migrants from Myanmar and Bangladesh, in abandoned jungle camps near the Thai border. In short, the regional response was sorely inadequate. Policing was thought to be the main way to tackle the crisis.[16] As in the Mediterranean, this aggravated the crisis. It is true, however, that the neighbouring countries provided some help in an irregular manner. And as the book demonstrates, India hosted a substantial number of Rohingya, although the government now seems to have made up its mind to deport the Rohingya.

One-off meetings became the norm for managing mass displacement events on the Andaman Sea. Regional institutions and processes – ASEAN, the Bali Process and the Jakarta Declaration – were largely muted during the crisis. Most crucially, the Bali Process did not have functioning mechanisms for officials and functionaries across the region to respond. Regional leaders made the right noises but took little concrete steps. Amidst all these came the 'New York Moment' in September 2016 when then US President Barack Obama and UN Secretary-General Ban Ki-moon spoke in high level discussions in New York on refugees and migrants.[17] The UN Summit for Refugees and Migrants was held on 19 September 2016 at the UN headquarters in New York. That was perhaps the last and a fleeting moment of attention.

Responsibility

To conclude, there are four dimensions to the Rohingya crisis: the root factors pushing a vulnerable community to undertake dangerous sea voyages and long marches across lands to gain protection and security of life; the economy of human trafficking in the Bay of Bengal; the policies of protection, asylum and hospitality of the respective countries in this region that fall short of the requirements of human rights protection and humanitarian care; and lack of a proper regional policy towards migration and refugee flows and the inability of the global protection regime to respond to the crisis. All these elements are present in the humanitarian tragedy that is under way in the Bay of Bengal.[18]

The Rohingya in Myanmar are fighting a daily battle for dignity. Even a cursory reading of reportages, commentaries, essays and articles on the precarious condition of the Rohingya refugees and asylum-seekers will tell us of the growing statelessness of people in protracted condition of displacement. As nationality issues get more ethnicized and securitized, we shall witness more the phenomenon of growing statelessness – de jure, but more de facto. The question is: When will international law recognise this crisis? When will the UNHCR and the international community in general become active to raise their response to the level the problem requires? Why don't the UNHCR and the international community prevail upon Australia so that the latter does not follow practices of warehousing, offshore detention, interception in mid-sea to prevent the boat people from seeking shelter, and then clamping security restrictions on people engaged in protection of the asylum-seekers? And, finally, when will the states – at least of South Asia – move beyond humanitarianism and attempt a regional or at least bilateral solution? More often than not, redress of injustice to the displaced caused by statelessness requires the cooperation of several states involved.

Why do not all of these happen? This is where we must recognize the unequal nature of power, influence, and responsibility in the global protection regime. In the light of this report and on the basis of the experiences of the Rohingya exodus from Myanmar, reflective of worldwide post-colonial experiences, we have to ask: What is the nature of this *power, influence and responsibility*? To ask this is important because through all these years following the convention on statelessness, the global protection regime has never questioned the dissociation between power and responsibility. This has been the case primarily for two reasons: first, in the age of majoritarian democracy responsibility lies with the minority groups to conduct themselves *responsibly* to be acceptable to the state; second, international responsibility is formally exercised by nation states, while power is vested with transnational agencies and empires which will exercise power without responsibility. In this situation of graded responsibility and its hierarchical history, it is important to ask: what is the nature of power and responsibility at the margins, rather than power and influence at the centre, which is called by that euphemism, a *protection regime*?

After all this there remains one more point. Is this so-called regime capable of addressing the issue of de facto statelessness? The present situation of flows of potential stateless groups of people is not marked by some mere discrimination and liminal violence, but brutal violence and stripping them of citizenship. The convention on statelessness barely touches the problem. Framed in the context of Europe and World War II, the question of responsibility for production of statelessness is stark today inasmuch as the ineffectiveness of the global protection apparatus.

We evaluate people and groups as responsible or not, depending on how they exercise their power. Often we exercise moral judgement. Sometimes we do this formally, for instance via legal judgement. The question will be how do we relate moral responsibility and legal responsibility – not only of individuals but of empires, global powers, states and other collectives? The current global protection regime has no particular idea of (a) what we may term as *responsible agency*, whereby an institution like the state is regarded as a moral agent; (b) *retrospective responsibility*, when a state is judged for its actions and is blamed or punished; or (c) *responsibility as a virtue*, when we praise a state as being responsible. Philosophical discussions of responsibility abound. However, we need in the context of post-colonial experiences a wider view of responsibility in order to explore connections between moral and legal responsibility, and between global and national responsibilities. After all, was it not the original philosophical invocation of the dual notions of power and responsibility that was constructed and amalgamated in political thought?

There is no way to close this book which focuses on India's engagement with the Rohingya crisis on an optimist note. India wants to deport the Rohingyas. Bangladesh seems to have had enough of humanitarianism. The regional framework only nominally exists. Australia wants to be a major economic actor in the region but would share none of its major problems. Other countries do whatever they decide they can, off and on. The international community, the UNHCR, and the IOM can only watch, spend a little money, and advise. The international law on statelessness is a piece of unusable paper as far as the Rohingya are concerned. And the state of Myanmar is being appreciated for her democratic advance with Aung San Suu Kyi hailed as the custodian of democracy there. Truth, lies, evasion, callousness, and some measure of human rights support and humanitarian protection seem to mark the state of statelessness of the Rohingya.

Notes

1 For details, please see https://www.baliprocess.net/membership/accessed on 30 April 2018.
2 https://www.baliprocess.net/regional-support-office/purpose-and-objectives/, accessed on 30 April 2018.
3 https://www.baliprocess.net/ad-hoc-group/, accessed on 30 April 2018.
4 https://reliefweb.int/report/myanmar/open-letter-governments-bangladesh-india-indonesia-malaysia-myanmar-and-thailand, accessed on 30 April 2018.
5 "Nope, nope, nope': Tony Abbott says Australia will take no Rohingya refugees', *The Guardian*, https://www.theguardian.com/world/2015/may/21/nope-nope-nope-tony-abbott-says-australia-will-take-no-rohingya-refugees, accessed on 30 April 2018.
6 *Ibid.*
7 *Ibid.*
8 James Griffiths, 'Australia accused of turning Nauru into 'open-air prison',' https://edition.cnn.com/2016/10/18/asia/australia-nauru-offshore-amnesty/index.html, accessed on 30 April 2018; and First four refugees from Nauru land in Cambodia in $40m resettlement deal, *The Guardian*, 4 June 2015, https://www.theguardian.com/australia-news/2015/jun/04/four-refugees-arrive-in-cambodia-from-nauru-under-deal-with-australia, accessed on 30 April 2018.
9 Australia closes door on persecuted Rohingya, Refugee Council of Australia, 21 may 2015, https://www.refugeecouncil.org.au/latest/australia-closes-door-on-persecuted-rohingya/, accessed on 30 April 2018.

10 'Why is the Manus detention centre being closed?' *Al Jazeera*, 29 October 2017, https://www.aljazeera.com/news/2017/10/manus-detention-centre-closed-171024212852806.html, accessed on 30 April 2018.

11 'Australia signs controversial refugee transfer deal with Cambodia', *The Guardian*, 26 September 2014, https://www.theguardian.com/world/2014/sep/26/australia-signs-refugee-deal-cambodia, accessed on 30 April 2018.

12 *Ibid.*

13 Marie McAuliffe, *Resolving Policy Conundrums: Enhancing Humanitarian Protection in Southeast Asia*, Migration Policy Institute, 2016, pp. 17–22, www.baliprocess.net/UserFiles/baliprocess/File/Bali%20Process%20SOM%202009%20-%20Thailand%20Presentation%20-%20The%20Rohingya%20Situation.pdf, accessed on 29 August 2017.

14 Richa Shivakoti, 'ASEAN's role in the Rohingya refugee crisis, *Forced Migration Review*, No. 56, October 2017, http://www.fmreview.org/latinamerica-caribbean/shivakoti.html accessed on 30 April 2018.

15 Summary: *Pathways to Employment: Expanding legal and legitimate labour market opportunities for refugees*, 1–2 September 2016, 15 September 2016. https://www.baliprocess.net/news/summary-pathways-to-employment-expanding-legal-and-legitimate-labour-market-opportunities-for-refugees/, accessed on 30 April 2018.

16 'Malaysia finds 139 graves at 'cruel' jungle trafficking camps', *The Daily Star*, Dhaka, 27 May 2015, https://www.thedailystar.net/world/malaysian-cops-find-139-suspected-migrant-graves-87100, accessed on 30 April 2018.

17 https://www.un.org/sg/en/subsite-section/ban-ki-moon?page=72, accessed on 30 April 2018.

18 K. Yhome. 'Rohingyas adrift, far from the shores of Asia's conscience', http://thewire.in/2015/05/21/rohingyas-adrift-far-from-the-shores-of-asias-conscience-2149/?relatedposts_hit=1&relatedposts_origin=11528&relatedposts_position=1, accessed on 11 October 2015.

AFTERWORD

Sabyasachi Basu Ray Chaudhury and
Ranabir Samaddar

As this volume was almost prepared for press, new developments began in the Rakhine State in Myanmar, with the military forces unleashing a new wave of repression on the Rohingya following an armed attack by a Rohingya insurgent group. This led to massive exodus of the Rohingya. At the same time, as if waiting for the moment, there was a chorus of voices regarding 'the threat from Islamic forces'. A new round of instability has started with no resolution of the Rohingya issue in sight, no promise of citizenship, and a continuing nightmare of de facto statelessness. The only way out of the crisis it seems is to somehow coax, cajole, or coerce the Rohingyas into going back to Myanmar.

The contemporary world has been witnessing 'mixed and massive flows' of population in different parts of the world – refugees, asylum-seekers, stateless population and undocumented migrants – all moving together for their survival, either for life or for livelihood. It was noticed recently also in case of the movement of people to Europe – people trying to cross the Mediterranean in rickety and leaky boats. In case of the Rohingya, the same was observed later. In such a situation, it may be difficult to categorize the forcibly displaced or voluntarily migrating people. Under such circumstances, even the refugees and stateless population are deprived of their basic right to life and shelter.

Second, the growing securitization of the displaced population in view of several 'terrorist' attacks in different parts of the world has, by and large, made the displaced people more vulnerable. The increasing 'Islamophobia' makes the 'refugees' and 'stateless' entirely defenceless if they happen to be Muslims. Quite easily, they are branded as potential terrorists, and potential threats to the 'national security' of a country, where this hapless population may be heading to. Therefore, providing them refuge may turn into a 'difficult' choice between 'national security' and 'compassion'. The policy-makers and statesmen tend to ignore the rights and entitlements of the displaced population. Therefore, it was not surprising when the Government of India talked about deporting the 40,000-odd Rohingya (official figures, while unofficial figures may be more) living in the country roughly for more than five years. This spectre of deportation hangs also on about 16,500 Rohingya, officially recognized and enlisted by the UNHCR. Mercifully, the decision to deport is temporarily on hold following Supreme Court's intervention.

The Supreme Court of India has called on the Government of India to approach the Rohingya issue with a judicious mix of concern for national interest and humanitarian values. The three-member bench consisting of Chief Justice Dipak Misra and Justices A. M. Khanwilkar and D. Y. Chandrachud has observed: the 'Constitution is based on humanitarian values'.[1] Unlike the government, which has a tendency to securitize every issue involving Muslims, the Honorable Court has urged it to also view it through the lens of the suffering of the refugees. According to the Division Bench of the Supreme Court, led by Chief Justice Dipak Misra, it is a 'large issue', and an 'issue of great magnitude', and therefore, the state has a big role to play, and that role of the state in such a situation 'has to be multi-pronged'.[2] It went on to mention that children and women 'do not know anything about it', and therefore, as a constitutional court, 'we cannot be oblivious to it.' The bench clearly stated that, 'We expect that the executive will not be oblivious to it,' and told the government: 'Do not deport. You take action if something wrong is found.'[3]

The government, however, keeps on saying that the Rohingya are a threat to national security. Even after the interim observation of the Supreme Court of the India, expressed on 13 October 2017, the Ministry of Home Affairs (MHA) said the issue of Rohingya migration had to be 'dealt with only by the Central government' as it is an executive function of the government. An MHA spokesperson stated that the central government 'is of the opinion that deportation of illegal immigrants has to be dealt with only' by the central government, because it is essentially an executive function of the government.[4] It is in tune with the statement in the parliament by Kiren Rijiju, in August 2017 that the central government had directed state authorities to identify and deport illegal immigrants including Rohingya. This statement by the minister was in response to a question in parliament on 9 August 2017.[5]

Thus, while the Tibetans can stay for decades and can even be allowed to form a government in exile, other select groups can stay for years and

Hindus from Pakistan can get citizenship here, 40,000-odd Rohingya have been found to be a problem. The whole talk of balancing national security and compassion now appears as a smokescreen for arbitrary judgements on whom to provide shelter and whom to refuse.

It therefore apparently may not matter if such deportation of Rohingya to Myanmar would entail the violation of two fundamental rights and one principle of international law. The fundamental rights in question are Article 14 (equality before law and equal protection of laws) of the fundamental right to equality and Article 21 (right to life and personal liberty) of the fundamental right to freedom. The fundamental principle of international law at risk is non-refoulement that prohibits any country from returning refugees or asylum-seekers to another country where there was a likelihood of persecution based on 'race, religion, nationality, and membership of a particular social group or political opinion'.

India is a signatory to several international conventions which include, inter alia, the principle of non-refoulement. India is also a signatory to the recent New York Declaration for Refugees and Migrants (2016) that recognized the rights of refugees to asylum and also affirmed the principle of non-refoulement. The UN General Assembly opined that, as set out in Article 14 of the Universal Declaration of Human Rights, everyone has the right to seek and enjoy in other countries asylum from persecution, and accordingly, called upon all states to refrain from taking measures that jeopardize the institution of asylum, particularly by returning or expelling refugees or asylum-seekers contrary to international standards. In 1977, the European Court of Justice ruled that there must be a genuine and sufficiently serious threat to the requirements of public policy affecting one of the fundamental interests of society (*Reg. v. Bouchereau*, 2CMLR 800). It follows from state practice and the convention *travaux* preparations that the criminal offences without any specific national security implications are not to be deemed threats to national security, and that, national security exceptions to non-refoulement are not appropriate in local or isolated threats to law and order. Moreover, the Directive Principles of State Policy of the Constitution of India require the state to 'promote international peace and security' (Article 51a) and 'foster respect for international law and treaty obligations' (Article 51c). Ignoring this would represent an abdication of moral and political responsibility towards the persecution of an ethnic minority the scale of which had been deemed as 'ethnic cleansing' and 'genocidal' by the UN observers.

In practice, while the Indian state did offer de facto protection to different groups of refugees, the absence of any specific legal framework for refugee protection in India has made the status of a refugee in the country a precarious one. This status is usually based on the goodwill and tolerance of the government in power. The ad hoc approach adopted by the Government of India towards refugees so far is reflected in the fact that many refugees have not been granted uniform rights and privileges or legal status. The Rohingyas taking shelter in India in the recent times have been fresh victims of such discrimination.

The Rohingya have a long history of unresolved political conflict for recognition of ethnic identity and citizenship in the wake of colonialism's retreat from Southeast Asia. Nearly half a million Rohingya have taken shelter in Bangladesh since 25 August 2017 due to crackdown by the Myanmar army. Including the earlier Rohingya refugees taking shelter in Bangladesh, the total number of Rohingyas has already exceeded 800,000, thus turning Cox's Bazar and the adjoining areas into the site of the world's largest refugee camp.

Religion and ethnicity have been the major focus in media coverage of the persecution of the Rohingya in Myanmar. Such persecution is part of a long and cruel history suffered by the Rohingya. But there are inadequacies to this explanation for the current phase of that long-standing violence. The Final Report of the Advisory Commission on Rakhine State (popularly known as the Kofi Annan Commission Report) rightly indicates the multi-dimensionality of the evolving crisis. It says:

> On one level, Rakhine represents a development crisis. The state is marked by chronic poverty from which all communities suffer, and lags behind the national average in virtually every area. Protracted conflict, insecure land tenure and lack of livelihood opportunities have resulted in significant migration out of the state, reducing the size of the work force and undermining prospects of development and economic growth . . . Although Rakhine is rich in natural resources, the development of extractive industries – such as oil and gas-related investments in Kyawkpyuh – have not generated a significant number of new jobs nor other benefits for local residents.[6]

It further mentions that:

> Rakhine also represents a human rights crisis. While all communities have suffered from violence and abuse, protracted statelessness and profound discrimination have made the Muslim community particularly vulnerable to human rights violations. Some ten percent of the

world's stateless people live in Myanmar, and the Muslims in Rakhine constitute the single biggest stateless community in the world. The community faces a number of restrictions which affect basic rights and many aspects of their daily lives . . . The community has been denied political representation, and is generally excluded from Myanmar's body politic. Efforts by the Government to verify citizenship claims have failed to win the confidence of either Muslim or Rakhine communities.[7]

Finally, the Kofi Annan Commission views the Rakhine issue also as a security crisis. Its report points out that:

As witnessed by the Commission during its many consultations across Rakhine State, all communities harbour deep-seated fears, with the legacy of the violence of 2012 fresh in many minds. While Muslims resent continued exclusion, the Rakhine community worry about becoming a minority in the state in the future. Segregation has worsened the prospects for mutual understanding.[8]

Taking cue from it, we can observe that the Government of Myanmar's 2016 decision to include a relatively significant three million acres of rural land in Rakhine in the national list of allocation of land for 'economic development' is a case in point. After all, so far in Myanmar, the government's language of 'economic development' describes allocations of land that the military has de facto control over, and have been selling to the firms of Myanmar and the foreign ones for the past almost two decades.

Despite the fact that Rakhine is not in Myanmar's heartland geographically, the state is crucial for the country's economy. In addition to the renowned Ngapali beach, Rakhine holds enormous economic potential because the state has oil, natural gas fields and maritime resources from the Bay of Bengal. But Rakhine remains the second poorest region or state in the country. Community and economic development are lagging behind, despite the prospect of several mega infrastructure projects, namely the Kyaukphyu project and the Kaladan multi-modal transit transport project. China's Kyaukphyu deep-sea port and Special Economic Zone (SEZ), which started under U Thein Sein's government, are currently being developed in Rakhine State. Subsequently, Aung San SuuKyi's government became party to China's Belt and Road Initiative when she visited Beijing in May. The Kyaukphyu project, which consists of both the port and the SEZ, is a significant part of the Belt and Road Initiative.

On the other hand, the Kaladan multi-modal transit transport project is supported by a grant from India. Sittwe jetty and Paletwa marine terminal have already been completed. When the jetty operates, India-Myanmar bilateral trade is likely to improve. In fact, there are more infrastructure projects connecting India with Myanmar than with any of India's other neighbours. This is not a mere coincidence that, the largest of them – the Kaladan multi-modal transport project – originates from the home state of the persecuted population of Rohingya. The fact is that these projects provide a crucial linkage to keep alive each of India's Look East initiatives. After all, without Myanmar, India cannot engage with any of the Asian nations to its east.

Other than Kaladan, there are seven more projects, including a trilateral highway – a 1,600-kilometre highway to connect India with Thailand through Myanmar – which is slated to be completed by 2020. The highway is part of the larger Mekong-India Economic Corridor project that envisages development of ports and more than one special economic zones over an 8,000-hectare area. A small port has been made operational, while the construction of a road link from Dawei in Myanmar to the Thailand border has just begun. The trilateral highway and the Kaladan multi-modal transport projects is supposed to be the bedrock for promoting India's connectivity with Myanmar and beyond into the ASEAN region. The Kaladan project aims to connect Kolkata by river and sea with the Myanmar port of Sittwe and further to Mizoram by road, and Sittwe is the capital of the disturbed Rakhine State in Myanmar. Under these agreements, Delhi has undertaken the construction of 69 bridges, including approach roads on the Tamu-Kyigone-Kalewa section of the IMT highway, and also upgrades the Kalewa-Yargi section of this highway. In addition, because Myanmar is India's land bridge to Southeast Asia, this infrastructure is aimed at linking India to markets in the region. It is expected to boost development in India's economically backward northeastern states, several of which share borders with Myanmar. Importantly, Myanmar provides landlocked northeast India with an outlet to the sea, a route that is shorter than the current one via the Siliguri Corridor to Kolkata port. In short, in Rakhine State, the Chinese and Indian interests are part of broader China-India relations. These interests revolve mainly around the construction of infrastructure and pipelines in the region. Therefore, the coastal areas of Rakhine State are of immense strategic importance to both India and China. The Government of Myanmar therefore has vested interests in clearing land to prepare for further development and to boost its already rapid economic growth. Accordingly, in 2011, Myanmar instituted economic and political reforms that led it to be dubbed as 'Asia's final frontier', and it opened up to larger foreign invest-ment. Almost immediately afterwards, in 2012, violent attacks escalated against the Rohingya in Rakhine State.

In other words, as the Rakhine State and its coastal areas have become strategically important for Myanmar, as well as for both China and India, the Muslim Rohingya have turned into the most unwelcome population in Buddhist-dominated Myanmar. In view of the above, the Kofi Annan Commission has recommended among many other things that the govern-ment needs to 'increase the participation of Rakhine's local communities in decision making affecting the development of the state, and find ways to ensure that local communities benefit from investments – including natu-ral resource extraction – in Rakhine State'.[9] Moreover, it suggests that, the 'Government should ensure adequate compensation for appropriated land.'[10] It has proposed that the

> Government should immediately ensure that those who are verified as citizens enjoy all benefits, rights and freedoms associated with citizen-ship. This will not only serve to strengthen the Government's rule-of-law agenda, but also demonstrate immediate tangible benefits of the verification exercise.[11]

It opines that the 'Government should establish a clear strategy and timeline for the citizenship verification process. This strategy should be transpar-ent, efficient, and with a solid basis in existing legislation.'[12] It suggests that to 'increase the accessibility of the process, the use of an uncle or aunt's documents (or other family members) should be permitted when the par-ent's documents are missing'.[13] Moreover, the 'Government should clarify the status of those whose citizenship application is not accepted.'[14] It clearly indicates that 'as a general rule, individuals will not lose their citizenship or have it revoked where this will leave them stateless.'[15] Furthermore, 'within a reasonable timeline, the Government should present a plan for the start of the process to review the citizenship law.'[16] However, as the Kofi Annan Commission Report was to be made public, the Rakhine State descended further into chaos, making more Rohingya into refugees/stateless. As the precarity of the Rohingya becomes more acute, as many countries in the region take a more 'inhuman turn', forgetting the 'responsibility to protect' members of the human race, the world looks forward to truly global and/or regional initiative(s) to ease the tensions in Myanmar and entire South and Southeast Asia, and ensure the 'human condition' of existence for the people facing the erasure of citizenship, and thereby, basic rights to be enjoyed by any human being in the world. It needs to be remembered that, without taking the interests of the human beings sincerely, the geo-strategic interests of the countries concerned cannot be fulfilled. In the end, the human beings are not mere cogwheels but the levers of growth, overall prosperity and inclusive development.

The chances of proper implementation of the Kofi Annan Commission Report appear dim. Likewise the efforts of the neighbouring countries do not have the teeth to make Myanmar see the reason of moderation, democracy, and equality of all nationalities in the country. The two big powers – Australia and India – are on the side of Myanmar for respective strategic and commercial reasons. China remains silent. In this milieu, Rohingya remain stateless, with provisions of the International Conventions (1954 and 1961) on Statelessness being of no avail.[17]

Notes

1 'Supreme Court has not stayed deportation of Rohingya refugees: What exactly happened', *India Today*, 14 October 2017, https://www.indiatoday.in/fyi/story/supreme-court-has-not-stayed-deportation-of-rohingya-refugees-from-india-1064580-2017-10-14, accessed on 30 April 2018.
2 *Hindustan Times*, New Delhi, 14 October 2017.
3 *Times of India*, New Delhi, 14 October 2017.
4 *Ibid.*
5 Krishna N. Das and Saneev Miglani, 'India says to deport all Rohingya regardless of U.N. registration', 14 August 2017, https://in.reuters.com/article/myanmar-rohingya-india/india-says-to-deport-all-rohingya-regardless-of-u-n-registration-idINKCN1AU0U2, accessed on 30 April 2018.
6 Advisory Commission on Rakhine State, *Towards a Peaceful, Fair and Prosperous Future for the People of Rakhine: Final Report of the Advisory Commission on Rakhine State*, August 2017, p. 9.
7 *Ibid.*
8 *Ibid.*, p. 10.
9 *Ibid.*, p. 24.
10 *Ibid.*
11 *Ibid.*, p. 27.
12 *Ibid.*, p. 28.
13 *Ibid.*
14 *Ibid.*
15 *Ibid.*, p. 31.
16 *Ibid.*
17 Please see the UNHCR document, H. Massey, *UNHCR and De Facto Statelessness*, 2010, www.unhcr.org/4bc2ddeb9.pdf, on *de facto* statelessness accessed on 15 October 2017.

REFERENCES

Books

Agamben, G. 1998. *Homo Sacer.* Stanford: Stanford University Press.

Amrith, S. S.2013.*Crossing the Bay of Bengal: The Furies and the Fortunes of Migrants.* Cambridge, MA: Harvard University Press.

Arendt, H. 1958. *The Origins of Totalitarianism.* Cleveland and New York: Meridian Books, World Publishing Company.

Arendt, H. 1963. *Eichmann in Jerusalem.* New York: Viking Press.

Arendt, H. 1994. 'We refugees', in M. Robinson (ed.) *Altogether Elsewhere: Writers on Exile.* London: Faber & Faber.

Banerjee, P., S. B. R. Chaudhury and S. K. Das (eds.). 2005. *Internal Displacement in South Asia.* New Delhi: Sage.

Basu, S. P. (ed.). 2014. *Forced Migration and Media Mirrors.* Kolkata: Frontpage.

Bhattacharya, S. 2015.*The Rakhine State (Arakan) of Myanmar: Interrogating History, Culture and Conflict.* New Delhi: MAKAIAS-Manohar.

Bose, P. K. (ed.). 2000. *Refugees in West Bengal: Institutional Processes and Contested Identities.* Kolkata: Calcutta Research Group.

Cheesman, N. and H. K. Win (eds.). 2015. *Communal Violence in Myanmar.* Yangon: Myanmar Knowledge Society.

Clive, J. C. 1996. *A Modern History of Southeast Asia: Decolonization, Nationalism and Separation.* New York: Tauris Academic Studies, and Singapore: Institute of Southeast Asian Studies.

Dhavan, R. 2004. *Refugee Law and Policy in India.* New Delhi: PILSARC.

Dupont, V. and D. Vacquier. 2013. 'Slum demolition, impact on the affected families and coping strategies', in F. Landy and M. C. Saglio-Yatzimirsky (eds.) *Megacity Slums: Social Exclusion, Urban Space and Policies in Brazil and India.* London: Imperial College Press, pp. 307–61.

Ghosh, P. 2000. *Brave Men in the Hills, Resistance and Rebellion in Burma, 1825–1932.* London: C. Hurst and Company.

Ibrahim, A. 2016. *The Rohingyas: Inside Myanmar's Hidden Genocide.* London: C. Hurst and Company.

Israeli, R. 1982. *The Crescent in the East: Islam in Asia Major.* London: Humanities Press.

Mayadas, N. S.1999. *The Marginal Nation.* New Delhi: Sage.

Mayadas, N. S. (ed.). 2003.*Refugees and the State: Practices of Asylum and Care in India, 1947–2000.* New Delhi: Sage.

Mayadas, N. S. (ed.). 2004. *Peace Studies: An Introduction to the Concept, Scope, and Themes.* New Delhi: Sage.

Mirowski, P. 2013. *Never Let a Serious Crisis Go to Waste: How Neoliberalism Survived the Financial Meltdown.* London: Verso.

Mutua, M. 2002. *Human Rights: A Political and Cultural Critique.* Philadelphia, PA: University of Pennsylvania Press.

Razzaq, A. and M. Haque. 1995. *Tale of Refugees: Rohingyas in Bangladesh.* Dhaka: Center for Human Rights.

Samaddar, R. 2009. 'Refugees and dynamics of hospitality: The Indian story', in U. A. Segal, D. Elliott and N. S. Mayadas (eds.) *Immigration Worldwide: Policies, Practices, and Trends.* New York: Oxford University Press, pp. 112–23.

Sassen, S. 1999. *Guests and Aliens.* New York: New Press.

Smith, M. 1991. *Burma: Insurgency and the Politics of Ethnicity.* London: Zed Books.

Taylor, R. H. 2015. *General Ne Win: A Political Biography.* Singapore: Institute of Southeast Asian Studies.

Trakroo, R. 2007.*Refugees and the Law.* New Delhi: Human Rights Law Network.

Journal articles and reports

Acharya, B. 2004. 'The law, policy and practice of refugee protection in India', www.researchgate.net/publication/256016766_The_Law_Policy_and_Practice_of_Refugee_Protection_in_India, accessed on 14 October 2015.

Akhter, S. 2014. 'Gender-based violence among documented Rohingya refugees in Bangladesh', *Indian Journal of Gender Studies*, 21(2): 225–46.

Anand, J. P. 1978. 'Refugees from Burma', *Economic and Political Weekly*, 13(27): 1100–1.

Anwar, N. H. 2013. 'Negotiating new conjunctures of citizenship: Experiences of "illegality" in Burmese: Rohingya and Bangladeshi migrant enclaves in Karachi', *Citizenship Studies*, 17(3–4): 414–28.

Apland, K., B. K. Blitz, C. Hamilton, M. Lagaay, R. Lakshman, and E. Yarrow. 2014. *Birth Registration and Children's Rights: A Complex Story*, www.planusa.org/docs/birth-registration-rights-2014.pdf, accessed on 14 October 2015.

Azad, A. and F. Jasmin. 2013. 'Durable solutions to the protracted refugee situation: The case of Rohingyas in Bangladesh', *Journal of Indian Research*, 1(4): 25–35.

Azis, A. 2014. 'Urban refugees in a graduated sovereignty: The experiences of the stateless Rohingya in the Klang Valley', *Citizenship Studies*, 18(8): 839–54.

Balazo, P. 2015. 'Truth and rights: Statelessness, human rights, and the Rohingya', *Undercurrent*, 11(1): 6–15.

Banda, S., Y. Vaidya and D. Adler. 2013. *The Case of Kathputli Colony: Mapping Delhi's First In-Situ Slum Rehabilitation Project*, CPR Working Paper 3. New Delhi: Centre for Policy Research.

Banerjee, P. 2016. 'Criminalising the trafficked: Blaming the victim', *Economic and Political Weekly*, 51(44–5): 62–8.

Basistha, N. and M. Mehrotra. 2011. 'Collective memories of repatriates from Burma: A case study of West Bengal', *Refugee Watch*, 37: 95–102.

Bhaumik, S. 2013. 'The East Bengali Muslims in Assam and Rohingyas of Myanmar: Comparative perspectives of migration, exclusion, statelessness', *Refugee Watch*, 41: 30–46.

Borren, M. 2008. 'Towards an Arendtian politics of in/visibility', *Ethical Perspectives*, 15(2): 213–37.

Brooten, L. 2015. 'Blind spots in human rights coverage: Framing violence against the Rohingya in Myanmar/Burma', *Popular Communication*, 13(2): 132–44.

Butler, J. 2012. 'Precarious life, vulnerability, and the ethics of cohabitation', *The Journal of Speculative Philosophy*, 26(2): 134–51.

Chan, A. 2005. 'The development of a Muslim enclave in Arakan (Rakhine) state of Burma (Myanmar)', *SOAS Bulletin of Burma Research*, 3(2): 396–420.

Cheung, S. 2012. 'Migration control and the solutions impasse in South and Southeast Asia: Implications from the Rohingya experience', *Journal of Refugee Studies*, 25(1): 50–70.

Chopra, K. 2014. 'Persecuted and unwanted: Plight of Rohingya refugees in India', *Refugee Watch*, http://refugeewatchonline.blogspot.in/2014/06/persecuted-and-unwanted-plight-of.html, accessed on 4 December 2014.

Choudhury, V. 1997. 'The Arakani governors of Chittagong and their coins', *Journal of the Asiatic Society of Bangladesh*, Dhaka, 42(2): 145–62.

Chowdhory, N. 2013. 'Marginalization and exclusion: Politics of non-citizen rights in postcolonial South Asia', *Refugee Watch*, 42: 1–16.

Datta, P., S. Sadhu and B. N. Bhattacharya. 2004. 'Impact of undocumented migration from Bangladesh to West Bengal', *Refugee Watch*, 23, www.mcrg.ac.in/rw%20files/rw22.doc, accessed on 14 October 2015.

Development and Justice Initiative. 2012. *National Consultation on the Right to Survival, Protection and Education of Children of Refugees, Migrants and Stateless Persons in India* (mimeo).

Dhavan, R. 2003. 'On the model law for refugees: A response to the National Human Rights Commission (NHRC)', *NHRC Annual Reports 1997–1998, 1999–2000*, New Delhi: PILSARC.

Dhavan, R. 2006. 'Refugee protection by executive action', *PILSARC* (mimeo).

Falise, T. 2001. 'On the trail of Burma's, internal refugees', *Refugee Watch*, (15).

Falise, T. 2010. 'On the run: In Burma's jungle hell', *World Policy Journal*, 27(1): 57–64.

Farzana, K. F. 2011. 'Music and artistic artefacts: Symbols of Rohingya identity and everyday resistance in Borderlands', *ASEAS: ÖsterreichischeZeitschrift fürSüdostasienwissenschaften*, (2): 215.

Ferguson, J. M. 2015. 'Who's counting? Ethnicity, belonging, and the National Census in Burma/Myanmar', *Bijdragen tot de Taal, LandenVolkenkunde*, 171: 1–28.

Ghertner, D. A. 2008. 'Analysis of new legal discourse behind Delhi's slum demolitions', *Economic and Political Weekly*, 43(20): 57–66.

Ghosal, S. 2000. 'Rohingya women: Stateless and oppressed from Burma', *Refugee Watch*, 10–11, www.mcrg.ac.in/rw%20files/RW10&11.DOC, accessed on 14 October 2015.

Ghosh, A. and S. Ghosal. 1999. 'What happened to the refugees in Bengal?', *Refugee Watch*, www.mcrg.ac.in/rw%20files/RW8.doc, accessed on 14 October 2015.

Ghoshal, A. 2012. 'Changing mentality of the Bengalee refugees: The story of Tripura (1946–1971)', *Refugee Watch*, 39–40, www.mcrg.ac.in/rw%20files/RW39_40/2.pdf, accessed on 14 October 2015.

Gill, F. S. 2014. 'Human rights and statelessness: The case study of the Rohingya in Myanmar', National Sun Yat-sen University, Taiwan, http://etd.lib.nsysu.edu.tw/ETD-db/ETD-search-c/getfile?URN=etd-0715114-125135&filename=etd-0715114-125135.pdf, accessed on 14 October 2015.

Green, P. 2013. 'Islamophobia: Burma's racist fault-line', *Race & Class*, 55(2): 93–8.

Guhathakurta, M. 2010. 'Cartographic anxieties, identity politics and the imperatives of Bangladesh foreign policy peace prints', *South Asian Journal of Peacebuilding*, 2(3): 1–10.

Harteleigh, R. 1999. 'Shattered lives, shattered homes', *Refugee Watch*, 7, www.mcrg.ac.in/rw%20files/RW7.doc, accessed on 14 October 2015.

Human Rights Watch. 2002. 'Crackdown on Burmese Muslims', www.hrw.org/legacy/backgrounder/asia/burmese_muslims.pdf, accessed on 3 December 2014.

Human Rights Watch. 2013. 'All you can do is pray: Crimes against humanity and ethnic cleansing of Rohingya Muslims in Burma's Arakan State', www.hrw.org/sites/default/files/reports/burma0413webwcover_0.pdf, accessed on 3 December 2014.

International Crisis Group. 2014. *Myanmar: Politics of Rakhine State*, Asia Report No. 261, 22 October, www.crisisgroup.org/~/media/Files/asia/south-east-asia/burma-myanmar/261-myanmar-the-politics-of-rakhine-state.pdf, accessed on 24 September 2015.

Karkala, S. 2012. *India and the Challenge of Statelessness: A Review of the Legal Framework Relating to Nationality*. New Delhi: National Law University, Delhi Press.

Kipgen, N. 2013. 'Conflict in Rakhine state in Myanmar: Rohingya Muslims' Conundrum', *Journal of Muslim Minority Affairs*, 33(2): 298–310.

Kipgen, N. 2014. 'Addressing the Rohingya problem', *Journal of Asian and African Studies*, 49: 234–47.

Kruthika, N. S. 2014. 'The Rohingya scenario: Role of Bangladesh and India in Myanmar's concealed tragedy', *Refugee Watch Online*, http://refugeewatchonline.blogspot.in/2014/04/the-rohingya-scenario-role-of.html, accessed on 4 December 2014.

Lewa, C. 2003. 'We are like a soccer ball, kicked by Burma, kicked by Bangladesh!', *Asia Forum for Human Rights and Development*, http://burmalibrary.org/docs/KICKED-June2003.doc, accessed on 3 December 2014.

Lewa, C. 2008. 'Asia's new boat people', *Forced Migration Review*, 30: 40–2, www.fmreview.org/en/FMRpdfs/FMR30/40-41.pdf, accessed on 11 March 2015.

Lewa, C. 2009. 'North Arakan: An open prison for the Rohingyas in Burma', *Forced Migration Review*,32: 11–13, www.fmreview.org/FMRpdfs/FMR32/11-13.pdf, accessed on 14 October 2015.

Morand, M. B., K. Mahony, S. Bellour and J. Rabkin. 2012. *The Implementation of UNHCR's Policy on Refugee Protection and Solution in Urban Areas, Global Survey–2012*, www.unhcr.org/516d658c9.html, accessed on 14 October 2015.

Nair, A. 2007. 'National refugee law for India: Roadblocks and benefits', *IPCS Research Paper*, 4–9, www.ipcs.org/pdf_file/issue/51462796IPCS-ResearchPaper11-ArjunNair.pdf, accessed on 27 December 2014.

Paasi, A. 1998. 'Boundaries as social processes: Territoriality in the world of flows', *Geopolitics*, 3(1): 69–88.

Pallis, M. 2002. 'Obligations of states towards asylum seekers at sea: Interactions and conflicts between legal regimes', *International Journal of Refugee Law*, 14(2/3): 329–64.

Palmer, V. 2011. 'Analysing cultural proximity: Islamic Relief Worldwide and Rohingya refugees in Bangladesh', *Development in Practice*, 21(1): 96–108.

Parnini, S. N. 2013. 'The crisis of the Rohingya as a Muslim minority in Myanmar and bilateral relations with Bangladesh', *Journal of Muslim Minority Affairs*, 33(2): 281–97.

Parsons, C. and P.-L. Vezina. 2013. 'Migrant networks and trade: The Vietnamese boat people as a natural', www.economics.ox.ac.uk/materials/events/12846/VEZINA_vietnam.pdf, accessed on 30 July 2015 (mimeo).

Pugh, M. 2004. 'Drowning not waving: Boat people and humanitarianism at sea', *Journal of Refugee Studies*, 17(1): 50–69.

Rahman, U. 2010. 'The Rohingya Refugee: A security dilemma for Bangladesh', *Journal of Immigrant and Refugee Studies*, 8(2): 233–9.

Rajpurohit, S. 2013. 'Rohingya refugees in India: Tales of endless persecution, torture and exploitation', *Countercurrents*, 13 July, www.countercurrents.org/rajpurohit130713.htm, accessed on 24 September 2015.

Ryan, C. 2013. 'The subjected non-subject: Security, subjectification and resistance in the occupied Palestinian territories', *Critical Studies on Security*,1(3): 295–310.

Samaddar, R. 2015. 'Human migration as crisis of Europe', *Economic and Political Weekly*, 50(51).

Shafer, C. B. 2013. 'The Rohingya: Impediments to inclusive citizenship', http://cosmopolistoronto.com/wp-content/uploads/2013/12/The-Rohingya-Impediments-to-Inclusive-Citizenship-by-Colin-Boyd-Shafer.pdf, accessed on 3 December 2014 (mimeo).

Sheikh, S. and S. Banda. 2014. 'The Delhi Urban Shelter Improvement Board (DUSIB): The challenges facing a strong, progressive agency', *Centre for Policy Research*, http://citiesofdelhi.cprindia.org/reports/the-delhi-urban-shelter-improvement-board-dusib/, accessed on 14 October 2015.

Smith, M. 1995. 'The Muslim Rohingya of Burma', paper presented at a Conference on Burma at Amsterdam, Nederland, 11 December 1995.

Sriraman, T. 2013. 'Enumeration as pedagogic process: Gendered encounters with identity documents in Delhi's urban poor spaces', *South Asia Multidisciplinary*

Academic Journal, 8, http://samaj.revues.org/3655, accessed on 24 September 2015.

Stanley, H. V. 2001. 'Journey from Burma to India', *Refugee Watch*, 13, www.mcrg. ac.in/rw%20files/RW13.DOC, accessed on 14 October 2015.

Tomas, L. 2013. 'When there's no place called home', *Tehelka*, 45(10), www.tehelka. com/when-theres-no-place-called-home/, accessed on 4 December 2014.

Tomas, L. and R. Rakshit. 2014. 'The art of statelessness', *Himal Southasian*, http://old. himalmag.com/vacancy/5233-art-of-statelessness.html, accessed on 4 December 2014.

Ullah, A. A. 2011. 'Rohingya refugees to Bangladesh: Historical exclusions and contemporary marginalization', *Journal of Immigrant and Refugee Studies*, 9(2): 139–61.

Van Joanne, S. and B. Cooper. 2005. *The New 'Boat People': Ensuring Safety and Determining Status*. Washington, DC: Migration Policy Institute.

Women's Refugee Commission. 2011. *Bright Lights, Big City: Urban Refugees Struggle to Make a Living in New Delhi*, http://womensrefugeecommission.org/resources/ document/733brightlightsbigcityurbanrefugeesstruggletomakealivinginnewde lhi, accessed on 24 September 2015.

Weblinks and websites

'Australia asylum: Dutton says Nauru is 'safe' for refugees', *Al Jazeera*, 6 October 2015, http://www.bbc.com/news/world-australia-34450776, accessed on 11 October 2015.

'Australia closes door on persecuted Rohingya', Australian Refugee Council, 21 May 2015, https://www.refugeecouncil.org.au/latest/australia-closes-door-on-persecuted-rohingya/, accessed on 30 April 2016.

'Australian government denies Cambodia refugee deal collapse', *Al Jazeera*, 31 August 2015, http://www.bbc.com/news/world-australia-34105064, accessed on 11 October 2015.

Burma Partnership. 2015. 'The Rohingya, the Citizenship law, temporary registration, and implementation of the Rakhine state action plan', www. burmapartnership.org/2015/04/the-rohingya-the-citizenship-law-temporary-registration-and-implementation-of-the-rakhine-state-action-plan/, accessed on 24 September 2015.

Goris, I., J. H. Reddy and K. Sebastian. 2009. 'Statelessness: What it is and why it matters', www.opensocietyfoundations.org/voices/statelessness-what-it-and-why-it-matters, accessed on 10 October 2015.

http://citiesofdelhi.cprindia.org/about/, accessed on 10 January 2016.

http://kindlemag.in/the-state-of-statelessness/, accessed on 20 December 2016.

Hukil, R. and N. Shaunik. n.d. 'Rudderless and drowning in tears: The Rohingyas of Myanmar', *IPCS Issue Brief*, www.ipcs.org/issue-brief/southeast-asia/rudderless-drowning-in-tears-the-rohingyas-of-myanmar-222.html, accessed on 6 June 2015.

Human Rights Watch. 2012. '"The government could have stopped this", sectarian violence and ensuing abuses in Burma's Arakan state', www.hrw.org/

report/2012/07/31/government-could-have-stopped/sectarian-violence-and-ensuing-abuses-burmas-arakan, accessed on 14 October 2015.

Human Rights Watch. 2013. '"All you can do is pray": Crimes against humanity and ethnic cleansing of Rohingya Muslims in Burma's Arakan state', www.hrw.org/reports/2013/04/22/all-you-can-do-pray-0, accessed on 11 March 2015.

Institute on Statelessness and Inclusion. 2014. *The World's Stateless*, www.institutesi.org/worldsstateless.pdf, accessed on 24 September 2015.

IOM. 2015. *IOM Sees Progress in SE Asia Migrant Crisis, But Warns More Must Be Done*, www.iom.int/news/iom-sees-progress-se-asia-migrant-crisis-warns-more-must-be-done, accessed on 24 September 2015.

Lewa, C. 2009. 'North Arakan: An open prison for the Rohingya in Burma', http://sayedarakani48.webs.com/rohingyaarticles.htm, accessed on 3 December 2014.

Matters India. n.d. 'Rohingya refugees in Hyderabad', http://mattersindia.com/rohingya-muslim-refugees-in-hyderabad/, accessed on 1 September 2015.

Najappa, V. 2015. 'Rohingya Muslims: Worry ahead for India', 4 June, www.oneindia.com/feature/rohingya-muslims-worry-ahead-for-india-1767313.html, accessed on 1 August 2015.

"Nope, nope, nope': Tony Abbott says Australia will take no Rohingya refugees', *The Guardian*, 21 May 2015, https://www.theguardian.com/world/2015/may/21/nope-nope-nope-tony-abbott-says-australia-will-take-no-rohingya-refugees, accessed on 30 April 2018.

'Rohingya refugee in Cambodia wants to go home', *Al Jazeera*, 7 September 2015, https://www.aljazeera.com/news/2015/09/rohingya-refugee-cambodia-home-150906113212848.html, accessed on 30 April 2018

Showkat Shafi, 'Rohingya refugees find safe haven in Kashmir', *Al Jazeera*, 30 December 2014, https://www.aljazeera.com/indepth/inpictures/2014/12/rohingya-refugees-find-safe-h-20141223163741968194.html, accessed on 11 October 2015.

Smith, M. 1995. 'The Muslim Rohingya of Burma', www.kaladanpress.org/index.php/scholar-column-mainmenu-36/36-rohingya/194-the-muslim-rohingya-of-burma.html, accessed on 24 September 2015.

'Tony Abbott rules out resettling Rohingyas in Australia, Indonesia says it is obliged to,' http://www.abc.net.au/news/2015-05-21/rohingyas-migrants-indonesia-says-australia-obliged-resettle/6486590, accessed on 30 April 2018.

'UN: Rohingya may be victims of crimes against humanity', *Aljazeera*, 20 June 2016, www.aljazeera.com/news/2016/06/rohingya-victims-crimes-humanity-160620131906370.html, accessed on 15 January 2017.

www.mha.nic.in, accessed on 10 January 2016.

www.pib.nic.in, accessed on 10 January 2016.

www.refworld.org, accessed on 10 January 2016.

www.unhcr.org, accessed on 10 January 2016.

Yhome, K. 'Rohingyas adrift, far from the shores of Asia's conscience', http://thewire.in/2015/05/21/rohingyasadrift-far-from-the-shores-of-asias-conscience 2149/?relatedposts_hit=1&relatedposts_origin=11528&relatedposts_position=1, accessed on 11 October 2015.

Newspapers

Ahmad, S. Z. 2012. 'Rohingya Muslims: A brief history of centuries long persecution', *Two Circles*, 29 July, http://twocircles.net/2012jul29/rohingya_muslims_brief_history_persecution.html#.VZDdzXW1Gko, accessed on 24 September 2015.

Aldama, Z. 2014. 'Myanmar's Buddhist-Rohingya ethnic divide', 4 February, www.aljazeera.com/indepth/features/2014/02/myanmar-buddhist-rohingya-ethnic-divide-20142211421962209.html, accessed on 2 December 2014.

Aljazeera. 2012a. 'Bangladesh orders halt in aid to Rohingya, 4 August, www.aljazeera.com/news/asia/2012/08/201284155353135194.html, accessed on 3 December 2012.

Aljazeera. 2012b. 'Bangladesh PM speaks out on Rohingya issue', July 27, www.aljazeera.com/video/asia/2012/08/201285113421146649.html, accessed on 3 December 2014.

Aljazeera. 2014. 'UN raises alarm over Rohingya Muslim abuse', 8 April, www.aljazeera.com/news/asia-pacific/2014/04/un-raises-alarm-over-rohingya-muslim-abuse-20144863638917587.html, accessed on 2 December 2014.

Al-Mahmood, S. Z. 2012. 'Burma's Rohingya refugees find little respite in Bangladesh', *The Guardian*, 29 June, www.theguardian.com/global-development/2012/jun/29/burma-rohingya-refugees-bangladesh, accessed on 24 September 2015.

Anandabazar Patrika. 2012. 'Gorishther Adhipatyo', 9 November, http://archives.anandabazar.com/archive/1121109/9edit2.html, accessed on 24 September 2014.

Anandabazar Patrika. 2013. 'Gonotontro O Myanmar', 3 June, http://archives.anandabazar.com/archive/1130603/3edit1.html, accessed on 24 September 2015.

Anandabazar Patrika. 2014a. 'ShonkyhyagururDapot', 24 June, www.anandabazar.com/editorial/%E0%A6%B8-%E0%A6%96-%E0%A6%AF-%E0%A6%97-%E0%A6%B0-%E0%A6%B0-%E0%A6%A6-%E0%A6%AA%E0%A6%9F-1.43751, accessed on 24 September 2015.

Anandabazar Patrika. 2014b. 'Shuchona', 24 September, www.anandabazar.com/editorial/%E0%A6%B8-%E0%A6%9A%E0%A6%A8-1.71907, accessed on 24 September 2015.

Anandabazar Patrika. 2014c. 'SoiritontrePhiribeki', 9 July, www.anandabazar.com/editorial/%E0%A6%B8-%E0%A6%AC-%E0%A6%B0%E0%A6%A4%E0%A6%A8-%E0%A6%A4-%E0%A6%B0-%E0%A6%AB-%E0%A6%B0-%E0%A6%AC-%E0%A6%95-1.485086%B0-%E0%A6%AC%E0%A6%B9%E0%A6%B0-%E0%A6%A6-%E0%A6%96-%E0%A6%9A-%E0%A6%A8-%E0%A6%A4-%E0%A7%9F-%E0%A6%95-%E0%A6%A8-%E0%A6%A6-%E0%A6%B0-%E0%A7%9F-%E0%A6%B8-%E0%A6%AC%E0%A6%B0-%E0%A6%B7-%E0%A6%9F-%E0%A6%B0-%E0%A6%AE%E0%A6%A8-%E0%A6%A4-%E0%A6%B0%E0%A6%95-1.9264#, accessed on 24 September 2015.

Azad, A. and A. Sakhawat. 2015. 'Why risk your life on the open seas?', *Dhaka Tribune*, 6 July, www.dhakatribune.com/bangladesh/2015/jul/06/why-risk-your-life-open-seas, accessed on 24 September 2014.

Bagchi, S. 2014. 'Rohingya influx: A brewing crisis', *The Hindu*, 17 March, www.thehindu.com/news/national/other-states/rohingya-influx-a-brewing-crisis/article5797314.ece, accessed on 24 September 2015.

Bangkok Post. 2015a. 'Thailand hunts trafficking suspects in blitz on people-smuggling trade', 8 May, www.bangkokpost.com/news/asia/555455/thailand-hunts-trafficking-suspects-in-blitz-on-people-smuggling-trade, accessed on 24 September 2015.

Bangkok Post. 2015b. 'Trafficking crackdown poses new dangers for victims', 6 May, www.bangkokpost.com/news/general/552783/trafficking-crackdown-poses-new-dangers-for-victims, accessed on 24 September 2015.

Baseerat, B. 2013. 'Riot-hit Rohingya Muslims take refuge in Hyderabad', *Times of India*, 15 April, Hyderabad, http://timesofindia.indiatimes.com/city/hyderabad/Riot-hit-Rohingya-Muslims-take-refuge-in-Hyderabad/articleshow/19551921.cms, accessed on 3 December 2014.

BBC. 2015. 'Why are so many Rohingya migrants stranded at sea?', 18 May, www.bbc.com/news/world-asia-32740637, accessed on 24 September 2015.

Bhalla, N. 2014. 'Myanmar's Rohingya stuck in refugee limbo in India', *Reuters*, 15 September 2015, www.reuters.com/article/2014/09/15/us-foundation-state less-india-rohingya-idUSKBN0HA07F20140915, accessed on 25 September 2015.

Bhattacharya, S. 2012. 'India's Myanmar refugees get visas after month of protests in Delhi', *The Nation*, 17 May, www.thenational.ae/news/world/southasia/indi asmyanmarrefugeesgetvisasaftermonthofprotestsindelhi, accessed on 24 September 2015.

Bhaumik, S. 2013. 'No country for Rohingyas', *India Today*, 22 March, http://india today.intoday.in/story/rohingya-muslims-rakhine-myanmar-bordering-ban gladesh/1/259014.html, accessed on 24 September 2015.

Biswas, T. 2013. 'Top Lashkar Terrorist Abdul Karim Tunda arrested by Delhi Police', *NDTV*, 17 August, www.ndtv.com/indianews/toplashkarterroristab dulkarimtundaarrestedbydelhipolice531895, accessed on 24 September 2015.

Boonyai, A. 2015. 'Southeast Asia nations agree on anti-trafficking task force', *Channel News Asia*, 29 May, www.channelnewsasia.com/news/asiapacific/southeast-asia-nations/1880868.html, accessed on 30 July 2015.

The Business Standard. 2015. 'Cops seek UNHCR help to monitor Rohingya refugees in Hyderabad', 31 July, www.business-standard.com/article/pti-stories/cops-seek-unhcr-help-to-monitor-rohingya-refugees-in-hyderabad-115073 100902_1.html, accessed on 14 October 2015.

Carrol, J. 2014. 'Myanmar's Rohingya deprived of education', 4 August, Sittwe: Aljazeera, www.aljazeera.com/indepth/features/2014/08/myanmar-rohingya-deprived-education-201484105134827695.html, accessed on 3 December 2014.

Cunningham, S. 2015. 'Do Myanmar's Rohingya really need citizenship now?', *Forbes Asia*, 7 April, www.forbes.com/sites/susancunningham/2015/07/04/dom yanmarsrohingyareallyneedcitizenshipnow/?commentId=comment_blogAnd PostId/blog/comment/2947239035, accessed on 24 September 2015.

Daily Excelsior. 2015. 'Government calls meet on Rohingya Muslims', 7 July, www.dailyexcelsior.com/govtcallsmeetonrohingyamuslims/, accessed on 24 September 2015.

Daily News and Analysis. 2014. 'Rohingya Muslim refugees in Hyderabad are under surveillance, say police', 27 December, www.dnaindia.com/india/report-rohingya-muslim-refugees-in-hyderabad-are-under-surveillance-say-police-2047456, accessed on 24 September 2015.

Datta, S. 2014. 'Arrested Rohingya trained Militants in Myanmar', *The Hindustan Times*, 23 November, www.hindustantimes.com/india-news/arrested-rohingya-trained-militants-in-myanmar/article1-1289131.aspx, accessed on 1 September 2015.

Davies, M. 2015. 'Rohingya and our rule-bending arrogance', *The Drum*, 18 May, www.abc.net.au/news/2015-05-18/davies-rohingya-and-our-rule-bending-arrogance/6477148, accessed on 24 September 2015.

Deccan Herald. 2012a. 'Bangladesh bans foreign charities helping Rohingya', 2 August, www.deccanherald.com/content/268792/bangladesh-bans-foreign-charities-helping.html, accessed on 24 September 2015.

Deccan Herald. 2012b. 'Refugees denied basic facilities', 20 October, www.deccan herald.com/content/286895/refugees-denied-basic-facilities.html, accessed on 24 September 2015.

Deccan Herald. 2012c. 'Refugees subjected to discrimination in India: Activists', 17 June, www.deccanherald.com/content/257575/archives.php, accessed on 24 September 2015.

Deccan Herald. 2013. 'SC notice to Centre on Myanmar refugees', 5 October, www.deccanherald.com/content/361432/sc-notice-centre-myanmar-refugees.html, accessed on 24 September 2015.

Dutt, N. 2015. 'Rohingya migrant recounts escape to India', *Al Jazeera*, www.aljazeera.com/blogs/asia/2015/06/mohammad-kareem-rohingya-refugee-150603175157381.html, accessed on 10 October 2015.

Fareed, M.A.R. 2014. 'Rohingya exiles struggle to survive in India', *Al Jazeera*, 6 January, www.aljazeera.com/indepth/features/2014/01/rohingya-exiles-struggle-survive-india-201416143243337187.html, accessed on 24 September 2015.

Fitzgerald, H. 2014. 'Held in Hyderabad: Rohingyas in the news', *New English Review*, 18 November, www.newenglishreview.org/blog_direct_link.cfm/blog_id/57598, accessed on 21 December 2014.

Fredrickson, T. 2015. 'Border camp horrors revealed, official arrested', *Bangkok Post*, 4 May, www.bangkokpost.com/learning/learning-from-news/549355/suspected-migrant-graveyard-discovered-in-songkhla, accessed on 24 September 2015.

Fuller, T. 2015. 'Boat with hundreds of migrants from Myanmar heads farther out to sea', *New York Times*, 15 May, www.nytimes.com/2015/05/16/world/asia/migrant-boat-myanmar-thailand.html?module=ArrowsNav&contentCollection=Asia%20Pacific&action=keypress &region=FixedLeft&pgtype=article, accessed on 5 September 2015.

Goodman, J. 2014. 'No respite for Rohingya in Bangladesh', *Al Jazeera*, 16 January, www.aljazeera.com/indepth/features/2014/01/no-respite-rohingya-bangladesh-201411675944519957.html, accessed on 2 December 2014.

Gupta, J. 2014. 'Khalid's arrest sparks off debate on Rohingyas in India', *The Times of India*, 20 November, http://timesofindia.indiatimes.com/india/Khalidsarrestspark

soffdebateonRohingyasinIndia/articlehow/45220794.cms, accessed on 24 September 2015.

Gupta, S. 2013. 'Lashkar Radicalises Rohingyas to wage war against India', *The Hindustan Times*, 2 August, www.hindustantimes.com/newdelhi/lashkarradical isesrohingyastowagewaragainstindia/article11102056.aspx, accessed on 24 September 2015.

Gupta, S. and A. Jatin. 2013. 'Was Bodh Gaya revenge for attack on Rohingya Muslims', *The Hindustan Times*, 8 July, www.hindustantimes.com/newdelhi/ was-bodh-gaya-revenge-for-attacks-on-rohingya-muslims/article1-1088843. aspx, accessed on 9 January 2015.

Hasan, S. 2015. 'Teen talikateishongshod Bodi', *Prothom Alo*, 18 June, www. prothomalo.com/bangladesh/article/556429/%E0%A6%A4%E0%A6%BF% E0%A6%A8-%E0%A6%A4%E0%A6%BE%E0%A6%B2%E0%A6%BF% E0%A6%95%E0%A6%BE%E0%A6%A4%E0%A7%87%E0%A6%87- %E0%A6%B8%E0%A6%BE%E0%A6%82%E0%A6%B8%E0%A6%A6- %E0%A6%AC%E0%A6%A6%E0%A6%BF, accessed on 24 September 2014.

The Hindu. 2012. 'India to open third mission in Myanmar', 16 December, www. thehindu.com/news/international/india-to-open-third-mission-in-myanmar/ article4204046.ece?ref=relatedNews, accessed on 24 September 2015.

The Hindu. 2014. 'Bangladeshi "infiltrators" would have to go back: Modi', 7 May, www.thehindu.com/elections/loksabha2014/bangladeshi-infiltrators-would- have-to-go-back-modi/article5986165.ece, accessed on 24 September 2015.

India Together. 2015. 'Seeking new homes in Hyderabad', *India Together*, 1 January, accessed on 10 January.

Jain, B. 2013. 'India alerts Bangladesh about Rohingya terror training camps in Chittagong Hill Tracts', *The Times of India*, 25 July, http://timesofindia.india times.com/india/IndiaalertsBangladeshaboutRohingyaterrortrainingcampsin- ChittagongHillTracts/articleshow/21320102.cms, accessed on 24 September 2015.

Janyala, S. 2015. 'Cyberabad Police seek UNHCR help to keep tab on Rohingya refu- gees', *The Indian Express*, 1 August, http://indianexpress.com/article/india/india- others/rohingya-muslims-in-hyderabad-and-cyberabad-come-under-scanner/, accessed on 10 October 2015.

Kei Nemoto. 'The Rohingya issue: A thorny obstacle between Burma (Myanmar) and Bangladesh', www.burmalibrary.org/docs14/Kei_Nemoto-Rohingya.pdf, p. 3, accessed on 10 October 2015.

Khan, A. Y. 2013. 'Hyderabad's Rohingya refugees fight language barriers', *The Hindu*, 1 July, www.thehindu.com/news/cities/Hyderabad/hyderabads-rohingya-ref ugees-fight-language-barriers/article4866622.ece, accessed on 10 October 2015.

Kumar, A. 2013. 'Nine explosions rock Bodh Gaya', *Deccan Herald*, 7 July, www. deccanherald.com/content/343424/nine-explosions-rock-bodh-gaya.html, accessed on 24 September 2015.

Mann, Z. 2012. 'Rohingya protesters in Delhi urged to leave', *Irrawaddy*, 16 May, www.irrawaddy.org/refugees/rohingyaprotestersindelhiurgedtoleave.html, accessed on 24 September 2015.

Mitra, A. 2014. 'Rajye Rohingya koyedir bohor dekhe chintay kendriyo swo-rashtro montrok', *Anandabazar Patrika*, 10 March, www.anandabazar.com/state/%E0%A6%B0-%E0%A6%9C-%E0%A6%AF-%E0%A6%B0-%E0%A6%B9-%E0%A6%99-%E0%A6%97-%E0%A6%95%E0%A7%9F-%E0%A6%A6-%E0%A, accessed on 24 September 2015.

Mizzima. 2015. 'UNHCR warns of sharp increases in boat people in Bay of Bengal', 10 May, www.mizzima.com/news-international/unhcr-warns-sharp-increases-boat-people-bay-bengal#sthash.jEvl4e3N.dpuf, accessed on 24 September 2015.

Mohammed, S. 2013. 'Rohingyas in Hyderabad live in fear', *The Times of India*, 9 July, http://timesofindia.indiatimes.com/city/hyderabad/Rohingyas-in-Hyderabad-live-in-fear/articleshow/20980972.cms, accessed on 24 September 2015.

Motlagh, J. 2014. 'These aren't refugee camps, they're concentration camps, and people are dying in them', *The Time*, http://time.com/2888864/rohingya-myanmar-burma-camps-sittwe/, accessed on 9 June 2015.

'Myanmar's war on the Rohingya', The Editorial Board, *The New York Times*, 21 November 2016, www.nytimes.com/2016/11/21/opinion/myanmars-war-on-the-rohingya.html, accessed on 2 January 2017.

Nanjappa, V. 2015. 'Rohingya Muslims: Worry ahead for India', *One India News*, June 4, www.oneindia.com/feature/rohingyamuslimsworryaheadforindia176731 html, accessed on 24 September 2015.

The New York Times. 2015a. 'Lost voices of the world's refugees', 13 June, www.nytimes.com/2015/06/14/opinion/lost-voices-of-the-worlds-refugees.html, accessed on 7 July 2015.

The New York Times. 2015b. 'Understanding Southeast Asia's Migrant crisis', 14 May, www.nytimes.com/interactive/2015/05/14/world/asia/Understanding-Southeast-Asias-Migrant-Crisis.html, accessed on 5 September 2015.

O'Connor, N. 2014. 'Bangladesh proposes interning, repatriating up to 270K Rohingya to Myanmar', *Al Jazeera*, 26 November, http://america.aljazeera.com/articles/2014/11/26/bangladesh-proposesinterningrepatriatingupto270krohing yatomyanma.html, accessed on 24 September 2015.

One India. 2014. 'Myanmar-Burdwan blast link: How Rohingyas cause blew out of Proportion', *One India*, November 18, www.oneindia.com/feature/myanmar-burdwan-blast-link-how-rohingyas-cause-blew-out-of-proportion-1564626. html, accessed on 14 December 2014.

Pagadala, T. 2015. 'Seeking new homes in Hyderabad', *India Together*, 12 August 2013, http://indiatogether.org/rohingya-human-rights, accessed on 1 September 2015.

Pearlma, J. 2015. 'Who are the Rohingya boat people?', *The Telegraph*, 21 May, www.telegraph.co.uk/news/worldnews/asia/burmamyanmar/11620933/Who-are-the-Rohingya-boat-people.html, accessed on 30 July 2015.

Perappadan, B. S. 2012. 'Rohingya asylum seekers back in Delhi', *The Hindu*, 18 May, www.thehindu.com/news/national/rohingyaasylumseekersbackindelhi/arti cle3433267.ece, accessed on 24 September 2015.

Pisharody, R. V. 2015. 'After terror threat in Hyderabad, cops step up vigil on Rohingyas', *The New Indian Express*, 23 July, www.newindianexpress.com/

cities/hyderabad/After-Terror-Threat-in-Hyderabad-Cops-Step-up-Vigil-on-Rohingyas/2015/07/23/article2935281.ece, accessed on 14 October 2015.

Radio Free Asia. 2015. 'Delhi slum better than life in Myanmar, Rohingyas say', 19 May, www.rfa.org/english/news/myanmar/indiarohingya05192015101001.html, accessed on 24 September 2015.

Rahman, S. A. 2014. 'Reporters face jail over Rohingya report', *Aljazeera*, 2 January, www.aljazeera.com/indepth/features/2014/01/reporters-face-jail-over-rohingya-report-2014111146216366.html, accessed on 3 December 2014.

Rajagopal, K. 2014. 'SC: Why is eastern border still porous?', *The Hindu*, 18 December, www.thehindu.com/todays-paper/tp-national/sc-why-is-eastern-border-still-porous/article6702655.ece, accessed on 24 September 2015.

Rediff. 2013. 'Around 1,500 Rohingya Muslims take refuge in Hyderabad', 11 July, www.rediff.com/news/report/around-1500-rohingya-muslims-take-refuge-in-hyderabad/20130711.htm, accessed on 10 October 2015.

Reliefweb. 2012. 'Iran offers cash assistance to Rohingya Muslim refugees in Hyderabad', 2 August, http://reliefweb.int/report/india/iran-offers-cash-assistance-rohingya-muslim-refugees-hyderabad, accessed on 10 October 2015.

Sengupta, S. 2016. 'Stateless, infiltrators, trafficked victims, Bangladeshis: Who are the Rohingyas', *Hardnews*, 7 January 2015, New Delhi, www.hardnewsmedia.com/2016/01/%E2%80%98stateless%E2%80%99-%E2%80%99infiltrators%E2%80%99-%E2%80%99trafficked-victims%E2%80%99-%E2%80%99bangladeshis%E2%80%99-who-are-rohingyas#sthash.XFZ4KRM2.dpuf, accessed on 10 December 2016.

Sengupta, S. and M. Chakraborty. 2015. 'Rohingyader Proti Day Achhe Amadero', *Anandabazar Patrika*, 2 June, www.anandabazar.com/editorial/we-have-to-responsible-for-rohingyas-1.153753#, retrieved http://archive.is/LjKns, accessed on 20 October 2016.

The Siasat Daily. n.d. 'Rohingya Muslims struggling for Rehabilitation in Hyderabad', www.siasat.com/english/news/rohingya-muslims-struggling-rehabilitation-hyderabad, accessed on 1 September 2015.

Syed, A. Z. n.d. 'Who cares for the Rohingyas?', *Kashmir Times*, www.kashmirtimes.com/newsdet.aspx?q=41261, accessed on 24 September 2015.

Thein, T. 2015. 'Green card meetings in Akyab and Maungdaw', *The Burma Times*, 16 July, http://burmatimes.net/greencardmeetingsinakyabandmaungdaw/, accessed on 24 September 2015.

Velath, P. M. 2015. 'The tragic case of the Rohingya refugees', *Deccan Herald*, 25 July, www.deccanherald.com/content/485583/tragic-case-rohingya-refugees.html, accessed on 7 September 2015.

Venkatraman, S. 2015. 'Humanitarian crisis: Darul Hijrat: A sanctuary for the Rohingya', *Dawn*, 14 June, www.dawn.com/news/1187553, accessed on 24 September 2015.

Yadav, A. 2013. 'Serial blasts rock Bodh Gaya temple', *The Hindu*, 8 July, www.thehindu.com/news/national/other-states/serial-blasts-rock-bodh-gaya-temple/article4891094.ece, accessed on 10 October 2015.

Case laws

Almitra Patel v Union of India 2000 (2) SCC 679.

Jaffar Ullah and Anr v Union of India, W.P(C) No. 859 of 2013, Supreme Court, pending.

Ram Jawaya v State of Punjab AIR 1955 SC 549.

Primary sources

Booklet of Development and Justice Initiative, undated. Available in file.

Fact Finding. *Socio Legal Information Centre*, Rohingya refugee Camp, Kalindi Kunj, New Delhi, July 2012.

Fact-Finding on Access to Contraception, *Socio Legal Information Centre*, Rohingya Refugee Camp, Mewat, April 2013.

Letter from Mahmood A. Madani to P. Chidambaram, 20 April 2012.

List of Districts, Townships, Cities/Towns, Wards, Village Groups and Villages in Union of Myanmar, Ministry of Home Affairs, Government of Union of Myanmar, 2001.

Lok Sabha, Corrigenda to the List of Questions for Written Answers on 15 July 2014/Ashadha24,1936 (Saka),Question No. 739 by Kodikunnil Suresh, http://164.100.47.132/questionslist/MyFolder/15072014.pdf, accessed on 1 September 2015.

Lok Sabha Debates, Question No. 4650 titled rehabilitation of Pakistani Migrants, by Udit Raj, Ashwini Kumar and Col. Sonaram Chaudhary, List of Questions for Written Answers Tuesday, 12 August 2014/Shravana 21, 1936 (Saka), http://164.100.47.132/questionslist/MyFolder/12082014.pdf, accessed on 1 September 2015.

Lok Sabha Debates, 'Situation arising due to the arrival of refugees from Myanmar in Delhi', Sumitra Mahajan, http://164.100.47.132/LssNew/psearch/Result15.aspx?dbsl=7319, accessed on 1 September 2015.

Press Information Bureau, Government of India, Ministry of Home Affairs, 'Law for Refugees in India,' 6 August 2014, http://pib.nic.in/newsite/PrintRelease.aspx?relid=108152, accessed on 1 September 2015.

Press Information Bureau Release titled, 'Facilities to minority nationals from neighboring countries to stay in India on Long Term Visa', Ministry of Home Affairs, Government of India, 16 December 2014.

Press Information Bureau Release titled, 'MHA to expedite LTV/Citizenship issues of minority nationals from neighbouring countries', Ministry of Home Affairs, Government of India, 15 December 2014, www.pib.nic.in/newsite/erelease.aspx, accessed on 1 September 2015.

Press Information Bureau release titled, 'Refugee determination system', Minister of State for Home Affairs, Government of India, 5 May 2015.

Press Information Bureau Release titled, 'Task force on citizenship/Long Term Visa (LTV) to visit Lucknow on October 16', Ministry of Home Affairs, Government of India, 9 October 2014, www.pib.nic.in/newsite/erelease.aspx, accessed on 1 September 2015.

Press Information Bureau Release titled, 'Teams to visit identified districts to expedite LTV/Citizenship issues', Ministry of Home Affairs, Government of India, 23 December 2014, www.pib.nic.in/newsite/erelease.aspx, accessed on 1 September 2015.

Question No. 6307, Lok Sabha Corrigenda to the List of Questions for Written Answers on 5 May 2015/Vaisakha 15, 1937 (Saka), http://164.100.47.132/questionslist/MyFolder/05052015.pdf, accessed on 1 September 2015.

Rajya Sabha Debates, Session 225, Short Notice Question, 16 May 2012, http://rsdebate.nic.in/bitstream/123456789/605960/1/IQ_225_16052012_SNQ8_p235_p240.pdf#search=refugees, accessed on 1 September 2015.

UN General Assembly. 1961. *Convention on the Reduction of Statelessness*, www.refworld.org/docid/3ae6b39620.html, accessed on 7 June 2015.

UNHCR. 2009. *Policy on Refugee Protection and Solutions in Urban Areas*, September, www.refworld.org/docid/4ab8e7f72.html.

UNHCR. 2011. *Basic International Legal Documents on Refugees*, Eighth Edition December.

UNHCR. 2012. *Summary Conclusions of Meeting with Representatives of Asylum-Seekers from Northern Rakhine State, Myanmar.*

UNHCR. 2013. *Urban Profiling of Refugee Situations in Delhi: Refugees from Myanmar, Afghanistan and Somalia and Their Indian Neighbours: A Comparative Study*, September 2013.

UNHCR. 2014a. *Rohingya Refugees and Asylum Seekers in India: A Situational Analysis*, February 2014. New Delhi: India.

UNHCR. 2014b. *Ending Statelessness within Ten Years*, www.unhcr.org/statelesscampaign2014/Stateless-Report_eng_final3.pdf.

UNHCR. n.d.a. *Figures at a Glance*, www.unhcr.org.in/index.php?option=com_content&view=article&id=3&Itemid=125, accessed on 24 September 2015.

UNHCR. n.d.b. *An Introduction to Stateless People*, www.unhcr.org/pages/49c3646c155.html, accessed on 10 October 2015.

UNHCR. n.d.c. *Refugee Protection in India*, www.hrdc.net/sahrdc/resources/refugee_protection.htm, accessed on 10 December 2014.

UNHCR. n.d.d. *Stateless People Figures*, www.unhcr.org/pages/49c3646c26.html, accessed on 24 September 2015.

Legislations referred

Application for Obtaining Birth Registration, Municipal Corporation of Delhi, Health Department, drawn up under Delhi Registration of Births & Deaths Rules, 1999, http://111.93.47.72/rbd/content/birth.pdf, accessed on 1 August 2015.

Birth Reporting Form in the State of Haryana, http://haryanahealth.nic.in/userfiles/file/pdf/Manual%20on%20Civil%20Registration%20System.pdf, accessed on 1 August 2015.

Birth Reporting Form in the State of Rajasthan, http://statistics.rajasthan.gov.in/Details/FORM_1.pdf, accessed on 1 September 2015.

The Burmese Constitution, 1947.

The Burmese Constitution, 2008.

Constitution of India.

FAQs on Registration of Births & Deaths, https://arogya.maharashtra.gov.in/Site/Uploads/GR/FAQsonRegistrationofBirthsandDeaths.pdf, accessed on 1 August 2015.

Foreigners Act, 1946.

Foreigners Order, 1948.

Ministry of Home Affairs Order titled, 'Case of registration in respect of Myanmar nationals' Claims to be refugees–reg.', No. 18029/23/2012FIV, dated 11.7.2012, Ministry of Home Affairs, Government of India. On file.

Myanmar–Bangladesh Pass issued by the Government of Myanmar to Rohingyas.

Powers delegated to State Governments/UT Administrations/FRROs/FROs for various visa related services, updated as on 16 September 2014, Foreigners Division, Ministry of Home Affairs, http://mha1.nic.in/pdfs/ForeigDPwrdlgtFRROs.pdf, accessed on 1 September 2015.

The Registration of Foreigners Act, 1939.

Right to Information Reply dated 12.3.2015 to the application by the author dated 15.1.2015 by Foreigners Division, Ministry of Home Affairs, Government of India.

The Union Citizenship Act, 1948.

The Union Citizenship (Election) Act, 1948.

INDEX

For Product Safety Concerns and Information please contact our EU
representative GPSR@taylorandfrancis.com
Taylor & Francis Verlag GmbH, Kaufingerstraße 24, 80331 München, Germany

www.ingramcontent.com/pod-product-compliance
Lightning Source LLC
Chambersburg PA
CBHW060036030426
42334CB00019B/2354